FREEDOM AND ORDER

Freedom and Order

A COMMENTARY

ON THE AMERICAN

POLITICAL SCENE

Henry Steele Commager

GEORGE BRAZILLER
NEW YORK

For information address the publisher:
George Braziller, Inc.
One Park Avenue
New York 16, New York

Library of Congress Catalog Card Number: 66-15755

Printed in the United States of America

Designed by Jennie R. Bush

ACKNOWLEDGMENTS

We wish to thank the following for permission to publish certain essays in
this volume:

Current History for The Right of Dissent
Daedalus for Leadership in Eighteenth-Century America and Today
Johns Hopkins Press for The United States and the Integration of Europe
(in European Integration, edited by C. Grove Haines, 1957)
The Nation for Washington Witch-Hunt
The New Republic for Red-Baiting in the Colleges
The New York Times for An Inquiry into "Appeasement," Yalta Recon-
sidered, "Yet the Nation Survived," Television and the Elections, Presi-
dential Age—and Youth, Change in History, Our Declaration Is Still a
Rallying Cry, "To Form a Much Less Perfect Union," and The Republican
Party Repudiates Its History
Saturday Review for What Ideas Are Safe?, Is Freedom Really Necessary?,
The Double Standard in Political Morality (originally titled A Historian
Looks at Our Political Morality), The Problem of Dissent: Vietnam, and
Tom Paine Talks Back to Providence.

"In a democratic nation, power must be linked with responsibility, and obliged to defend and justify itself within
the framework of the general good."

Franklin D. Roosevelt,
Last annual message to Congress, January 6, 1945

Preface

It is surprising, almost disconcerting, to look back from the perspective of over thirty years and discover how early you entered on those paths which you have long trod so familiarly, how long you have been preoccupied with those problems which still, in one way or another, excite your interest and stir your imagination and require your participation.

It is a quarter of a century now since I wrote *Majority Rule and Minority Rights*; the issue which I undertook to analyze in that small book—the place of judicial review in a democracy—has continued to enlist my interest, and I returned to it with, I trust, a somewhat livelier concern for its complexities in the Sperenza Lectures which I delivered at Columbia University in 1960, and which are here published for the first time. When, some fifteen years ago, McCarthyism enveloped us like some noxious London fog, I wrote (and spoke) those papers later collected under the title *Freedom, Loyalty, Dissent*. That book is out of print, but the issues to which it was addressed are, alas, neither out of date nor out of style, for the excommunication of Senator McCarthy did not carry with it the repudiation of his philosophy. In one form or another the spirit and practices of McCarthyism have infiltrated both federal and state administration, and a good many private organizations as well: witness the persistence of "security" checks in both government and industry, the enormous and growing power of the FBI, the habit of equating hostility to the Vietnam War with disloyalty or Communism.

I have returned to this problem again and again in the attempt to make clear the logic and necessity for rather than to argue the abstract right of freedom in our kind of society—freedom to inquire, criticize, and to dissent; freedom to travel, freedom from censorship, academic freedom—freedom as a method, probably the only method, of avoiding error and arriving at truth. It was in the atmosphere of the Cold War that the myths of "appeasement," of betrayal at Yalta, of a conspiracy against nationalist China, emerged and flourished, and found expression in such follies as the Loyalty program, the antics of the House Un-American Activities Committee, and the Bricker Amendment, and during the postwar years I assailed these with unremitting ardor. While the form of the follies thus dramatized is, let us trust, a thing of the past, the kind of thinking about politics—what Richard Hofstadter has happily called the Paranoid Style in American politics—is not at all a thing of the past but still very much with us, thinking which derives not from history or experience, but from abstractions, hypotheses, and fantasies.

Indeed as I have re-read these essays, I have been struck anew with the way in which the old familiar problems emerge in new guise, in which old and hackneyed arguments are directed into new channels. Thus the loyalty-security complex is still with us; applicants for federal jobs are still required to testify that they do not belong to any one of some hundreds of organizations, and though the Smith Act and the McCarran Act are thoroughly discredited, their victims still languish in jail. Even as I write we learn that the State Department and the FBI are bustling about Europe shadowing American tourists suspected of harboring dangerous thoughts, and that letters to the White House protesting the war in Vietnam are turned over to the security branch of the Justice Department.

The issues of academic freedom are still with us, though in altered form; now it is the question of the right of students to protest against an unjust war, or to demonstrate for civil rights. Censorship, private and official, is still with us, private censorship by self-appointed guardians of patriotism and morality who keep a sharp eye on textbooks and local libraries; official censorship of "obscenity" by local and state officials; censorship even in the government itself. The day of book burning is happily gone, but Ambassador Galbraith has just told us that the USIA solemnly compiles lists of books which give a "favorable" and an "unfavorable" picture of the United States for the guidance of overseas libraries.

Judicial review has taken on a new vitality and scope; for the first time in our history it functions efficiently to preserve civil liberties and enlarge the guarantees of the Bill of Rights, but the old problem of the role of the judiciary in the democratic process remains unsolved. The problem of bigness in government, too, has taken on not only new dimensions but new character; we can see now that fragmentation has dangers no less than centralization, and that not only war but the welfare state and the protection of civil liberties implacably require bigness and centralization. The problem is no longer one of a simple choice between the particular and the general, but rather that of holding in Behemoth, of bridling Leviathan, without making them impotent.

The pattern of the political kaleidoscope changes, too, but the ingredients remain much the same. Thus the relevance of the principles of our own Revolution to revolutions in the newly emerging nations of the world; thus our ability to survive what we are tempted to suppose are ultimate crises but which are more often routine crises of our own making; thus the power and presumptuousness of what President Eisenhower called the "industrial military establishment." Even in the realm of foreign policy, though the objects of our concern have changed, the vocabulary and the thinking remain much the same as they were twenty years ago. Although the Cold War with the Soviet has thawed perceptibly in the past decade or so, the freeze seems to have moved halfway around the globe to the Pacific; where twenty years ago it was the Russians' Communism that was atheistic, immoral, and ripe for destruction, now it is China's which invites all of these moralistic labels, and which is the ultimate enemy we must destroy or contain.

These essays may seem, at first glance, somewhat miscellaneous in character, but they have a unity of theme and, I believe, of philosophy as well, if that is not too pretentious a word. The theme is, in a broad sense, political; all of these essays are addressed to the overarching problem of the reconciliation of liberty and order in a world troubled, as ours is, by the eccentricities of both. They deal with the claims of freedom as a method of working out solutions to intractable problems, with political institutions and practices; it is chiefly the practices that interest me, such as federalism, or judicial review, or leadership in a democracy, or the conduct of foreign policy. They concern themselves with the national character—if there is such a thing—as a product of historical and social experience.

The concluding essays are inspired by and addressed to some of the problems that have grown out of our tragic involvement in Vietnam. That cloud, when it first appeared on the distant horizon, was no bigger than a man's hand; now it spans the horizon and fills the skies, and threatens to envelop all of us in its storm and turbulence. It is discouraging to close this collection on a note so melancholy, but it is reassuring that we have the kind of society and government where an aroused and enlightened public opinion may yet save us from the ultimate catastrophe of a world war.

Instead of saying that these papers have a "philosophical" unity it might be better to say that they seem to express a pretty consistent point of view. That point of view is the somewhat unfashionable one which used to be called Jeffersonian liberalism. I cheerfully confess an abiding faith in democracy as the best kind of government which has yet been developed, and in majority rule; in freedom as a method of arriving at truth and avoiding error; in working out solutions in politics, as in most other areas, by the pragmatic method of experimentation. I continue to believe in toleration for those ideas which we may think "loathsome and fraught with death"; in a single standard of morality and of political conduct for great nations and for small, for Western nations and for Eastern—a doctrine observed now chiefly in the breach; in the necessity of big government and in eternal vigilance as the price of liberty under such a government. And I continue to abhor the pernicious danger of doctrinaire principles like the perfectability of man, or philosophical ultimates like "better dead than Red," or shibboleths of states rights or of *laissez faire*.

These essays, written over a stretch of a quarter of a century, reflect my "can't help but believes." I have not attempted to bring them up to date, but have let them stand as they were originally written.

I am deeply grateful to my son, Steele Commager, of Columbia University, who took on the drudgery of the selection and organization of the contents. And I am happy to find that while he is innocent of responsibility for the opinions and sentiments which I have voiced here, he is quite ready to associate himself with them.

HENRY STEELE COMMAGER

Amherst, Mass.
April 6, 1966

Contents

PART FOUR

PART FIVE

PART SIX

PART ONE

Democracy and Judicial Review

It is difficult to know whether to be more astonished at the boldness and courage, or at the resourcefulness and
originality, of the generation that won our independence, established the nation, and wrote the Constitution and the Bill of
Rights. The American nation was launched under the auspices of
two remarkable experiments. The first, the boldest, was the experiment in self-government on a scale and with a vigor heretofore
unknown in history: neither the imperfect democracy of Periclean
Athens nor the limited democracy of the Swiss cantons and Ice-
land were genuine antecedents. The second—and most original—
was the contrivance of an elaborate system of self-imposed limitations on self-government, limitations designed to prevent those
abuses almost universally supposed to be an inevitable attribute of
democracy.

Americans of that generation not only formulated the
principles of democracy and of limited government; they institutionalized them. For centuries, philosophers had imagined governments which derived their authority from the people: Americans
translated that ideal into the institution of the Constitutional Convention and, on a more mundane plane, the political party. For
centuries philosophers had designed governments whose powers
were limited by God, by Nature, by Reason—or by Revolution;
Americans institutionalized all of these in such practical devices as
written constitutions, bills of rights, the system of checks and
balances, the distribution of powers in a federal system, and judicial review, and provided for all of these devices the sanction of
the Law.

Both of these experiments challenged history and experience. In the eighteenth century the conviction that the masses were incapable of self-government was matched in ardor only by the conviction that if the experiment were tried it would inevitably fail. And not in the eighteenth century alone: until the end of the American Civil War the upper classes of the Old World watched with malign dissatisfaction the progress of American democracy, confidently anticipating that almost any moment it would degenerate into despotism or collapse into anarchy.

Even more striking, perhaps, than the deliberate flouting of history and of logic was the paradox, implicit and even explicit, in these two American achievements—the paradox of democracy and limited government or, if you will, of majority power and minority rights. And it is relevant to observe that while, in the course of the following century, some nations adopted the American practices of self-government, and many the American techniques of limited government, very few successfully combined the two. Most of the governments of the Western world in the nineteenth century were parliamentary—that is, with no explicit constitutional limits on majority will—or oligarchical, with express limitations on the majority will; or—as with many of the states of Latin America—a combination of democracy that mocked at true self-government and of constitutional limitations that rarely worked.

It was the Americans who first formulated the paradox, and then institutionalized it; it remained for Americans to resolve it.

And what a paradox it was, a paradox that still, after almost two centuries, haunts our political philosophy and vexes our judicial practice. The voice of the people is the voice of God, or of Nature, but it may speak only on stated subjects, in calm and respectable accents, at given occasions; and even then it is not really a voice but a confusion of tongues, and therefore need not be taken too seriously. It is the right of people to alter or abolish governments and to institute new ones, or to change the rules of government, but only in a fashion at once so orderly and so complex that it hardly ever happens. The majority is to govern, but it is not permitted to govern in all matters, and sometimes it is not even permitted to express itself at all.

The paradox was most eloquently put by the greatest of democracy's philosophers, the very man who gave immortal form to the doctrine of self-government. Absolute acquiescence in the decisions of the majority, said Thomas Jefferson, was "the vital principle of republics, from which there is no appeal but to force"; but in the same Inaugural Address he celebrated the "sacred principle" that "though the will of the majority is in all cases to prevail, that will to be rightful must be reasonable," and "that the minority possess their equal rights which equal laws must protect, and to violate would be oppression." And, again, he wrote to his friend Madison that "it is my principle that the will of the majority should always prevail" (1787) but a decade later cooperated with the same Madison in vigorous opposition to majority will as expressed through the Alien and Sedition laws with the observation that "it would be a dangerous delusion were a confidence in the men of our choice to silence our fears for the safety of our rights. Confidence is everywhere the parent of despotism; free government is founded on jealousy, not confidence; it is jealousy, not confidence, which prescribes limited Constitutions to bind down those whom we are obliged to trust with power." (Ky. Resolutions of 1798.)

What is surprising is that this paradoxical system, and philosophy, worked so well, and for so long a time, thus illustrating here as elsewhere the great historical principle that Americans can have their cake and eat it too. Notwithstanding the almost hysterical fears of those bred to Old World notions, democracy did not get out of hand, strike down constitutional limitations, overthrow established institutions, flout law and order, and take refuge in anarchy. Nor on the other hand did the complex network of self-imposed limitations prove unduly restrictive. American democracy has managed to get on with the job, most of the time. Certainly it has never felt so hampered or frustrated that it has been tempted to exchange its system of self-imposed limits for one more permissive or more responsive to majority will.

From the beginning, and during most of the nineteenth century, it was majority rule that was most imperiously challenged. Only rarely—as with Calhoun—did that challenge take the form of a positive justification of minority rule; for the most part it took the negative, but none the less aggressive, form of the charge of majority tyranny. The doctrine of majority tyranny has been a constant in our history, and merits more attention than it has received. It has gone through a series of rather well-defined phases, each with its own rationale. What is perhaps most curious about these successive responses to the alleged tyranny of the majority is that they have so rarely been inspired by anxious concern for the moral and intellectual rights of the individual, and have so rarely addressed themselves to the central issue of the reconciliation of liberty and order.

Almost the whole generation of the Founding Fathers had deep misgivings about the principle of majority rule. Their doubts and reservations were, perhaps, more objective and more philosophical than those entertained by later generations; they were certainly more general. For to a John Adams, a Hamilton, a Jefferson, a Henry, a Pinckney, it was not that the lower orders—or the upper—were not to be trusted; it was Man who was not to be trusted. All history—and the Fathers studied history assiduously to justify their hypotheses—all history taught that all men alike were greedy of power, and that none could be trusted with power. Kings and nobles, the church and the army, the rich and the powerful, all abused power; the people—in those fitful episodes when they happened to enjoy power—were equally wicked and despotic. Alas for mankind! none were to be trusted, not the one, nor the few, nor the many; one could only put one's trust in mechanical devices guaranteed to frustrate the natural depravity of man. Freedom under government, John Locke had said, is to have "a standing law to live by," and John Dickinson put it more concretely when he defined a free people as "not those over whom government is reasonably and equitably exercised, but those who live under a government so constitutionally checked and controlled, that proper provision is made against its being otherwise exercised." There was no special animus here against a particular class or race, though sometimes, in the heat of controversy, a Hamilton, a John Adams, a Jefferson, or a Paine might give that impression. In constructing bulwarks against tyranny all the Founding Fathers were veritable Vaubans, but the enemy was not the Aristocracy or the Demos, it was Human Nature.

The first quarter, or third, of the nineteenth century witnessed the passing of leadership from what Adams and Jefferson liked to call a Natural Aristocracy, to the people themselves, and this shift in the center of political gravity brought with it a shift in the anti-majoritarian argument. A vote of no-confidence in human nature was no longer useful and, except for Calhoun, who was something of a specialist in futility, statesmen and philosophers abandoned that gesture and shifted instead to doubts about democracy itself. It was the magisterial Tocqueville who most persuasively formulated these doubts; he had consulted Webster and Story and Kent and Jared Sparks, but he had consulted most of all his own fears and misgivings. All these he crystallized in two famous chapters on "The Tyranny of the Majority," in his *Democracy in America*. The argument, though vigorous and incisive, was theoretical and deductive. Majority tyranny was not something that Tocqueville saw spread out before him, but something that he anticipated, and his conclusions were based not on evidence or experience but on logical necessity. Aware of this sobering inadequacy, Tocqueville confessed that the tyranny of the majority was not harsh and brutal, as in the Old World, but pervasive and suffocating, a tyranny not over the bodies but over the minds of men. "I know of no country in which there is so little true independence of mind and freedom of discussion as in America," he wrote, conveniently forgetting Italy and Spain and Russia, and concluding drearily that

> if ever the free institutions of America are destroyed, that event may be attributed to the unlimited authority of the majority, which may at some future time urge minorities to desperation and oblige them to have recourse to physical force. Anarchy will then be the result, but it will have been brought about by despotism.

Here was the strongest, as it has been the most persistent, of the anti-majoritarian arguments, for it was conceived not in anger but in sorrow, and directed not to the preservation of special privilege, but to the preservation of individualism and culture. It was objective, it was disinterested, it was almost scientific; and it had the enormous advantage that it could not be readily disposed of by submitting counter-evidence drawn from a democratic culture, for to cite evidence of cultural elegance or sophistication was itself a confession that both were wanting.

The Tocquevillian argument that democracy levels down was not abandoned, but after the Civil War something new was added to the anti-majoritarian arsenal. The generation of William Graham Sumner and Justice Field, of Joseph Choate and Thomas Bailey Aldrich, continued to be impressed by the innate vulgarity of democracy. Indeed, what with the emancipation of the Negro and the coming of all sorts of people from abroad they were more conscious of this than ever; but they were impressed, too, by its greed—a greed no longer characteristic of mankind as a whole, but peculiar to the poor. These are the two themes, not too subtly interwoven, in much of the literature of the closing decades of the century: that democracy is dangerous because it is no longer the good old American democracy of our forebears, but something new and strange; and that it is dangerous because it will not respect the arrangements and commitments of the past, but threatens to reopen every question of status and of right, and to carry equalitarianism from the social realm to the economic.

The first theme can be read in the fastidious lamentations of Aldrich about our "Unguarded Gates":

> Wide open and unguarded stand our gates
> And through them presses a wild motley throng—
> Men from the Volga and the Tartar steepes. . . .
> Malayan, Scythian, Teuton, Kelt and Slav,
> Flying the Old World's poverty and scorn . . .
> O liberty, white Goddess, is it well
> To leave the gates unguarded. . . . ?
>   Have a care
> Lest from thy brow the clustered stars be torn
> And trampled in the dust.

The second, that democracy threatens vested interests, can be followed in the arrogant pages of William Graham Sumner's essays, in Joseph Choate's passionate argument against the income tax in the Pollock case, or in Theodore Roosevelt's letters telling how to dispose of Governor Altgeld and the Chicago anarchists. It can most luminously be traced in that long series of Supreme Court opinions identifying liberty with property, and the Fourteenth Amendment with social statics that weighs so heavily on the judicial conscience today.

Yet even at a time when the tide of anti-democratic argument was running most swiftly, that most judicious of all foreign observers, James Bryce, rejected it, and like some philosophical Canute commanded it to retreat. *The American Commonwealth*, published almost fifty years after Tocqueville's *Democracy*, denied that American majorities exercised tyranny, either legal or social. "The tyranny of the majority," Bryce stated flatly, "is no longer a blemish on the American system, and the charges brought against democracy from the supposed example of America are groundless." And as for tyranny over the minds of men,

> If social persecution exists in America of today, it is only in a few dark corners. One may travel all over the Northern and Western States, mingling with all classes and reading the newspapers, without hearing of it.

The geographical distinction was crucial, and doubtless gratifying to Boston Irish, if not to Alabama Negroes.

Notwithstanding the tenacious strength of those democratic forces which Bryce celebrated, the growth of democracy at home and its spread into new quarters of the globe, anti-majoritarian doctrines did not disappear. Instead, in the twentieth century, they gained new strength and respectability. For in the second quarter of the century two developments, immense, impressive, and ominous, seemed to justify, if not to require, skepticism toward majority claims and resistance to majority impositions. Those who watched majorities in Germany and Italy, and in lesser states, commit suicide by turning government over to dictators concluded, not without reason, that there should be some limits to the majoritarian principle. And—not to bemuse ourselves overmuch with examples from other lands—those who contemplated the never-ending audacity of our own elected persons, and the implacable expansion of their claims, in cold war as in hot, over the minds as well as the bodies of men, asked once again: Who shall hold in Behemoth, who bridle Leviathan? The new critics of majority rule, then, take their stand not so much on old considerations of property as on new considerations of politics. Democracy, they feel, is too serious a business to be left to the people—or if not too serious, at least too complex and exacting. The people—so they have learned from Freud, Le Bon, Pareto, or McDougall—are well-meaning but simple, and easily deceived. Buffeted by fear, torn by prejudice, distracted by trivia, misled by propaganda, they must be protected against themselves.

Yet even those who are most alive to the dangers of Big Government are not prepared to return to small government—to a government that divests itself of its responsibilities, a government dedicated to *laissez faire* in social and economic realms, a government therefore incapable of functioning effectively in the realm of international relations. Nor, except during the stress of campaigns, do they seriously believe that state and local governments are more effective instruments for the reconciliation of order and liberty. The notion that there is some descending scale of freedom from the Federal government to local units, and some ascending scale of tyranny from the town meeting to the Federal government, is without support in history or experience. Certainly it would be asking a good deal to ask Negroes to subscribe to the idea that the Federal government was dangerous to their liberties, but that they could with confidence look to the states. It would be asking a great deal to ask organized labor to forget half a century of history and trust the state governments to champion and protect its freedom. It would be asking a great deal to ask scholars and scientists to agree that the government which has maintained the Library of Congress, the National Archives, the Coast and Geodetic Survey, the Geological Survey, the Smithsonian Institution, and the National Gallery of Art is less to be trusted to maintain the traditions of intellectual and scientific freedom than the miscellaneous authorities that support local universities, schools, libraries, and museums throughout the United States.

Thus the paradox of self-conscious and even vainglorious democracy and deep distrust of majority rule persists down to our own day. And today, too, as so often in the past, that paradox pervades the thought and character of the entire body politic. Our society is not sharply divided between men of faith and men of little faith, between the triumphant champions and the sullen critics of democracy. It is the same men who are both champions and critics, the same men who are sure that democracy is one of the ultimate values of our society and who are prepared to restrict and defeat it, often at the slightest provocation. And—except on the Court—they seem to accept with equanimity what seems to the disinterested observer a bad case of political schizophrenia.

Thus those who held their mandate from majorities and professed confidence in democracy nevertheless voted a constitutional amendment designed to prevent future majorities from exercising their own judgment in voting for the most important office in their control. Thus those who professed to fear government and who cherished individual rights voted—in 1940, in 1950, and in 1954 —for ever stricter security measures, ever more comprehensive surveillance of associations, education, reading, travel, and even beliefs of citizens.

Perhaps the most ostentatious example of the paradox is the State of Georgia, which in the name of democracy reduced the voting age to eighteen, yet which also built into its constitutional framework a guarantee that no urban majority would ever outvote a rural minority.

So the paradox is still with us, and the problem as well: the problem of the balance of order and liberty, the most ancient, the most recent, and in many ways the most difficult of all political problems. But may we not have reached the point where we can contemplate our political world not as divided and fragmented, but as united and harmonious, where we are confronted not with a series of conflicting choices but with a progression of interrelated ideas? Our concern is not with liberty as such, but with liberty as the essential condition for order, and with those liberties that take on meaning only when directed to social ends. Our concern is not with order as such—after all, the Nazis promised that—but with order as the essential framework for liberty. Have we not arrived at the point where much of the antinomy between majority rule and minority rights has become meaningless? We have set majority and minority off against each other, as if we could maintain our republican system with less than both, as if we could flourish with a unanimous majority or without any working majority at all. After all, it should not be too difficult for us to realize that we cannot have either order without freedom or freedom without order, any more than we can have the body without the mind or the mind without the body.

2

How then are we to resolve this paradox?

The habitual—perhaps I should say the instinctive—reaction of Americans to the paradox has been to ignore it. We assume that all alleged majorities are in fact real majorities and, accepting their credentials at face value, we accord them the respect due a sovereign people in our philosophy; we either circumvent mechanical limitations upon majorities or accommodate ourselves to them without too much thought, just as we accommodate ourselves to other inconveniences in life that we cannot really control—the ailments of our bodies, for example. So, too, we go on pretending that every invasion of minority rights, every violation of freedom, every departure from constitutional due process, is a special case, justified by extraordinary circumstances, one that will never happen again and that we can therefore safely ignore. Thus we avoid the burden and the embarrassment of consistency and enjoy the luxury, or the release, of self-indulgence.

But when forced, as we so often are, to rationalize what we do, or at least to palliate it, we try to transfer the whole issue to the judiciary department. Thus we free the political branches of our government (that is, ourselves) from the reproaches of a guilty conscience, and satisfy the ceremonial requirements of our constitutional system. That the judiciary was not created for this purpose, that it is not competent to the task (I mean, of course, technically and constitutionally competent; outside the South where standards are doubtless exceptionally high, no one questions its intellectual competence), that it cannot possibly satisfy the conflicting demands of our society, that it would prefer not to exercise the responsibility—all this is beside the point. The judiciary is our church, our confessional, our sanctuary, our safety valve, our preceptor, our palladium; we are insatiable in the demands that we make upon it and grudging in the demands we permit it to make upon us.

Confronted by these demands, the judiciary has responded with varying degrees of reluctance. It is not, to be sure, wholly without resources, and it can—and does—take refuge in the almost trackless waste of the doctrine of "questions of a political nature," or in the labyrinths of procedural exemptions. But these escapes are not always open to it, nor do all judges share Justice Frankfurter's ardent passion for judicial continence. As Justice Cardozo wrote:

> Judges march . . . to pitiless conclusions under the prodding of remorseless logic which is supposed to leave them no alternative. They deplore the sacrificial rite. They perform it none the less, with averted gaze, convinced as they plunge the knife that they obey the bidding of their office. The victim is offered up to the gods of jurisprudence on the altar of regularity.

In the circumstances it is not surprising that their performance is not always consistent, that even individual judges do not always wear the garments of consistency; in the rejection of this hobgoblin they are Emersonian, though not elsewhere transcendental.[1*] To the perplexing questions that cluster themselves about the issue of the limits of majority rights in our constitutional system, judges have returned not a clear answer, but a chorus of answers, or even of evasions, and we must draw from them such conclusions as we may.

What are the answers which the judiciary has formulated to this vexatious problem? Reading from left to right, as it were, we can distinguish these arguments:

One: The majority has no right to violate the provisions of the Constitution or the Bill of Rights, and it is the function of the Courts to supervise and restrain the political branches of the government. I hasten to add that this extreme position belongs to the pre-1937, or Dark Ages, of judicial history, and has no spokesmen on the Supreme Court today and not many elsewhere.

Two: Where the prohibitions of the Constitution are inescapably clear, as they are in some of the provisions of the Bill of Rights, they are absolute. Thus the Congress may make *no* law respecting religion, or abridging freedom of speech or of the press or the right peaceably to assemble, and it is the duty of the Court to strike down all laws that appear to invade these areas, regard-

* This note and subsequent notes for this essay appear on pp. 317–318.

less of alleged emergencies or extenuating circumstances. This is, most of the time, the Black-Douglas position.

Three: The Constitution is not always clear, many of its provisions are vague and even conflicting, and it is not the business of the Court to impose its interpretation of these provisions on the majority will in any ordinary matters. But the rights guaranteed by the First Amendment are essential to the exercise of all other rights, and enjoy therefore a preferred position in the Constitution. Majorities may be permitted to make mistakes elsewhere, but not here, for mistakes here might undermine and destroy the very principle of majority rule. Foreshadowed by Justice Cardozo in the Palko case,[2] this position was enshrined by Justice Stone in the most famous footnote in judicial literature;[3] it is now accepted, off and on, by not only Justices Black and Douglas, but by Justices Warren and Brennan as well.

Four: There are no preferred, and therefore no deferred or common, parts of the Constitution; all parts of that document speak with equal authority and command the same respect. Where there are conflicts within the Constitution itself, or in different interpretations of the Constitution by majorities, it is the duty of the Court to balance one interest against the other and to embrace that which, in the particular circumstance of the legislation, seems to have the most compelling claim on its common sense and intelligence. If the Court does more than this it will inevitably fail. This may be called the Frankfurter position (most of the time) out of Holmes and Learned Hand.

Five: Whatever the interests may be, the appropriate political majority has already weighed them in the balance and made its choice, and it is not up to the Courts to put these interests back on some judicial scales and weigh them over again. The Court neither can nor should substitute its own judgment for that of Congress and President, or of the states where they confine themselves to matters of internal policy, on what takes priority among the conflicting claims of the Constitution. This extreme position is perhaps most succinctly stated by Professor H. B. Mayo: "Restraint and forbearance, as they operate in the free political process, is the only protection a democracy can offer against tyranny; to seek more is to seek the unattainable: a government legally powerful enough to do right but powerless to do wrong."[4] It has some support, too, from Justices Clark and Harlan.

I hasten to add that these are the judicial answers to our problem of the limits of majority rule, and that even if they do run the gamut of judicial ingenuity, they do not thereby exhaust the possible solutions to the problem.

It is very difficult to say anything about these judicial explications of the problem of majority power and minority rights that the Court itself has not said better. It is relevant to note that our generation is writing a new chapter in American judicial history (which is, by the way, the most interesting volume in the library of judicial history), a chapter that expounds a change—one might almost say a revolution—quite as dramatic as that which came with the passing of Marshall and Story and the ascendancy of Taney in the eighteen-thirties and forties, and quite as significant as that which unfolded in the eighteen-eighties with the assumption by judges of the role as regulator of the economy. Since 1937, if we must choose a date, the Court has returned to earlier habits of judicial continence, has abandoned attempts to restrain Congressional legislation or to "go behind the returns" of regulatory commissions or administrative bodies in the economic arena, and has allowed the states greater leeway in experimentation than had been customary in the past.

The controversy over the role of the Court in the protection of minority rights against majorities has been greatly narrowed, but it has also been greatly sharpened. Because the Court still suffers from a bad conscience for its imperialism of the half-century from the eighteen-eighties to the nineteen-thirties, it is now reluctant to interfere in ordinary legislation, eager to avoid the faintest appearance of substituting its own judgment for that of the political branches in those areas where the political branches are authorized to make judgments, and quick to refuse jurisdiction where excuses can be made to sound plausible. Yet, perhaps because it has so ostentatiously retired from the marketplace of social and economic legislation, some of its members bring to the narrower but blood-stained battlefield of civil liberties a special belligerence and passion.

We can dismiss the two extreme arguments—that the function of the Court is to censor the political branches of the government and to prevent majorities from making mistakes, or that Courts are bound in all but extreme (and therefore highly improbable) cases to accept the decisions of majorities. For there is no likelihood that the Court will return to the chauvinism which dictated *Pollock v. Farmer's Loan, Adair v. U.S., Hammer v. Dagernhart, Adkins v. Children's Hospital* or even *U.S. v. Butler*. Nor is there any serious likelihood that it will surrender its historic role of interpreting the Constitution and refusing to recognize laws or administrative acts that clearly impair the machinery of the federal system, or flagrantly violate specific provisions of the Constitution or historic principles of procedural rights mortised in the Bill of Rights.

Nor is there any strong indication of growing support, on the bench or off, for the position associated with Justice Black, that the prohibitions of the Bill of Rights are absolute.

The area of controversy then is chiefly between the preferred position doctrine and the balance of interest doctrine. These two doctrines take us to the very heart of the problem of majoritarianism, and therefore demand our most earnest consideration. We are not, however, required to exhaust the differences between them nor to explore all of their ramifications; it is sufficient that we note their relations to the issue of majority rule and minority right.

3

First, then, the "preferred position of the First Amendment" doctrine. That doctrine was most simply put by Justice Black in the case of *Marsh v. Alabama*: "When we balance the Constitutional rights of owners of property against those of the people to enjoy freedom of press and religion . . . we remain mindful of the fact that the latter occupy a preferred position." (326 U.S. at 509, 1946.) And three years later Justice Rutledge—who had formulated the principle in *Thomas v. Collins* (323 U.S. 516 at 529, 1945)—was able to point out that "the First Amendment guarantees of the freedoms of speech, press, assembly, and religion occupy preferred positions not only in the Bill of Rights but also in the repeated decisions of this court." (*Kovacs v. Cooper*, 336 U.S. 77 at 106, 1949.)

The antecedents were in fact respectable and imposing. If they did not clearly go back to *McCulloch v. Maryland*, as Justice Stone implied (letter to C. J. Hughes, qt. Mason, Stone, 514) they did go back to Holmes, Brandeis, and Hughes himself,[5] and to the universally respected Cardozo, whose dicta anticipated Stone's by two years:

> We reach a different plane of social and moral values when we pass to the privileges and immunities that have been taken over from the earlier articles of the federal bill of rights and brought within the Fourteenth Amendment by a process of absorption. These in their origin were effective against the federal government alone. If the Fourteenth Amendment has absorbed them the process of absorption has had its source in the belief that neither liberty nor justice would exist if they were sacrificed. This is true, for illustration, of freedom of thought and speech. Of that freedom one may say that it is the matrix, the indispensable condition of nearly every other form of freedom. . . . So it has come about that the domain of liberty, withdrawn by the Fourteenth Amendment from encroachment by the States, has been enlarged by latter-day judgments to include liberty of the mind as well as liberty of action. . . . The extension indeed became a logical imperative when once it was recognized, as long ago it was, that liberty is something more than the exemption from physical restraint, and even in the field of substantive rights and duties the legislative judgment, if oppressive and arbitrary, may be overridden by the courts. (*Palko v. Connecticut*, 302 U.S. 319.)

It was from Justice Stone's Carolene Products Company footnote that the principle of the preferred position derived its inspiration, and its weight as well, for it was Stone who had warned the Court against a "tortured construction" of the Constitution, who pointed out that the Courts were not to be assumed to be the only branch of the government conscious of responsibility, and who admonished it that the only check upon its power was its own sense of self-restraint. The warning was clothed with modesty and with grace:

> There may be narrower scope for operations of the presumption of constitutionality when legislation appears on its face to be within a specific prohibition of the Constitution, such as those of the first ten amendments, which

are deemed equally specific when held to be embraced within the Fourteenth.

It is unnecessary to consider now whether legislation which restricts those political processes which can ordinarily be expected to bring about repeal of undesirable legislation, is to be subjected to more exacting judicial scrutiny under the general prohibitions of the 14th Amendment than are most other types of legislation. . . .

Nor need we inquire whether similar considerations enter into the review of statutes directed at particular religious . . . or national . . . or racial minorities . . . whether prejudice against discrete and insular minorities may be a special condition, which tends seriously to curtail the operation of those political processes ordinarily to be relied upon to protect minorities, and which may call for a correspondingly more searching judicial inquiry. (304 U.S. 144, 152–4 n.4.)

Another three years, and notwithstanding the implied repudiation of this position in the Gobitis case (310 U.S. 586) Attorney General Robert H. Jackson could invest Justice Stone's footnote with the dignity of a constitutional provision:

There is nothing covert or conflicting in the recent judgments of the Court on social legislation and on legislative repressions of civil rights. The presumption of validity which attaches in general to legislative acts is frankly reversed in the case of interference with free speech and free assembly, and for a perfectly cogent reason. Ordinarily legislation whose basis in economic wisdom is uncertain can be redressed by the processes of the ballot box or the pressure of opinion. But when the channels of opinion or of peaceful persuasion are corrupted or clogged, these political correctives can no longer be relied on, and the democratic system is threatened at its most vital point. In that event the Court, by intervening, restores the processes of democratic government; it does not disrupt them. (*Struggle for Judicial Supremacy*, 284–5.)

This was the view of Mr. Roosevelt's Attorney General. But twelve years later, Justice Jackson, now a veteran of more than ten years on the Supreme Court, concluded that the "libertarian cult" of the preferred position was

a doctrine wholly incompatible with faith in democracy, and in so far as it encourages the belief that the judges may be left to correct the result of public indifference to issues of liberty, in choosing Presidents, Senators and Representatives, it is a vicious teaching. (*The Supreme Court in the American System of Government*, 58.)

Justice Frankfurter, who had never accepted the implications of the Carolene Products footnote, and had parted company with both Justices Stone and Jackson in the flag salute cases—cases involving legislation which, by the way, did not "corrupt or clog the channels of opinion or of peaceful persuasion"—formally rejected the "preferred position" doctrine in a concurring opinion in *Kovacs v. Cooper*. "This is a phrase," he wrote fastidiously,

> that has uncritically crept into some recent opinions of this Court. I deem it a mischievous phrase, if it carries the thought, which it may subtly imply, that any law touching communication is infected with presumptive invalidity. . . . I say the phrase is mischievous because it radiates a constitutional doctrine without avowing it. (*Kovacs v. Cooper*, 336 U.S. 77 at 90, 1949.)

It is of course an error to imply that because Mr. Justice Frankfurter was not prepared to concede a preferred position to First Amendment rights he was disposed to neglect them; he believed, simply, that all parts of the Constitution were created equal. Even in his Gobitis opinion he insisted that "education in the abandonment of foolish legislation is itself a training in liberty" only "where all the effective means of inducing political changes are left free from interference," (310 U.S. at 600) and he thought, quite rightly, that in these cases the means were free. And in *Sweezy v. New Hampshire* he observed that "in the political realm, as in the academic, thought and action are presumptively immune from inquisition by political authority." (345 U.S. at 266.) Yet if the wound which he has inflicted on the "preferred position" doctrine is not so deep as a well, nor so wide as a church door, it is enough, and will serve.

By 1950, then, the "preferred position" doctrine, so hopefully submitted as an acceptable substitute for the rejected "clear and present danger" principle, was all but bankrupt. That year the most revered figure in American law decisively repudiated "clear and present danger" and, by implication, the preferred position as well. Sustaining the conviction of twelve Communists under the Smith Act (*Dennis v. U.S.*, 183 Fed. 2nd at 212), Judge Learned Hand formulated what we may call the "discount" formula as a substitute for the Holmesian doctrine, and this the Supreme Court hastened to embrace. "In each case we must ask whether the gravity of the 'evil' discounted by its improbability, justifies such invasion of free speech as is necessary to avoid the danger." It was, said Chief Justice Vinson, "as succinct and inclusive as any other [principle] we might devise at this time." (341 U.S. 494 at 510.) And Justice Frankfurter, concurring, took time out to preside somewhat elaborately over the obsequies of "clear and present danger" and briefly to foreshadow that balance of interest doctrine which he later perfected: "On the one hand is the interest in security. . . . On the other hand is the interest in free speech." (341 U.S. at 546 and 548.)

We need not inquire too importunately what had happened between *Palko v. Connecticut* and *Dennis v. United States* to discredit that aggregation of formulae—clear and present danger, Carolene Products, preferred position, and so forth. What had happened was the War. What had happened was the world-wide threat of Communist subversion. What had happened was, more practically, the Smith Act of 1940 and the Internal Security Act of 1950. But deeper than these was the progressive disillusionment with the capacity of the courts to save democracy from its follies or its self-indulgence, a disillusionment whose philosophical origins might be traced to considerations and sentiments not wholly consistent. One was a deep respect for the democratic processes and for the therapeutic value of mistakes. Another was an almost mystical feeling that for the judiciary to stand aloof from the emotions and passions of mankind was almost an indulgence in spiritual vanity, that in a democracy the judiciary must share, at least vicariously, in democracy's guilt. This view reflected, perhaps it derived from, Justice Holmes's admonition that "as life is action and passion, it is required of a man that he should share the passion and action of his time at the peril of being judged not to have lived" (Memorial Day Address, 30 May 1884, in Lerner, ed. *Mind and Faith of Justice Holmes*, 10), and more deeply, his warning that "no man can set himself over against the universe as a rival god, to criticize it or to shake his fist at the skies, but that his meaning is its meaning, his only worth is as a part of it, as a humble instrument of universal power." (*Ibid.* p.37.)

For "universe" read "democracy" and we are not far from Judge Learned Hand's rejection of those "stately admonitions" with which the Court consoles itself; for

> thrown large upon the screen of the future as eternal verities, they are emptied of the vital occasions, which gave them birth, and become moral adjurations, the more imperious because inscrutable, but with only that content which each generation must pour into them anew in the light of its own experience. If an independent judiciary seeks to fill them from its own bosom, in the end it will cease to be independent. And its independence will be well lost, for that bosom is not ample enough for the hopes and fears of all sorts and conditions of men, nor will its answers be theirs; it must be content to stand aside from these fateful battles.

4

In the decade of the fifties, then, what may be loosely and inadequately called the "balance of interest" doctrine replaced the "preferred position" doctrine in adjudications involving rights claimed under the First and Fourteenth Amendments. In one way or another, to be sure, the Court had been engaged in balancing interests from the beginning of its history—the interests of state and nation, for example, in the interpretation of the commerce clause, or of military and civilian claims in time of war, or of "fundamental" and "formal" rights in the "Insular" cases at the turn of the century, or of police power and due process in hundreds of state regulations. Perhaps all we can say of the process of balancing in recent civil liberties cases is that it has been applied here somewhat more confidently to substances that had heretofore appeared to have moral rather than natural weight, and therefore to elude traditional measurements and frustrate familiar balancing techniques.[6]

The most succinct statement of the principle comes from Justice Harlan in the Barenblatt case:

> When First Amendment rights are asserted to bar governmental interrogation, resolution of the issues always involves a balancing by the courts of the competing private

and public interests at stake in the particular circumstances shown. These principles were recognized in the Watkins case where, in speaking of the First Amendment in relation to Congressional inquiries, we said, "It is manifest that despite the adverse effects which follow upon disclosure of private matters, not all such inquiries are barred. . . . The critical element is the existence of and the weight to be ascribed to the interest of the Congress in demanding disclosures from an unwilling witness. . . . In the last analysis this power [to compel disclosure] rests on the right of self-preservation. (354 U.S. at 198 and 360 U.S. at 126.)

But it is two cases which came up from the courts of New Hampshire that—like the two flag salute cases some twenty years back[7]—most dramatically present the problems that cluster around the balancing process like steel filings that form lines of force around a magnet. Both are monuments to the tireless zeal of New Hampshire's Baron Jeffreys, that Louis Wyman who doubles as a one-man investigating committee and as prosecutor of those he investigates.[8]

Although these two New Hampshire cases have a superficial resemblance to the two flag salute cases of the early forties, both in the general nature of the issues presented and in the quick reversal of the judicial position on what appear to the layman to be the same legal issues, for our purposes of weighing the claims of majorities the differences are more suggestive than the similarities. First the requirement of a flag salute represented, in West Virginia certainly, the will of the legislative body (in the Gobitis case it represented merely the will of the local school district board), while the citation for contempt against Professor Paul Sweezy and the Reverend Willard Uphaus was the personal decision of Mr. Louis Wyman who in his capacity of one-man investigator of un-American activities recommended contempt action to himself in his capacity as Attorney General. Whatever the nature of the legal authority here—and of course it is valid—it is difficult to assert with a straight face that these actions come to us with all the moral authority of a majority mandate. Second, where the requirement of a flag salute would not interfere directly with those political processes which might be trusted to form newer and wiser majorities, the challenge to academic freedom and to unterrified participation in legally-recognized political parties explicit in the Sweezy case, and to the right of privacy, the right of association, the right of interstate travel, and the rights of free speech implicit in the Uphaus case, clearly does threaten to clog or corrupt the processes of political appeal.

In both the New Hampshire cases the Attorney General—and those who sustained him—balanced the interest of the state in self-preservation against the lesser interests of defendants in their alleged rights; both arguments, too, followed the familiar House-that-Jack-built logic. In the first it was this: the state has a paramount interest in self-preservation; this interest requires the discovery and exposure of all subversive persons and organizations within the state; such discovery calls for an investigation of the now defunct Progressive party and those who were associated with it because it might be ascertained that this party was subversive; this in turn justifies an inquiry into the political activities and affiliations of professors who lecture at the State University, and this justifies an inquiry into the character of the lectures themselves!

The Chief Justice, in striking down the New Hampshire verdict which sustained this remarkable train of logic, did not find it essential to balance the interests that were here conjured up, but his brother Frankfurter, concurring, did after a careful exercise in balancing. Justice Frankfurter concluded that

> for a citizen to be made to forego even a part of so basic a liberty as his political autonomy, the subordinating interest of the State must be compelling. Inquiry pursued in safeguarding a State's security against threatened force and violence cannot be shut off by mere disclaimer, though of course a relevant claim may be made to the privilege against self-incrimination. But the inviolability of privacy belonging to a citizen's political loyalties has so overwhelming an importance to the well-being of our kind of society, that it cannot be constitutionally encroached upon on the basis of so meagre a countervailing interest of the State as may be argumentatively found in the remote shadowy threat to the security of New Hampshire allegedly presented in the origins and contributing elements of the Progressive Party and in petitioner's relations to these. (354 U.S. at 265.)

But Mr. Justice Clark, to whose enraptured ears every *cri de coeur* of officialdom had at that time the irresistible lure of the songs of the maidens of Lorelei, dissented. "We have no right" he said,

> to strike down the state action unless we find not only that there has been a deprivation of Sweezy's constitutional rights, but that the interest in protecting those rights is greater than the State's interest in uncovering subversive activities within its confines. (354 U.S. at 269.)

In the second of these cases a bare majority of the Court held that the interest of New Hampshire in preserving itself against subversion overbalanced the interest of Mr. Uphaus and his associates in refusing to make available membership lists and correspondence relating to a World Fellowship summer encampment five years earlier. If at first glance the relationship between the two is not apparent, we should recall Mr. Dooley's observation that what looks like a stone wall to a layman is a triumphal arch to a corporation lawyer; what looks like a harmless activity by a kindly and benevolent clergyman can easily be transformed into a monstrous and incendiary conspiracy by an Attorney General bent on ends that have only the remotest connection with justice. Once again the Attorney General submitted a House-that-Jack-built argument; once again Mr. Justice Clark agreed with him, and this time had the happiness to speak for a majority in preserving the foundations of the Granite State from the erosions of clerical correspondence.

> What was the interest of the State? The Attorney General was commissioned to determine if there were any subversive persons within New Hampshire. The obvious starting point of such an inquiry was to learn what persons were within the State. . . . The Attorney General had valid reason to believe that the speakers and guests at World Fellowship might be subversive persons within the meaning of the New Hampshire Act. . . . The Attorney General sought to learn if subversive persons were in the State because of the legislative determination that such persons, statutorily defined with a view toward the Communist party, posed a serious threat to the security of the State. The investigation was therefore undertaken in the interest of self-preservation. (360 U.S. at 78, 79.)

These opinions, together with the opinion of the Court in the contemporary Barenblatt case (360 U.S. at 109), reveal the inadequacy of the balance of interest doctrine as a formula for resolving the conflict of majority rule and minority right. Indeed, from this vantage point the most conspicuous feature of the constitutional landscape is the fog that has settled upon it.

The most ostentatious of the inadequacies of the "balance of interest" formula may readily be seen. In the first place, the balance of interest as submitted by the Court and, almost inevitably, as accepted by the public, is not a true balance. It is a loaded one. On the one scale is, visibly, the prodigious, even the absolute interest of the state in self-preservation, "the ultimate value" as the Court says, "of any society." On the other scale is, presumptively, the claim of an individual right—a poor and selfish thing at best, peculiarly odious in the circumstances of our time, and in these particular cases: the right to be self-indulgent, to be private, to be eccentric, to be churlish, to deny the state information that the state asserts it desperately needs, to indulge in dubious political activity, to associate with publicans and sinners, to agitate dangerous ideas, to travel where travel is prohibited, to speak of things best left in the limbo of silence, to violate the rules of the game fixed by society, to make trouble for the rest of us in a thousand ways. Who are these men who, in the words of Holmes, set themselves up against the universe—or even against society—as rival gods, and shake their fists at the skies? What folly to indulge in sympathy here for the claims of privacy or of individual rights!

Clearly, this is not a true picture of the "balance of interest" as Justice Black pointed out in his dissenting opinion in the Barenblatt case, this kind of presentation

> mistakes the factors to be weighed. In the first place it completely leaves out the real interest in Barenblatt's silence, the interest of the people as a whole in being able to join organizations, advocate causes and make political mistakes without later being subjected to governmental penalties for having dared to think for themselves. . . . The obloquy which results from investigations such as this not only stifles "mistakes" but prevents all but the most courageous from hazarding any views which might

at some later time become disfavored. . . . It is these interests of society, rather than Barenblatt's own right to silence, which I think the Court should put on the balance against the demands of the Government, if any balancing process is to be tolerated. Instead they are not mentioned, while on the other side the demands of the Government are vastly overstated and called "self-preservation." . . . Such a result reduces "balancing" to a mere play on words. (360 U.S. at 144.)

It does indeed. For if we examine more closely the claims of the parties in these disputes—not those of the state and the individual, but those of the state and society—we see a very different set of interests and strike a very different balance.

What then is the real interest here—in the Uphaus, the Barenblatt, and in the Nelson and the Perez cases as well? It is of course the interest of our whole society, future as well as present, in the exercise of those fundamental rights traditionally, and correctly, thought essential to the preservation of our security and our happiness: the right of assembly, the right to join voluntary organizations, the right to worship—or not to worship—as we wish, the right of speech and publication, the right of the mind to roam where it will and to make known its discoveries, all of those miscellaneous rights that go to make up the fabric of our free society. This is what should be balanced against the claims of the state.

It is no more valid to balance the rights of an individual, as if it were merely that, against the interests of the state, than it would be to balance the interest of a criminal in due process with the vast interest of the community in maintaining order, and thus justify the flouting of due process or the use of torture. If we weaken procedural safeguards in the realm of public inquiry, of access to employment, of academic freedom—in those areas that can be denominated political or administrative rather than legal—we are in danger of weakening them everywhere. This has already brought a more amiable view of what Justice Holmes called the "dirty business" of wire-tapping, or an easy-going attitude toward search and seizure, or ready acquiescence in a double standard for orthodox Brahmins and Communist untouchables in a wide range of "loyalty" and "security" investigations. But the same considerations obtain in the realm of civil liberties as in the realm of procedural rights: every Uphaus, every Barenblatt, every Dorothy Bailey, every Thomas Nelson (*Nelson v. County of Los Angeles, 80 S. Ct. 527*) represents society's interest in the preservation of freedom, not as an absolute but as the quintessential condition of survival.

There is a second consideration, familiar enough, yet not always given the weight it deserves. Most of the cases which have come before the Court involving a balance of interest come up from the state courts (there are of course important exceptions). They involve, therefore, in the balance, rights that are attached to or inherent in citizenship in the United States, and in which the *whole* people have—or should have—an ardent interest. James Madison originally hoped that the Bill of Rights would apply to the states as well as to the Congress, and this hope was realized indirectly and tardily through the Fourteenth Amendment. The whole people—not just the people or the government of New Hampshire (*Sweezy* and *Uphaus*), or of Alabama (*NAACP v. Alabama*), or of California (*Nelson v. Los Angeles,* and *Unitarian Church v. Los Angeles*), or of Pennsylvania (*Belian v. Philadelphia*) or of New York (*Lerner v. Casey*)—have a stake in the preservation of those rights guaranteed by the First and Fourteenth Amendments, and have a stake, too, in the preservation of, and extension of, all those rights that may contribute to wisdom in the performance of the duties of United States citizenship. Whether an Uphaus has a right to carry on pacifist propaganda, whether a Lerner has a right not to be dropped arbitrarily from his job on the New York subway, whether a Belian can be dismissed from the school system of Philadelphia, whether the Unitarian Church of Los Angeles is to be deprived of tax exemption on capricious grounds, is no more the exclusive concern of the people of New Hampshire, New York, Pennsylvania, or California than the question of whether Negro children are entitled to go to unsegregated schools or their parents entitled to vote is a matter that concerns only the people of Alabama and Louisiana. Sometimes—the Uphaus case is a melancholy example—this larger interest of the whole people in the rights and freedoms of the individual is overlooked or disparaged, and the narrower and more parochial view obtains. When there arises a question involving state taxation of the instrumentalities of the Federal government, or state regulation of commerce that is interstate in character, the Courts do not permit the state to plead its own interest in self-preservation as against the larger interests protected by the Federal Constitution, and they subject even claims under the broad canopy of the police power to skeptical scrutiny if these appear to challenge Federal laws or rights. But here there appears to be a double standard.

Judicial intervention in these sensitive areas of state activity —especially when one state appears as the champion of an entire section—do sometimes raise a hue and cry of judicial usurpation. It did after *Brown v. Topeka* (1954) struck down segregation in public schools, and again after *Pennsylvania v. Nelson* (1956) barred state competition in the area of national loyalty and security. Over the years, however, the Courts have learned to weather these outbursts of discontent. Even those most eager to have the Courts withdrawn entirely from the political arena or to abdicate earlier powers of judicial review are inclined to agree with the famous observation of Mr. Justice Holmes that though the United States would not come to an end if the Court lost its power to declare an act of Congress void, "I do think the Union would be imperiled if we could not make that declaration as to the laws of the several States." ("Laws and the Courts," quoted in Lerner ed. *The Mind and Faith of Justice Holmes*, 390.)

Nor is it irrelevant to call attention to one provision of the Constitution commonly ignored, but not without comfort to those who are concerned for the preservation of the states against subversive organizations or ideas. The *whole* people have an interest in the survival of every state, and that interest is written into the Constitution itself. The United States, no less, guarantees to every state a republican form of government (Art. IV, sec. 4). While that clause stands in the Constitution it is absurd for New Hampshire to tremble for its survival, or for the survival of its constitutional system. The United States will not permit the Reverend Mr. Uphaus and the World Fellowship to undermine New Hampshire's republican form of government. The position of New Hampshire—and of other states similarly exposed—is not a desperate one, and she need not resort to desperate expedients to assure self-preservation. If states never created a single un-American activities committee, if they never engaged in a single safari for subversives, if they never dismissed a single Lerner from the subway system or jailed a single Uphaus, they could still rest assured that their government would be sustained by the mighty arm of the United States.

We cannot, in short, think of majorities in the insulated chambers of the states. The majority will that we are committed to sustain is the majority will of the American people, not just of a single state or community. It is the whole people that have a paramount interest in the effective functioning of the majoritarian principle.

The "balance of interest" doctrine is too frail to bear the weight that is put upon it by the Court—the weight of preserving fundamental rights that will enable majorities to function with wisdom and with virtue. As formulated, it concedes to the state authority to make decisions that may impair or even destroy the capacity of the majority to rule, for by yielding to easy claims of emergency or to presumptuous claims of self-preservation it permits the states to silence dissidents and thus to discourage or impair those delicate and sensitive processes whereby majorities and minorities reconcile their differences and educate each other.

5

It will not be denied that whatever the advantages of the "preferred position" doctrine—advantages of logic, of history, even of drama—it suffers from one sobering drawback. It asks society to take a chance; it asserts that the dangers that are generally anticipated are in fact neither clear nor present, and that the improbability of the evil which legislation, or administrative action, seeks to cure is so great that its gravity can indeed be discounted. "The balance of interest" doctrine, however, makes no such demands upon the good sense or the moral heroism of society. It does not set up against the majority judgment a counter-judgment of moderation; it does not assert that the Court knows best; without too much beating about judicial bushes, it accepts the argument of necessity.

And a plausible argument it is. For except in the matter of representation, it is rare indeed that our political authorities, state or national, openly and deliberately flout rights guaranteed in the Constitution, or the rights of minorities, if white. And where legislative action does impair such rights, it is almost invariably on the plea of necessity—the necessity of avoiding some grave evil such as subversion or military defeat, the necessity of achieving some transcendent end, such as self-preservation. This plea of necessity is, of course, one of the factors weighed by the Court when it balances interests, and it is not the least weighty.

This is, as will be recognized at once, the argument put so succinctly by President Lincoln at a time when crisis did indeed strain the Constitution. "Are all the laws but one to go unexecuted, and the government itself go to pieces, lest that one be violated?" he asked, in his message of 4 July 1861—that same message where he put the basic question of politics: "Must a government of necessity be too strong for the liberties of its own people, or too weak to maintain its own existence?" All this in extenuation, if not in justification, of acts that went to the very verge of constitutional propriety, if they did not overstep it: suspension of the writ of habeas corpus, establishment of martial law, arrests without warrants and detention without trial, and other acts that seemed equally arbitrary.

That is the way our present-day legislators and administrative officials reason, when they bother to reason, and that is the way counsel for state and national governments put the matter to the Court, though rarely so pithily or with such humility as Lincoln put it to Congress. Whatever is done, they insist, is necessary to the self-preservation of the state,[9] or necessary to the conduct of sound foreign policy,[10] or necessary to the process of ridding government of security risks,[11] or necessary to detecting traitors[12] and exposing conspiracies and preventing the spread of dangerous teachings,[13] or necessary to encouraging those sentiments of patriotism and of loyalty essential in time of crisis.[14]

Who are we, say the Judges, in effect, to challenge a legislative finding that communism is a world-wide conspiracy dedicated to the overthrow of democratic government everywhere? Who are we to challenge the finding that the Communist party is not an ordinary political party, but an integral part of the Communist conspiracy? Who are we to challenge the conclusion that the danger from Communist agitation if not always clear and present, is grave and not wholly improbable? Who are we, even, to challenge the argument that the safety of New York City may hinge on the employment of Mr. Lerner as a subway guard, that the very existence of New Hampshire may depend on access to the Reverend Mr. Uphaus's correspondence, that the successful conduct of foreign policy may be imperiled because Clemente Perez voted secretly in a Mexican election, that the nation itself is in danger if John Zydoc is allowed out on bail a single day before trial for deportation—poor Zydoc who had lived thirty-nine years in America, sold $50,000 worth of war bonds, contributed blood to the Red Cross seven times, and boasted two sons in army uniform, and who had not "violated any law or engaged in . . . any subversive activities" (342 U.S. 524)?

Who indeed?

6

It is asking too much to ask the Courts to investigate the validity of each legislative claim of the necessity for self-preservation; that, after all, is a realm where the political branches are presumed to know best. So said Justice Holmes in a famous opinion on martial law: "The plaintiff's position is that he has been deprived of liberty without due process of law. But it is familiar that what is due process of law depends on circumstances. It varies with the subject matter and the necessities of the situation." (*Moyer v. Peabody*, 212 U.S. 78, 1909.) And if other martial law decisions—*Sterling v. Constantin* (287 U.S. 378) and the local but not unimportant *Hearon v. Calus* (178 South Carolina 381) —suggest that this generalization might be a bit too generous, the judicial acquiescence to Japanese relocation (*Hirabayashi v. U.S.*, 320 U.S. 81, and *Korematsu v. U.S.*, 323 U.S. 214) reasserted and dramatized the Court's reluctance to challenge the political or the military claim of necessity in time of war.

Nor is this cause for surprise. It is not only that, as Justice Hughes observed, "we have a fighting Constitution," but that, as Professor Rossiter has somewhat sardonically remarked, "the

Court likes to win wars, too." The difficulty goes even deeper. The Court learned by hard experience the folly of trying to go behind the arguments in legislative decisions on rate-making, labor relations, the regulation of commerce, and those broad areas of public policy where expert knowledge is essential. Why then should it attempt to do so in more vital areas; why should it venture onto those historic battlefields where contending forces fight out the great issues of national survival?

Yet neither of these antecedents or analogies—those drawn from the realm of war, or those drawn from the history of the exercise of the police power in highly technical areas of the economy—are entirely valid for the arenas of civil liberties. The analogy from wartime emergency is not wholly valid because it equates "crisis" with war, and thereby ratifies limitations on freedom during "crisis" as well as during war. But "war" is a recognized legal term, as it is a fact; whereas "crisis" belongs to that long and growing category of words almost drained of meaning: un-American, loyalty, subversive, security risk, sympathetically-affiliated-with, and so forth. The differences are more than semantic. The immediate and imperative task, in time of war, is victory; the most pressing task, in time of crisis, is the avoidance of war— in our own time the avoidance of a war that in the nature of things cannot assure victory to any of the participants. The necessities of military victory doubtless put a premium on action uninhibited by legal restraints; the necessities of crisis or of cold war (to use that now popular term), put a premium above all on those qualities that flourish best in an atmosphere of constitutionally protected freedom. The argument used to justify, let us say, Japanese relocation in time of war—that the danger seemed great and that "the government was not constitutionally bound to be proved right in its estimates of these dangers, it was only bound to have a reasonable basis for taking the action which it did at the time at which it took it" (Cushman, "Some Constitutional Problems of Civil Liberty" Bacon lecture, 2 April 1943), is not valid for, let us say, the jailing of an Uphaus, the dismissal of a Dorothy Bailey, the persecution of a Lattimore, the deportation of a John Zydoc, the harassment of newspapers, of scientists and scholars; for these acts are not dictated by any pressing emergency, and the consequences of these acts cannot but impair the capacity of the nation to work out solutions to the great public problems on which survival itself may depend.

Nor is the analogy with regulatory or police legislation involving a high degree of expertise a valid one. For in almost every instance of this kind, what confronts the Court is not an unsupported expression of legislative will on matters of public utility regulation, commerce, communications, or labor relations, but legislation filtered through impartial commissions whose business it is to evaluate the facts, whose work is presumed to be objective, and who are, in any event, required to observe due process in all their investigations and findings. To put the matter briefly, a decision of a legislative body, or more commonly of a public utility commission, in these areas not only involves far less consequential issues than decisions about rights of speech or press or association, but comes to the Courts with credentials of fact more substantial, and credentials of necessity more respectable, than those which customarily support the work of, let us say, state or Federal un-American activities committees. If the Court is content to accept the findings of fact that support most utility or police regulations, and if society is content that it should do so, that is because legislatures and administrative commissions have learned, over the years, to base their decisions on factual evidence. And it is, too, because (we return here to the Carolene Products Company principle) in these realms mistakes, no matter how serious, can be more easily remedied by the ordinary political processes.

But in the delicate, the sensitive, the vulnerable, the vastly more vital realms of freedom—in those realms where not just time or money but democracy itself may be lost—there are no expert or impartial commissions to guide legislatures or to make independent decisions. The findings which Courts feel obliged to accept about the crisis of self-preservation against the machinations of an Uphaus in New Hampshire, about the imminent danger of allowing a Zydoc to be free on bail, about the irreparable damage to the conduct of foreign policy if Paul Robeson is granted a passport—these are not precisely of the same character as those which come to it from independent regulatory commissions. It is sufficient, perhaps, if we contrast the investigations conducted by, let us say, the Tenney Committee in California, or the Broyles Committee in Illinois, or the one-man Wyman Committee in New Hampshire with the kind of investigations conducted by the Public Utility Commissions of those states. If telephone and electric rates were determined with the same insouciant disregard for evidence, and for due process, that characterizes the work of these and other un-American activities committees, conservatives everywhere would be up in arms. Unless Courts are prepared to apply the same standards to rulings affecting freedom that they apply to rulings affecting public utilities or communications, the task of assuring fair play for freedom may go by default.

What a commentary it is on our society that not only are the Courts without guidance of impartial legislative or committee findings in the realm of civil liberties; almost without guidance, even from scholars. The history of commerce has been more elaborately explored than the history of freedom; the data on public utility rate-making is mountainous—nay Himalayan—when compared with the little mounds of materials on the regulations governing liberty thrown up by the spadework of historians. Few historical, or legal, enterprises could be more rewarding than that of surveying and charting the history of freedom in America with a view to illuminating the validity of the claim of necessity so regularly submitted as justification for oppression and suppression.[15]

7

In a broad way we can distinguish eight chapters in the history of the denial of minority rights and the limitations on freedom that would repay careful investigation: I arrange these chronologically, rather than topically:

First is that associated with the enactment of the Alien, Sedition, and Alien Enemies Acts of 1798, against which those two champions of freedom, Madison and Jefferson, protested so eloquently in the Virginia and Kentucky Resolutions.

Second is that associated with the comprehensive and headstrong campaign of the slavocracy to assure support to the "peculiar institution" by stopping inquiry, silencing discussion, intimidating criticism, and punishing dissidence.

Third is that which was a product—and a byproduct—of the Civil War, particularly in the North: the impairmen of constitutionally guaranteed rights that the Union government and the military countenanced in their zeal to put down the rebellion.

Fourth is that which accompanied Reconstruction—what Harold Hyman calls the Era of the Oath: the radical program of the North which threatened the executive power and turned Southern states into military satrapies; and the Ku Klux Klan and other instruments and devices whereby the South sought to frustrate radical Reconstruction.

Fifth is that which embraces the Sedition and Espionage Acts of the First World War; the crusade against "hyphenated Americans," against German language, music, and cooking; and the quasi-official campaigns of self-constituted "patriotic" organizations like the American Protective League. Closely related to this is:

Sixth, that which grew out of the fears and oppressions of the war and took the form of a "Red scare" and the Palmer raids, and was speedily metamorphosed into a crusade against pacifism, liberalism, socialism, and almost any other "ism."

Seventh is that associated with the events leading up to the Second World War, and with the war itself: the Dies Committee and its shabby successors, the Smith Act, Japanese relocation, and other manifestations of governmental and private determination to take no chances on even the shadow of subversion or disloyalty in any form.

The eighth is one with which this generation is familiar, and which is indeed still with us: a fear of Communist subversion whose various manifestations embrace the vast loyalty-security program, the McCarran Act of 1950, the Communist Control Act of 1954, the activities of Federal, state, and local un-American activities committees, and that complex of public and private misconduct which goes by the name of McCarthyism.[16]

All of these chapters of our history should be investigated with a view to discovering whether those dangers which we conjured up as justification for suspending the exercise of freedom did exist, or whether they were the creatures of panic and of fear, or of extraneous economic or political purposes. We should try to find out whether methods formally adopted (as the Alien and Sedition Acts or Japanese relocation), or the pressures informally applied (as in the ante-bellum South or during the period of McCarthyism), had any valid relation to the alleged dangers, and we shall attempt to ascertain what have been the costs and the consequences of these exercises in suppression—the costs in tangibles that can, perhaps, be computed (e.g. the costs of investigations, or security clearances, of the loss of talent in civil service or in science) and the consequences in those intangibles that defy computation.

It would be most uncritical to anticipate the findings of historical scholars in all of these areas, but perhaps I may be permitted to indulge in a generalization based on such investigations as have been made by those scholars who have worked in this field. It is this: that in only two of these eight chapters of our history is there any persuasive evidence that there were in fact disloyal or subversive activities that imperiled government, or dissident or critical views that threatened the integrity of the social order. One of these is the Civil War: secession and war and the danger of losing the Border States, plots and conspiracies, the Copperheads and the Knights of the Golden Circle, draft riots and sabotage—all of these were realities, not figments of imagination or the projections of neurotic fears and hatreds. Lincoln, who had no instinct either for dictatorship or for oppression, seems to have been justified in suspending the writ of habeas corpus and probably even in his (still somewhat obscure) program of arbitrary arrests. Even at that it is worth keeping in mind that Lincoln put down the greatest of rebellions without recourse to Alien or Sedition Acts, or the use of concentration camps, or any general censorship. A second is the attempt of the ante-bellum South to preserve a way of life based on the "peculiar institution." Criticism of slavery was real, too, and doubtless it posed a threat to that institution—as enlightenment and the free mind inevitably threaten oppression and slavery. If, as slaveholders contended, slavery was a blessing, then Southerners were not without some justification in burning books, censoring the mails, driving editors from their offices, clergymen from their pulpits, and professors from their academic chairs for the crime of agitating a question which had been settled on moral grounds once and for all. As Justice Holmes was later to say in the Abrams dissent:

> If you have no doubt of your premises, or your power, and want a certain result with all your heart you naturally express your wishes in law and sweep away all opposition. . . . To allow opposition by speech seems to indicate that you think the speech impotent . . . or that you do not care wholeheartedly for the result or that you doubt either your power or your premises.

The Old South suspected that speech was not impotent, and did not doubt its premises or its power. But if slavery was not in fact a blessing but a curse on white and black, on North as on South, and if there was even the slightest chance that the dread issue might have been settled peaceably by keeping open the channels of discussion and criticism and the consideration of viable alternatives, instead of by recourse to the awful arbitration of war, then the policy of the Old South in silencing criticism and putting down dissent was one of criminal folly.

These two chapters, one a Civil War unlikely to recur, the other an attempt to preserve the anachronistic institution of slavery which ended in catastrophe, do not afford much comfort to those who raise the banner of necessity every time they want to silence criticism or strike at some alleged danger by riding roughshod over constitutional guarantees.

But these dramatic chapters in the history of freedom by no means exhaust the subject, or answer the questions that we now raise about abuse of power by majorities. Broad surveys may make bad history. Even more illuminating, and perhaps more convincing, would be a careful inquiry into the scores and indeed hundreds of particular cases involving the infringement of constitutional rights on the plea of necessity. Such an investigation into particulars has one signal advantage over the larger inquiry into general history, that it can address itself more circumspectly to what happened rather than broadly to what might have happened. For it may, of course, always be alleged that we cannot in the nature of things know what would have happened in the past had it not been for restrictive or punitive legislation. Congressman Matthew Lyon might have overthrown the John Adams adminis-

tration had he not been jugged for four months. It is improbable—
and Congress later made amends by refunding his fine—but perhaps this bold action by government prevented more dangerous
criticism from other editors! Jacob Abrams, and others, might
have slowed up arms production, and thus crippled our conduct of
the war with Russia, had he not been sentenced to twenty years in
jail as a fit punishment for distributing his pitiful leaflets. Secretary Acheson—and after him Secretary Dulles—might have filled
the State Department and the foreign service with subversives had
it not been for the sleepless vigilance of Senator McCarthy. It all
seems pretty improbable now, just as the fears conjured up
throughout our history look improbable in the perspective of time:
the fear of the consequences of manhood suffrage in New York in
1821; the fear of the "rebel" Thomas Dorr in Rhode Island
in 1842; the fear that the income tax law of 1895 would usher in
communism, that woman suffrage would destroy the purity of
womanhood and the sanctity of the home, that social security
legislation would sap the moral fiber of the American people. An
assiduous student could perhaps ransack the past to discover some
danger whose materialization was a bit more probable.

In a host of recent—and not so recent—episodes that have
come before the Courts we do have something like true laboratory
tests. For there are numerous instances where governments have
confidently asserted that the silencing of criticism, or the punishment of dissenters was essential to self-preservation. But in some
cases defendants preferred prison to cooperation, and thus criticism persisted, or dangerous activities continued. In other cases
the Courts did not agree with the arguments advanced by the
government, and thus again governments were denied their way,
and exposed to all the dangers that were conjured up. Did the
dangers materialize?

In 1925 Benjamin Gitlow was sent to jail for distributing a
Left Wing Manifesto; Justice Sanford held that it was the "language of direct incitement," and that "a single revolutionary spark
may kindle a fire that, smoldering for a time, may burst into a
sweeping and destructive conflagration." That particular fire has
been smoldering for a long time now; did it in fact burst into a
conflagration, or do we instead quote Judge Cardozo's comment

that "historians may find hyperbole in the sanguinary simile." Rosika Schwimmer and Professor MacIntosh were denied citizenship on the ground that their pacifism made them undesirable citizens, and not to be trusted to protect and defend the United States; those decisions were reversed in the Girouard case (328 U.S. 61, 1946); did Girouard or any other pacifists in fact prove dangerous members of the body politic? It was alleged by government counsel that book after book, from *Ulysses* to *Lady Chatterley*, would corrupt the minds of those who read them and lead to criminal conduct; the books have circulated now for many years; is there any instance of corruption or of incitement to criminal conduct? The government of New Hampshire alleged that without access to the papers of the Reverend Mr. Uphaus its very survival was imperiled, and the Court agreed. The papers have not been forthcoming. Has New Hampshire survived? The State Department asserted that to grant passports to dangerous men like Paul Robeson or Roger Kent would gravely embarrass the conduct of foreign policy. They received passports—as did many others in the same category; what embarrassments has our State Department experienced? Again and again Congressional committees have alleged that without information wrung from reluctant witnesses it would be impossible for Congress to legislate on matters of subversion. In many instances witnesses have preferred to go to jail rather than to give the information; has Congress in fact been unable to legislate in this area? Alabama asserted that without access to the membership lists of the NAACP it would experience "irreparable injury to the property and civil rights of citizens of the State." Alabama was denied access to those lists; have the injuries in fact been irreparable, have there, indeed, been any injuries at all?

Attorney General Brownell asserted, after the Jenckes decision (353 U.S. 657, 1957) that that decision, requiring the government to make available FBI and other secret testimony in criminal prosecutions where such reports were the subject of oral testimony, "created a grave emergency in law enforcement, an emergency so grave it is necessary to have new legislation." The new legislation was forthcoming, but it sustained the Court, not the government, and it is relevant to ask whether the emergency really proved to be both grave and continuing. When in *Cole v. Young* the Court refused to sanction the dismissal of a Federal meat inspector on the ground that he was a security risk, Representative Walters of the House Un-American Activities Committee asserted that the decision had the effect of opening the government "to the infiltration of our mortal enemies." That was almost five years ago; have the mortal enemies infiltrated? When in the case of *Pennsylvania v. Nelson* the Court struck down state sedition statutes on the ground that the United States had pre-empted the field, thirty-five state attorney generals declared that the decision was "dangerous to public safety" and that it "left the states impotent to regulate acts of sedition or subversion occurring within state borders." That, too, was five years ago; have the states in fact been exposed to sedition and subversion because thus naked to their enemies?

Surely it is superfluous to cite further examples, for it is the historical method rather than the particular case that is relevant to our inquiry. Clearly what is needed is an investigation of every important instance where government conjured up dire consequences as the inevitable result of the exercise of particular freedoms in time of alleged emergency, in order to determine whether those consequences did prove dire. If it should be discovered (as I very much suspect it would be) that the malign consequences of freedom are invariably exaggerated, that would not decide the legal question of the right of majorities to act, even to act foolishly. But it would justify the Court in regarding with a good deal of scepticism the insistent arguments of calamity and catastrophe, and even in asking for evidence that the alleged dangers have some existence outside the world of imagination, and of politics. And it would throw some light on the claims which majoritarians make for the authority which sanctifies their conduct, and on the intellectual and moral respect we must accord to those claims.

8

This brings us to a second major inquiry which should be concluded before we accept too uncritically the credentials of majorities in state and national politics—an investigation of the claims and the facts of majorities in the legislatures of American states.

I do not propose here to embark upon the familiar, even the hackneyed, arguments against what passes for the majority:

That the concept itself is too vague and too elusive to be useful: we never in fact know whether we are concerned with a majority of voters, of potential voters, or of the entire population.

That ours is not, and is not designed to be, a majoritarian system, but rather one cunningly contrived to balance numerical against sectional and other interests: thus federalism itself in all of its manifestations; thus the equal representation of states in the Senate; thus the complicated method of electing a President; thus the separation of powers, and the complex system of appeals from legislative to executive and from executive to judicial branches.

That in our system (unlike the parliamentary) majorities cannot and do not hold any clear mandate for specific policies, and therefore do not speak with the authority of true majorities on specific issues. That our elections do not present clear-cut alternatives, but may be variously interpreted or misinterpreted by the political branches. That our representatives and executives have in any event the right—and may even have the duty—to go counter to the majority will whenever their judgment dictates such action.

That there are immense differences in the intensity of desire or will of majorities which are not subject to ordinary political rules; that, let us say, the desire of a majority of Louisiana whites for some ostentatious manifestations of their superiority does not come to us with the same moral claims as does the desire of a minority of Negroes for the right to vote or the right to an education. That there are qualitative differences in the subject-matter of majority will; thus, a majority vote for sheriff, even for a very bad sheriff, does not raise the same philosophical questions as a majority vote to do away with the Bill of Rights.

All of these objections have some substance. But the danger of this kind of attack upon the majority principle is that it proves too much; we end up by rejecting the principle altogether and settling for minority government instead, because it is simpler and presumably easier to manage. But there is no evidence that minorities are in fact either more just or more efficient than majorities, and a good deal of evidence that they are not.

There is, however, one valid consideration relevant to the central purpose of our inquiry—to determine what degree of authority, or of sanctity, we should assign to decisions that come to us from legislative or administrative bodies claiming to represent majority will. This consideration goes to the very heart of the matter: the numerical basis of current majority claims. It does not challenge the majority principle, but it does question the illogical, impudent, and even illegal claims made under cover of that principle.

It insists first on the elementary fact that most state legislatures do not represent majorities at all. I refer not to the fact that in some states a substantial proportion of the population does not vote; that is their fault, and their right. I refer rather to the fact that in many Southern states large numbers of citizens constitutionally entitled to vote are prevented from doing so by illegal means—by violence, intimidation, economic pressures, quackery and knavery in the administration of voting laws.[17]

It submits the glaring fact that in most states representation is not based upon population at all. Almost everywhere in the United States the rural population is heavily over-represented and the urban population scandalously under-represented. As recently as 1955 in twenty-six state legislatures less than 40 per cent of the population elected a majority of both Houses. Thirty-two states had legislatures in which one House represented only one-third of the population; in twelve states a majority of one house represented less than one-fifth the total population.

Some American states indeed flaunt a misrepresentation which would have shocked thick-skinned defenders of the unreformed House of Commons of the eighteenth century, and deeply embarrassed those earlier Americans who thought they suffered from taxation without representation. Thus Alabama provides by Constitution for one Senator from each county; Birmingham which has almost 20 per cent of the state's population has 3 per cent of the representation in the Senate and not quite 7 per cent in the House, and one-third of the population controls a majority in both Houses. Thus Georgia is equally notorious for its disregard of the majority principle: here no county may have more than one member in the Senate or six votes in the House: thus one vote in sparsely settled Chattahoochee County equals 114 votes in Fulton County. Nor is this situation confined to the South. In New

Hampshire, which has distinguished itself as a Yankee rival of Georgia and Alabama in the abuse of majority will, representation in the Senate is based on direct taxes actually paid, and 37 per cent of the people control a majority of the House; the ratio between the largest and the smallest district is 136 to 1, and the last reapportionment was in 1915. In Connecticut less than 10 per cent of the people elect a majority in the lower House; in California it is 12 per cent; in Rhode Island 14 and in Florida 18 per cent.

Many of these incongruities are written into state constitutions, but elsewhere they flourish in open defiance of the constitutional mandate. The constitutions of Alabama, Tennessee, Kentucky, Louisiana, and Mississippi all require reapportionment every ten years; the last reapportionment was 1901 in Alabama, 1901 in Tennessee, 1921 in Louisiana and 1916 in Mississippi. And just to prove that the South has no monopoly on constitution-flouting, Indiana, where the American Legion wages ceaseless war on all un-American activities, provides by constitution for reapportionment every ten years, but indulged in that enterprise for the last time in 1921.

Under majoritarian theory, then, we are not obliged to accept every claim put forward under color of majority right, for the claims are sometimes counterfeit. For practical purposes we must accept what the states provide in the way of representation until we can change it, and certainly we cannot go behind the returns on each piece of legislation to determine the nature of the majority that enacted it: just so, Justice Marshall ruled a century and a half ago that the Courts could not look into charges of bad motives or bad faith on the part of legislative majorities (*Fletcher v. Peck*, 6 Cranch 87). No political contrivances can achieve either mechanical or mathematical perfection, and for practical purposes of getting on with the job of government we must settle for such working arrangements as we have developed over the years. But this is very different from saying that these working arrangements, some of them merely awkward, some defective, some palpably unconstitutional, can so impose upon our credulity that we are stopped from challenging their morality.

If the American people really believe in majority rule they

can have it, for as Justice Frankfurter said in *Colgrove v. Green,* "the Constitution of the United States gives ample power to provide against the evils" of unfair or illegal apportionment (328 U.S. at 554). If the Congress is not prepared to enforce the guaranty clause of the Constitution, or even section two of the Fourteenth Amendment (enjoining a reduction in Congressional representation proportionate to the denial of the vote on any ground except crime), it is asking a great deal to expect the Courts to impose democracy and justice on states indifferent to both. "The Constitution," wrote Justice Frankfurter, "has left the performance of many duties in our governmental scheme to depend on the fidelity of the executive and legislative action, and ultimately on the vigilance of the people in exercising their political rights." (*Ibid* at 556.)

9

"The vigilance of the people." In the end everything comes back to that. But vigilance is not automatic, and certainly it cannot be taken for granted. It requires a convulsive effort to persuade even a bare majority of Americans to participate in electing their President once in four years, and in most elections, state and local, less than one-half of those entitled to vote bother to go to the polls. If it is this difficult to excite the people to an interest in the most elementary and dramatic of all democratic activities, how are we to inspire in the people a sense of vigilance for such complex, subtle, and elusive concepts as the nature of freedom and the nature of the majority principle?

The task is fundamentally educational, for it is an assumption basic to our whole culture that given all the facts the American people prefer majority to minority rule, and freedom to tyranny. But just as government cannot be left entirely to formal political institutions, so education cannot be assigned exclusively to formal educational institutions—certainly not education in self-government. Happily in our voluntaristic and pluralistic society both enterprises are carried on by scores and hundreds of organizations and institutions.

What then are the institutions to which we should turn for guidance and help, institutions sufficiently powerful to exercise influence, and sufficiently enlightened to exercise that influence benevolently for the enlargement of freedom and of democracy? What are they, and to what extent may we count on them?

Any list of such institutions would of necessity include the following: the major political parties; labor unions; veterans' and fraternal organizations such as the American Legion or the Masonic Order; business and professional organizations such as the Chamber of Commerce or the American Medical Association; the churches, Protestant, Catholic, and Jewish; the newspaper and periodical press; agencies of communication—radio, television and the films; the varied institutions that contribute so richly to our cultural life—libraries, publishing houses, museums, musical societies, foundations and so forth; education, which embraces schools and universities and research organizations of almost every kind; and finally government itself, but particularly the Law.

We have only to imagine what would happen if, by some convulsion of nature or of politics, all of these, and similar voluntary organizations, ceased to function, and the entire burden of government, at every level, were left to officials. As Tocqueville pointed out well over a century ago, "Wherever at the head of some new undertaking you see the Government in France, or a man of rank in England, in the United States you will be sure to find an association." In the United States voluntary associations have operated, not only to fragment governmental power and diffuse authority, and to provide training in public service and in the democratic process, but as quasi-sovereigns in many realms. Labor unions, bar and medical associations, parent-teachers associations, churches, and scores of other institutions participate actively in the business of government and must be included in any realistic survey of practical democracy.

The record of these institutions in the development, expansion, and vindication of freedom is far from encouraging; it is, indeed, bleak. These great and powerful organizations, so alert to the necessity of self-government, seem at times blind to the necessity of freedom. They are ready enough to participate in politics, but delude themselves that politics concerns only material things, ignoring Aristotle's admonition that "the basis of a democratic state is liberty, which [is] the true end of every democracy."

Let us ask which of these institutions is assuming responsibility for the vindication of freedom in our society today.

Not the great political parties. They compete with each other in ignoring or evading the issue of the preservation of minority rights except where particular minorities are politically powerful. In recent Presidential elections—those of the fifties and the sixties —neither the Republican nor the Democratic party concerned itself with any rights except those of the Negro; those complex questions of the reconciliation of liberty and order with which our Courts have wrestled throughout this decade have not been thought worthy of mention.

Not the labor unions. They are inextricably involved in the problem of freedom, and their own welfare is dependent on the fortunes of freedom. But they are for the most part narrow and parochial in their views, and they did not even rally against so blatant a threat to their own interests as McCarthyism; they have displayed neither interest in nor sympathy for minority groups or minority rights, and they have contributed nothing to the prosperity of the Negro or of Civil Rights.

Not the veterans' and fraternal organizations, who number their members by the tens of millions. The great veterans' organizations who presume to speak with the voice of patriotism are not only indifferent to most of the freedoms guaranteed in the First and Fifth Amendments, but wage ceaseless warfare upon them; while the sprawling fraternal organizations such as the Masonic Order, the Rotary, the Kiwanis, the Knights of Columbus, the Woodsmen of the World, the college fraternities—these and hundreds of others, for all their charities and good works, show not a glimmer of interest in the preservation of minority rights.

Not the substantial representatives of the business and professional community: the Chambers of Commerce, the National Association of Manufacturers, the medical, engineering, and architectural organizations. These are deeply concerned with the preservation of private enterprise, but their concept of private enterprise is narrow and selfish; they have yet to discover that all enterprise begins in the minds and hearts of men, and that there can be no enterprise in business or the professions unless there is freedom to inquire, discuss, criticize, invent, to be different, and to revolt.

Not the churches. With some exceptions—the Unitarian, the Quaker, the Catholic in the South—they have displayed little interest in freedom, and little recognition of the relation between religious and intellectual freedom; not one of the major churches championed the Jehovah's Witnesses in their day of trouble; not one of them appeared as *amicus curiae* in the crucially important cases seeking to deny tax exception to the Unitarian Church of Los Angeles on grounds that struck at the very foundations of religious freedom.

Not, astonishingly enough, the press—the great newspapers and newspaper chains (there are honorable exceptions here—the *New York Times*, the New York *Herald Tribune*, the St. Louis *Post-Dispatch*, the Washington *Post*, the *Milwaukee Journal*, the Louisville *Courier-Journal*, the *Denver Post*), the weeklies and monthlies with circulations into the millions. These all depend for their very existence on the guarantees of the First Amendment but concede its vindication to others. Few of them responded even to the attacks on the freedom of the press implicit in Congressional investigations of editors and reporters, in denial of passports to journalists, or in the policy of official secrecy in high places. Indifferent to the dangers that threaten them, they have been shamefully remiss in their duty to the public to report, analyze, and expound the problems of freedom.

Not the radio, the television, and the films—organizations which should be in the forefront in the battle for freedom; these, as the Fund for the Republic's report on blacklisting made clear, confessed themselves more sensitive to intimidation from pressure groups than any other major institution; more pusillanimous in their eagerness to appease, more craven in their cowardice; they welcomed with alacrity the prison of self-imposed censorship and learned to love the chains that bound them.

Yet somehow we must manage to enlist all of these institutions in the great enterprise of the reconciliation of liberty and order, or that enterprise will fail, and with it some of the noblest hopes of mankind. Yes, how persuade businessmen and labor leaders, churchmen and doctors, Legionnaires and politicians, publishers and those who control the great networks of communication, of what seems so clear and elementary? How make clear to them that if majorities recklessly impede the formation of new and different majorities, democracy will commit suicide? How bring home to them that freedom is not a form of self-indulgence, but the price of survival?

Responsibility for educating all of these groups to their own obligations rests on the Academy and on the Law—the two great institutions that by their very nature are not only dedicated to freedom but pervaded by it.

What then of the complex institutions of scholarship, science, literature and the arts that we call the Academy? Their record is incomparably better than that of the far more powerful, and therefore less vulnerable, institutions of organized business or organized labor. Yet it has not been without its surprises and its disappointments. Even in the universities there was timidity and confusion. There was a readiness—sometimes an embarrassing eagerness—to make themselves unofficial adjuncts of governmental agencies, and to inflict punishment on those whom the law could not reach by firing recalcitrant teachers who refused to testify before legislative committees. There was, and is, a willingness to acquiesce in loyalty oaths for scholars and in loyalty affidavits as the price of student loans, to accept the propriety of legislative investigation of the moral or patriotic credentials of their scholars, to surrender to claims of pressure groups to censor teaching materials and books, to bow to demands of scientific secrecy laid upon them by short-sighted bureaucrats.

And how ineffectual, on the whole, our cultural leaders have been in the vindication of freedom against the claims of necessity brought forward so confidently by state and national governments and even by private filiopietistic organizations. It is too much, perhaps, to ask for a Jefferson in the Presidential chair, a Theodore Parker in the pulpit, a Horace Greeley at the head of our greatest papers, a Wendell Phillips on the platform, a William Lloyd Garrison in the field of race relations, a Thoreau to counsel civil disobedience.

It is to the institutions of learning and science and the arts with their venerable traditions of freedom and their ample arsenals that we must look for the education of the rest of society. Are those institutions capable of providing that education, and are they courageous enough to undertake the task?

We come back, then, to government, and to that department of government concerned with education in freedom: the Courts. Even if the Courts follow those paths of judicial self-restraint marked out for them by Learned Hand and Justice Frankfurter, they are certainly not precluded from playing an active, even a decisive, part in the preservation of liberty. They can do this ultimately not by their power to strike down laws, but by their ability to expound them. It is as an educational institution that the Court may have its greatest contribution to make to the understanding and preservation of liberty.

By great good fortune our Courts took on (for it is too much to say that they were assigned) at the threshold of our history the task of expounding not only laws but the Constitution itself, and not only the Constitution but a universe of political philosophy: the contrast here with British courts and, even more, with Continental ones is instructive. The American Courts were expected to preside over litigation, work out solutions to conflicts of laws, create international law, maintain and umpire a federal system, set the bounds of majority will, and—in the course of fulfilling all of these exacting duties—to educate a swarming and heterogeneous people to an understanding of the most complicated government ever devised by the ingenuity of man. Thanks to the wisdom of the makers of our Constitution, the men assigned these Herculean tasks were protected, if not immunized, from the worst buffetings of politics. And throughout our history our highest Court has been safe from the ultimate pressures and storms of politics, and has attracted men of ability and integrity.

How astonishing was their achievement; without precedent in history, and without parallel. Without a specific mandate, without compelling antecedents, without adequate tools or facilities, with no assurance of support but what came from the weight of their own decisions, they took on, with courage and with dignity, the task of settling great constitutional disputes between states that thought themselves sovereign, reconciling through adjudication prodigious economic and social interests, illuminating profound problems of political philosophy, and educating the people and their chosen leaders to an understanding of the true nature of Law and the Constitution.

With deep wisdom judges adopted at the beginning the habit of the seriatim opinion and clung to it even against the powerful will of John Marshall; with touching faith in the ultimate triumph of reason they wrought their dissenting opinions—opinions unknown to Continental jurisprudence and rare in English—appeals from present to future that were to be of inestimable educational value. With infinite patience they accorded to every case, and to every plaintiff who came before them with a legitimate problem, their most scrupulous attention, their most faithful concern, their ripest wisdom. Over the years they built up, case by case, the most imposing body of constitutional law known to history. If we confine ourselves to secular literature we can say that there is nothing in history to compare with this enterprise. When we contemplate this record and this achievement we can say, with Justice Holmes, that our eyes dazzle.

Sometimes it is said that America has contributed little to formal political philosophy. The charge is true enough, but almost irrelevant, for it is the Court that has supplied much of our political as well as our constitutional philosophy. Sometimes it is said that for a people dedicated to freedom we have contributed but feebly to the literature of freedom: no *Areopagitica*, no Mill *On Liberty*, no Acton, no Croce even. Less true—considering Jefferson—but once again, almost irrelevant, for surely no other people owns a literature on the nature and the daily life of freedom comparable to that which can be read in the United States *Reports* from *Chisholm v. Georgia* to *Uphaus v. Wyman*, or *Baker v. Carr*, some three hundred and eighty volumes of treatises and commentaries, each one a torch of reason lighting the American people down the path of freedom.

Seventy-five years ago James Bryce concluded his magisterial *American Commonwealth* with the observation that "the masses of the people are wiser, fairer, and more temperate in any matter to which they can be induced to bend their minds, than most European philosophers have believed it possible for the masses of the people to be." Have we not ground for hope, as we contemplate our experience with self-government and with freedom, and weigh our intellectual and moral resources, that if the American people can but be induced to "bend their minds" to the great issues of democracy and freedom, they will prove themselves wise, fair, and temperate?

1960

The United States
and the Integration
of Europe

My theme is not so much America *and* the Union of Europe, but America *as* the Union of Europe. For in the perspective of distance and of time perhaps the most remarkable thing about America is precisely this, that it does vindicate in so many ways the promise of the motto first contrived by Benjamin Franklin, John Adams, and Thomas Jefferson: *E Pluribus Unum*. It is many in one; it is all Europe in one. More, it is all mankind in one. The fact is elementary, but its very obviousness sometimes prevents us from appreciating it, for we all tend to be chary of the obvious. It has furnished the theme for a hundred novels, plays, songs, and a thousand learned monographs. Europeans are doubtless most familiar with what might be called their part of the story, with the fact that the Irish in America outnumber the Irish in Ireland, that New York and Chicago are among the largest of Italian cities, Cleveland and Buffalo of Polish, Minneapolis and Omaha of Scandinavian. It is perhaps appropriate to observe that the process of assimilation has embraced non-Europeans as well. We boast a million or more French-Canadians, over a million Mexicans, more than a million Puerto Ricans, hundreds of thousands of Orientals, to say nothing of the sixteen to seventeen million Americans of African origin whose presence confronts Americans with that dilemma so perspicuously explored by a great European, Gunnar Myrdal.

What we have here is a continuous unification of Europe. The "American Farmer," Hector St. John Crèvecoeur, described the process (he called it Americanization) in the third of his *Letters*. The European, he said, when he finds himself an independent farmer, becomes an American almost overnight. He throws off his Old World allegiance, and with this he throws off, too, his Old World habits of thought, his Old World prejudices and hostilities and antagonisms. The description, written about 1780, is perspicuous and prophetic. For what is most remarkable about European unification in America is that it has come about so easily and so peaceably, that it has come from within rather than from without, that it has come voluntarily and by democratic processes. Unification of Europe in America has been achieved without religious wars, without racial wars, and without even that class war so confidently predicted by Marxist dialecticians. And for the overwhelming majority it has come not as a series of sacrifices, but as a fulfillment, not as a traumatic experience, but as a creative experience.

It is not only in the obvious physical—almost physiological—sense that America unified Europe. In the cultural and intellectual sense, too, the United States achieved and is still in process of achieving a sort of amalgamation or synthesis of European civilization. It is not merely that America inherited (as a matter of nature and of right) the whole of European civilization—the ancient traditions from Judea and Greece and Rome, the modern contributions from England and France and Germany and Italy—but that in a characteristically energetic fashion Americans undertook to acquire the best of each current European culture and to assimilate it to American culture. It is an instructive story and a moving one, too, and although it sometimes had vulgar aspects (as in the bodily transplanting of European castles to America), it is fair to say that if a great power is to display imperialism, it is well that that imperialism should be concentrated on the aggrandizement of culture rather than on its destruction.

At the end of the eighteenth century it was to London that the American artists went for study, and for patronage. Early in the new century the sculptors descended on Florence and Rome—at one time there were over fifty American sculptors with studios in Italy—and some remained. The philosophers turned to the Germany of Kant and Fichte, but happily transformed and Americanized their doctrines; the theologians studied at Tübingen and later at Marburg and Basle; the painters shifted from London to Paris, to Barbizon, and some went to Dusseldorf (which gave us "Washington Crossing the Delaware"). America led the world in popular education, but in the eighteen-forties, educators like Horace Mann and Henry Barnard were studying the educational systems of Prussia, and a little later it was Switzerland that inspired the American kindergarten. American doctors and surgeons studied in Edinburgh and Leyden and Paris. Architects levied, almost indiscriminately, on every age and country: on classical Greece and Rome, on Georgian England, and, alas, on Victorian, on Gothic, on Renaissance France, and even on medieval Germany. And American men of letters levied, similarly, on every country for the content and style of literature—classical, romantic, and naturalistic, imaginative and critical and scholarly.

Perhaps the ultimately important thing about all this is not that Washington Irving drew on Granada for romanticism and Longfellow took the meter of Kalevala for "Hiawatha"; that Hiram Powers and Horatio Greenough studied sculpture in Rome and Allston and Page painted in that same center of art; that the jurist Joseph Story drew on Mansfield and Eldon for the law merchant and William Livingstone on Beccaria for a more humane penal system; that theologians like Theodore Parker could rejoice in Strauss and translate De Wette, and philosophers like Ripley and Hedge bathed themselves in Kantian idealism, and antislavery reformers like Garrison found inspiration and support from a Wilberforce or a Granville Sharp. Perhaps the important thing is rather that these and others were able to carry their findings back with them to America without embarrassment or difficulty, and fitted them to American needs and put them to American work without suspicion or opposition.

Canada and Australia offer analogous rather than comparable histories. Both countries have fused disparate elements into a national unity, although it is proper to add that the fusion between the French and the British north of the Canadian-American boundary is rather less complete than the fusion to the south, and that Australian immigration policy has been less hospitable than

American in the last century or so. Yet who can doubt that in both of these vast and rapidly growing nations, as in the United States, we are witnessing the process of European unification.

There is, needless to add, one other nation which has successfully organized a European union. When Sir Winston Churchill gave that great speech which, in a sense, inspired the present movement for European unity, it was to this state that he referred as an example and a model for the whole of Europe. "All the while," he reminded us, "there is a remedy which, if it were generally and spontaneously adopted, would, as if by a miracle, transform the whole scene and would, in a few years, make all Europe . . . as free and as happy as Switzerland is today." Here, in this remarkable Swiss laboratory, we have a European microcosm of the American macrocosm—a small country with two faiths, three languages, and a score of separate histories and traditions, all bound together in a common nation and a common loyalty. And, although Switzerland is far and away the most encouraging example of what Europeans can do when they have the will to harmonize their differences in larger unity, it is not the only example; there is Belgium with its Walloon and Flemish elements, and Finland with Finnish and Swedish, and Britain herself with the Scots, the Welsh, and at least some of the Irish living happily together under a single flag and crown.

There have been, of course, ambitious efforts to unify Europe, or efforts to unite it on an ambitious scale. The achievements of the Universal Church of the Holy Roman Empire, and of the all-European Crusades come to mind, but we can dismiss them as largely irrelevant to our problem because they flourished before the rise of modern nationalism. There was something of a union, or at least a community, in the eighteenth century, too. During the era we call the Enlightenment it was possible for philosophers and scholars and artists and scientists, and for the aristocracy, too, to move freely from country to country. It was an age when the claims of learning and science and art, and even of class (if the upper) took precedence over the claims of the nation; when Frederick the Great could use French as the language of his court while fighting the French; when George III could retain the American, Benjamin West, as painter to his court while fighting the Americans; when Turgot and Franklin could decree during the

Revolutionary War that no harm should come to Captain Cook, because he was engaged in work useful to humanity; when the American-born Benjamin Thompson could emerge as Count Rumford of the Holy Roman Empire, organize the Royal Institution, reorganize the kingdom of Bavaria, and leave his fortune to create the Rumford Chair of Natural Science at Harvard College; when Napoleon's mother could, with impunity, invest her money in British securities; when during the height of war Jefferson could remind his compatriot, the scientist David Rittenhouse, that it was never the intention of Providence to waste the genius of a Newton on the affairs of state, and urge that he give up public service and go back to his experiments. It was a very real community, this empire of reason, but it was one that functioned on a small stage and for but a brief moment, and whose benefits were limited to a narrow circle of the elect. It was not an international community strong enough to resist the rough impact of nationalism.

The era of nationalism itself has witnessed three major attempts at unification: Napoleon's effort to establish a European imperium; Hitler's attempt to impose Nazi rule on the Western world; and the current drive of the Communists to establish not only a European, but a global, hegemony. These three enterprises have two things in common: they are imposed from without and not from within, and they are imposed by force and not by reason. Perhaps we may already say that they have a third thing in common—that they are unsuccessful. The really successful unifications remain, then, on a small scale Switzerland and on a large scale the United States. Can Europe unify on a small scale only in Switzerland, or can Europe unify on a large scale only outside Europe?

If we look at this problem from the perspective of the United States, the difficulties seem to be not so much economic or military, or even political, as historical, cultural, and psychological. It is, apparently, easier for Europeans to achieve at least partial unity in the economic, military, and political realms than in the social and cultural. It is easier to reduce tariff barriers than to reduce the barriers between universities; easier to do away with visas than to do away with the hurdles that get in the way of recognition of professional degrees or certificates; easier to arrange monetary agreements than to standardize library classifications or practices. Belgium joins cheerfully in a program of economic and military cooperation, but the ancient university at Louvain must maintain in effect two faculties to satisfy the demands of the Walloons and the Flemings, although each student group knows well the language of the other. Skane was for centuries part of Denmark, but now Danish books have to be translated into Swedish if they are to be read ten miles from Elsinore, and though Norway and Denmark have had a common language for some centuries, the Norse seem as eager as the Irish to encourage a language, or languages, of their own. Or, to turn from the particular to the general, the United Nations Educational, Scientific and Cultural Organization seems to have done less to mitigate nationalist misunderstanding than the European Economic Community, and European intellectuals have, in the past decade, contributed rather more than their normal share to accentuating and exacerbating differences within the community of Western civilization, especially the differences between the European and American branches of that community.

How have Europeans in America managed to avoid so many of the misunderstandings, prejudices, enmities, and wars that afflicted them in Europe? How did it happen that Europeans, who repudiated or shattered their very genuine community of culture in the Old World, nevertheless carried that community with them and reconstructed it in the New? How did it happen that Europeans, unable to avoid religious conflicts in Europe, achieved religious tolerance in America; unable to mitigate the ravages of chauvinistic nationalism and aggressive imperialism in Europe, built up in America a nation free of the most characteristic manifestations of nationalism, a colonial power that abjured colonialism, and a world power that is not yet imperialistic?

There is no pat set of reasons for the success of European unification in America, but there are historical processes, habits, and institutions that help to explain it.

One of the elementary and most important of these is the federal system. The Dutch historian, Pieter Geyl, recently said, with understandable impatience:

> I may seem dangerously near the conclusion that only trained historians are fit to rule the world. In all sincerity that is not what I mean, although I can't deny that I have

sometimes wished that, for instance, American statesmen who now exercise so direct and profound an influence on the destinies of the world, knew more about the history of Europe. They might not, in that case, talk so lightly about European federation.

True enough, but one might express the wish, too, that European statesmen knew more about American history. They might not in that case talk so desperately about European federation. It is not by chance that the great European statesman who knows most about history, including American history (I mean, of course, Winston Churchill), is also the one who is the inspiration of the movement for European union.

It is, of course, folly to suggest American federalism as a pattern for Europe. The situations are profoundly different. But the important thing about federalism is not so much the particular form of organization, as the techniques for reconciling and balancing general with local interests. American history represents the triumph of the general over the particular, whereas in Europe the particular triumphed over the general. But this triumph has not come, in America, through the creation of a highly centralized or militarized state, nor through the sacrifice of local cultural or economic interests. It has come through a distribution of authority among governments which, in the end, has strengthened rather than weakened the constituent parts of the union. While it is unlikely that a scheme like the American could be adapted to the needs of western Europe, it is not at all difficult to imagine a number of small federations—Benelux, the Scandinavian countries, the Iberian peninsula, the Balkans—which may some day furnish the ingredients for a larger federation.

And if the familiar and traditional methods will not do, we must invent new ones. The last fifteen years have been among the most inventive in modern history. In these years we invented Lend-Lease, UNESCO, the United Nations, Marshall Plan, EEC, Benelux, the Coal and Steel Community, NATO, technological assistance, international atomic research, and a host of other international organizations and devices. There is no reason to suppose that these remarkable inventions have exhausted European or American ingenuity. As Arthur MacMahon has written, "Europe, while conserving the beauty of the past, must invent and is inventing forms of organization and economic policies novel in the world."

American federalism may not, in itself, serve as a pattern for Europe, but what I call the reverse side of federalism is not without interest to Europeans looking for a pattern. For federalism is, in a sense, the repudiation of statism. Although the tradition of the state is relatively new in Europe, it is immensely powerful, and nowhere more so than in those central bastions of European civilization, France and Germany. Americans have never known statism—the state as a mystical entity, a religious symbol, a brooding omniscience in history. The American attitude toward government was, from the beginning, disrespectful and almost supercilious. "Government, like dress," said Tom Paine, "is the badge of lost innocence." They made a state—by contract—and determined to keep it in its place, which was a subordinate one. They devised a constitution designed to make sure that government could not become too strong. They created neither army nor navy in any real sense. They did not put their officials in uniforms or give them titles or honors—or even pay them very well; they created no *droit administratif*; they established no national system of education and no national university; they scarcely had a national capital, until the twentieth century, and still lack, in a sense, a national name.

Because they do not worship and scarcely respect the state, it is not difficult for Americans to concede equality to all other states, even the smallest and weakest; and since the adoption of the Northwest Ordinance in 1787 they have stitched the principle of the coordinate state into the fabric of their governmental and philosophical system. Federalism here is both cause and effect. Because the Americans did not want a powerful state, they created a federal system; because they started with a federal system —started indeed with thirteen states that thought themselves sovereign and independent—they looked with suspicion upon a powerful national state.

There is one analogy between the American experience and the current European problem that is not without interest. Whereas in the Old World nationalism customarily developed long before the organization of the political state—as in Italy, Germany, Norway, Greece, Finland, Bohemia, Poland, and Ireland—in America the political organization of the nation came first, and the other ingredients of nationalism were added afterward. In this respect present-day Europe is closer to the United States of 1787 than to its own constituent parts. The political organization of Europe can be completed by acts of federation and of union. It will still remain to fill in the cultural and the emotional ingredients, to create a sense and a sentiment of union. That this task is difficult will be readily conceded, but it should not be greatly more difficult for Europeans to recapture and reanimate a cultural unity that once flourished than it was for Americans to create one out of miscellaneous ingredients of history and experience.

An important part of American history has been what might be called a series of exercises in avoidance. One thing that the United States has avoided until now is clearly relevant to our problem. We have avoided dependence on the military, on wars, on the nursing of national antipathies. We have never had, in the United States, a military class, a class that played a political and social as well as a professional role; and we certainly have never had an officer class, nor even a permanent general staff which has influenced the conduct of foreign policy. During the whole of the nineteenth century our army was smaller than that of Switzerland or Sweden. When it was enlarged to fight wars, as in 1861, it was enlarged as a citizen, not a professional, army, and speedily disbanded.

It was our good fortune, perhaps, rather than our virtue that permitted us to avoid having, or nursing, national antipathies. Every Frenchman, every Italian, every Irishman, every Finn knows who is the traditional enemy of his people, but the Americans would be hard put to it to think of any candidate for that post. Britain was a candidate for a short time, but it is always easy for the victors to forgive the vanquished, and the British, on their part, were inclined to apologize for the War of Independence and to forget entirely the War of 1812. Aside from Britain there were no other national enemies, and the inability of Americans to think of the Germans as enemies after two years, or to treat them the way victors in the past treated the vanquished, has been something of an embarrassment to America's erstwhile allies. What this meant was that in the United States nationalism could flourish without resort to war, without glorification of the military, or the creation of a military class. The greatest of American heroes are not primarily military; the greatest American military hero is the leader of an unsuccessful rebellion against the United States, Robert E. Lee. American literature has no military tradition. The only American battle songs come from the Civil War and are heavily sentimental. Serious American painting is almost as innocent of battle scenes as of nudes. We need only contemplate the role played by the military and by war in the development of European nationalism, or the role of antipathies in the nationalism of newer nations like Ireland, China, or the Arab States, to appreciate how fortunate the American experience has been in this realm.

National enmities are a product of history, as indeed the fragmentation of Europe is a product of history, and history cannot be exorcised by incantations. But national enmities and the fragmentation of Europe are also, in a sense, the product of historians. All through the nineteenth century, and in almost every country of Europe, historians were the willing and zealous apologists for the most parochial and chauvinistic nationalism. The German historians, from Dahlmann and Droysen to Von Syvel and the egregious Treitschke, were doubtless the worst offenders, but they were not alone in the sorry business of forcing Clio to speak in the vulgar accents of nationalism. Michelet and Thiers and Masson in France, Arneth and Klopp in Austria, Botta in Italy, Lafuente in Spain, Geijer in Sweden, Palacký in Bohemia, Paparrhegopoulos in Greece—all these displayed the same enthusiasm for nationalism and confessed the same confusion in distinguishing between patriotism and history.

And not only did historians celebrate nationalism for the most part uncritically. Even quantitatively they concentrated on a national and parochial version of history. Instead of instructing their readers that nationalism was a new and in many respects an artificial thing; that all nations had much the same origins and each was but a part of European society; that the notion of a distinct national character was something of a myth and the notion of the natural superiority of any one people or nation a pernicious myth; and that every citizen was a citizen not only of a state but of the larger community of Western Christendom, historians did their utmost to inflame nationalism and chauvinism.

Although the worst excesses of nationalist historiography are happily a thing of the past, historians still force histor into a national framework, and concentrate attention upon the l ory of the individual nation. Thus to this day historians of Denmark are preoccupied with the problems of Danish history, and those of Holland with Dutch history, and so forth. If this preoccupation were merely a matter of the study it would not be so serious, but it carries over into the university, and from the university it percolates down to the secondary and the elementary schools, so that in almost every country of Europe the young are trained, from childhood, to an astigmatic view of history.

The United States has been fortunate in escaping the worst ravages of nationalistic history. We have never had a "nationalist" school of historians in the United States, nor have our historians concentrated unduly upon the history of the United States. Of the leading historians of the nineteenth century only Bancroft is an exception to this generalization, and even Bancroft was more concerned with vindicating democracy than with celebrating nationalism, and did not in any event carry his studies past 1789. Prescott wrote of the Aztecs and the Incas and of the Spain of Philip II; Motley celebrated the rise of the Dutch Republic; Parkman described the struggle between Spain, France, and England for North America; and Admiral Mahan, the most nationalist of all these, traced the influence of the sea upon history; while Henry Adams, who did write nine brilliant volumes on the administrations of Jefferson and Madison, began and ended his literary career as a medievalist. Nor has the twentieth century brought a reversal of this tradition of interest in the history of other peoples and times.

It is not only the absence of nationalism in American historical writing that is noteworthy, but the early, continuous, and pervasive interest in history outside America. It is only recently that American history has made its way into the curriculum of the schools, and in some states it has required legislation to assure the study of American history in the secondary schools. Our universities, too, address themselves assiduously to the history of other nations and civilizations. Thus Columbia University maintains professorships in the history of Britain, Canada, Latin America, Scandinavia, Germany, Italy, Spain, France, Russia, China, and Japan.

Perhaps the New World historian can say what it seems difficult for Old World historians to admit—that history is too often a refuge for and an enticement to nationalist sentiment. Where it emphasizes the particular rather than the general, where it teaches the superiority of each national state and culture, it blinds rather than enlightens. The sense of the past is always with us, but we may become prisoners of the past to a degree where we are not masters of the future. Winston Churchill spoke as a great historian when he reminded us just a decade ago at Zurich that "there must be a blessed act of oblivion." He had in mind oblivion of the cruelties and wickedness of the immediate past, but may we not say there must be an act of oblivion for the long heritage of national egocentricity and vanity as well?

One other feature of American life has made it easy for Europeans to live together in America without rivalry or hostility —the historic separation of church and state. The United States was the first Western nation to try the bold experiment of separating church and state and ordaining complete equality in religion, and almost the only modern nation to have escaped religious wars and conflicts. We have in America today some thirty-five million Catholics, perhaps seventy million Protestants subdivided into over a hundred different denominations, and perhaps five million people of Jewish faith. All these live peacefully side by side and, except for minor lapses, they have always done so. Had the United States attempted to guarantee one religion a privileged position, the consequences would have been fatal. Had Europeans been encouraged or permitted to indulge in religious rivalries and animosities in the New World, the consequences would have been fatal. What is most interesting, however, is not that the Founding Fathers made the right decision in 1787— they could scarcely have made any other—but that the decision has been accepted and implemented so effortlessly. Europeans, accustomed for centuries to religious conflicts, persecutions, and wars, found it the easiest and most natural thing in the world to live with rival religions. There has been some anti-Catholicism in the United States, but it evaporated very early. There has been anti-Semitism in the United States, but it has never been allowed to take overt or a great deal of violent form. And the *kulturkampf* had little meaning in a society where each denomination was free to establish its own churches and maintain its own schools and colleges, and where those who were not devout could be as independent as they pleased.

Separation of church and state in America not only made it possible for Europeans to abandon age-old religious rivalries; it also broke that historic connection between religion and the state which has done so much to inflame aggressive nationalism elsewhere in the world. It is difficult to imagine the national states of Ireland, Pakistan, Israel, even Spain, without the religious ingredient, and it is tempting to speculate on the dazzling possibilities of economic and social progress in the Near East which technology makes available, but religion vetoes. It is not irrelevant to ask why men and women of different religious faiths can live together in Ohio and Pennsylvania, but not in Ireland, Spain, Egypt, or Pakistan and their neighbors. Are religious conflicts unavoidable? If they are, there can be no European union, but the experience of the United States, and of some other nations as well, suggests a happier answer.

Alexis de Tocqueville devoted two chapters of his *Democracy in America* to what he considered perhaps the most remarkable of American characteristics, the practice of voluntary association. He saw clearly the role of the voluntary association in stimulating self-government and dispersing the power of the state, but even he did not fully appreciate one of the major functions of the voluntary association—its harmonizing and unifying function. Voluntary association is the institution that has done most to cut across the boundary lines of state, race, religion, class, and interest, and bind together by a thousand strong though invisible ties a numerous and heterogeneous people.

For almost all of our organizations are nation-wide; some, like the Rotary or the Boy Scouts or the Red Cross, transcend national boundaries. Almost all of them are unifying rather than nationalizing. They cut across boundaries to form an intricate network of new and highly personal unions. Lawyers can compare cases from state to state; fishermen of Vermont tell fish stories to fishermen of Oregon; Rotarians and Lions find friends and companions in every town in the country.

In short, Americans have formed, over the years, this ingenious system to fragment government and to superimpose social and professional loyalties upon political and class and religious loyalties. These new associational loyalties are nowhere strong enough to threaten the state (as some of the class or religious loyalties of nineteenth- and twentieth-century Europe have done), but they are strong enough to create or enlarge bonds of interest and affection. They mitigate nationalism without impairing it; they fragment the big government without undermining it; they stimulate social and economic democracy without discouraging political democracy. Because they are so many and so diverse, they unify without standardizing.

Americans have no monopoly on the habit of voluntary associations. The English are almost as adept as the Americans in this practice, and every European nation boasts its scores and hundreds of private organizations. Two considerations, however, are relevant. First, the tradition of state direction of religion, education, medicine, social services, and many other things has tended to give less scope to the practice of voluntary association in European nations than in the United States. And second, precisely because so many of these activities are directed by the state, it is difficult to organize across national boundaries, and the habit of forming European, as distinct from Danish or Italian, organizations is therefore still weak. Nothing would contribute more to creating a spirit of unity among Europeans than a vigorous growth of this practice. Scholars, men of letters, and scientists now commonly enjoy their European congresses, but the habit of meeting together has not percolated down to the average man and woman. When rose-growers of England organize with those of Switzerland, when the school teachers of Sweden join with those of Italy, when veterans of the Resistance movements can meet together and know each other, they will discover that the things that unite them are stronger than the things that divide them.

The very suggestion of national organization—particularly

fraternal or professional—conjures up that bogy of the European intellectual, standardization. I say bogy, because so far as it affects the problem of European union it is largely a figment of the imagination; I say European intellectual, because we are not so standardized in the United States as to have any group who can be called "intellectuals."

The very term *standardization* is a semantic trap, for it conjures up a sort of Orwellian nightmare. But some standardization is a very good thing, even in the cultural realm. We do not want a standardized literary style, but a standardized typewriter keyboard facilitates creative writing. The notion of a peculiarly American standardization is, too, a somewhat exaggerated one, for American society is less standardized and European society more so than most Europeans realize. Compare the monolithic religious landscape of Sweden and Italy with the diversity of the American religious scene, or the uniformity of higher education in France or Spain with the diversity in the United States.

What is important, however, is to keep in mind that there is no necessary connection between European union and European cultural standardization. Not only can union be achieved without standardization—after all, there is as much variety in the literature of the English-speaking world as in the literature of twenty European countries—but standardization can and will advance without union. Indeed, I am not being merely paradoxical if I suggest that cultural standardization may advance faster without European union than with it. Standardization within a single nation is potentially more dangerous than over a large area embracing many countries. Witness what happened in Germany under the Nazi regime. And this kind of standardization is a product of those forces that are generated by chauvinistic nationalism or the monolithic and intolerant church, of war and preparation for war, or a rigidly controlled economy. The chances are far less of any of these forces operating on a united Europe than on single states—especially if they are hostile states.

Finally I return to the point I raised at the very beginning, that because (by good fortune, it now appears) America started without a culture of its own to protect and exalt, it largely escaped the ravages of cultural chauvinism and could serve therefore as a cultural clearinghouse for the Old World.

In the tiny square of Bellosguardo, Italy, looking down on the gleaming domes of Florence, stands a granite shaft with the simple inscription:

> JAMES FENIMORE COOPER
> NATHANIEL HAWTHORNE
> LOUISA MAY ALCOTT
> HENRY JAMES
> *Loved this Place*

For well over a century now Americans have been making that declaration of love not to Florence alone, but to the hundreds of centers of art and learning and beauty which constitute, in Hawthorne's phrase, "our old home." They have done so with no sense of unfaithfulness to their own country. For over a century America has accumulated the culture, art, architecture, music, science, and scholarship of the Old World and welcomed and assimilated, at the same time, each successive generation of European artists, scientists, and scholars. The process has gone so far that we can almost say that while French culture flourishes only in France and Italian culture only in Italy and Irish culture only in Ireland, European culture flourishes best in America. This is what Lewis Mumford had in mind when he wrote that the uprooting of Europe was the settlement of America. It is what Professor Panofsky has in mind when he argues that European historians of art are so circumscribed by national prepossessions that the artistic history of Europe can best be studied and written in the United States. Certainly our formal institutions of culture, universities and libraries and museums, represent not the loot of the European past, but a genuine assimilation and continuation and enrichment of that past.

One form of the continuation and enrichment is of immediate interest—the colleges and seminars devoted to the study of the unity of the West. Most of the support for this has come, in recent years, from America, particularly from great foundations like the Rockefeller, the Carnegie, the Ford, and the Guggenheim. There is no reason why Europe should not create and maintain a dozen flourishing centers of study devoted to the recovery of the cultural unity of this "noble continent."

It is useless to say that European union *cannot* be achieved, because it *has*, in a very real sense, been achieved in America. What is impressive about the achievement is how readily the peoples of the Old World adapted themselves to it, how cheerfully they abandoned the nationalist and religious antagonisms, the class consciousness, the cultural vanity, even the linguistic commitments, which had been second nature to them in the Old World. What is impressive is how easily they accepted a common language, common education, common practices of voluntary association, common social habits and standards, and a common culture. It is granted that the situation in the Old World is different from that in the New, and that the boundary which separates France from Germany is not like that which separates Indiana from Illinois; it is granted, too, that a common language and a single government immensely facilitate understanding. But some of the boundaries of the Old World seem quite as artificial as those of the New; a common language has not yet reunited Norway with Denmark or Belgium with Holland and France; and racial heterogeneity is greater in the United States than in all Europe. The explanation of the unification of Europe in America and the fragmentation of Europe in Europe does not lie so much in these hard facts of language or race or politics as in the realms of history, philosophy, religion, and psychology.

It is here that the scholars, the artists, the men of letters, the moral leaders, can play a decisive role in the weakening of those historical and psychological forces that so powerfully inhibit cultural and moral unification. So far, over a period of a century or more, they have not done so. So far they have contributed more to the cult of the particular than to the religion of the general, more to fragmentation than to unity. So far they have seemed more sensitive to what President Eisenhower has called "the intense fear of losing cherished local traditions and cultural and political institutions," than to the values inherent in the enlargement of cultural horizons for hundreds of millions of men and women. They have been, many of them, like secular priests so determined to cultivate the dogma of their particular denomination that they ignore the common moral values of all religion. The prison in which so many Europeans, even European intellectuals, live is one of their own making. It is a prison fabricated from the fears, the disappointments, the suspicions, the vanities, and the timidities of the past. Let us say what the venerable Justice Holmes wrote to one of his younger disciples—that it would be well if we were to consult our hopes and not our fears.

1957

PART TWO

Washington
Witch-Hunt

It is not improbable that President Truman's executive order on disloyalty in the executive branch was designed to steal the thunder of the Thomas Committee or head off such extreme bills as that proposed by Representative Rankin—that it was intended, in short, to furnish some protection to persons in government employment wrongfully accused of disloyalty. If so, it is a pity that it was not more carefully drawn, that it does not more scrupulously observe legal and constitutional proprieties. For as it stands it is an invitation to precisely that kind of witch-hunting which is repugnant to our constitutional system. And as it stands, it should be added, it is liable to instigate persecution not only of radicals by red-baiters but of reactionaries by radicals.

The crucial clauses are in Part V: *Standards*, and these merit close attention. Most striking is the looseness, the almost unbelievable looseness, with which standards are fixed. Here are the "activities and associations" of an employee which are to be considered as a test of loyalty:

> Membership in, affiliation with, or sympathetic association with any foreign or domestic organization, association, movement, group or combination of persons, designated by the Attorney General as totalitarian, fascist, Communist, or subversive, or as having adopted a policy of advocating or approving the commission of acts of force or violence to deny other persons their rights under the Constitution of the United States, or as seeking to alter the form of government of the United States by unconstitutional means.

Note first how all-embracing these terms are. It is not only membership in or affiliation with subversive organizations that is proscribed, but "sympathetic association" with them. What is sympathetic association, and how is it to be distinguished from unsympathetic association? Is a member of the Democratic party in New York sympathetically or unsympathetically associated with the Democratic party of Mississippi, which denies Negroes their rights under the Constitution of the United States? Note, too, the connection—it is difficult to use a more precise word—that is made suspect. It is not only membership and so forth in actual organizations but membership in and sympathetic association with a "movement" or a "group or combination of persons." What is a movement? Is the Wave of the Future a movement? Is anti-Semitism a movement? Is hostility to organized labor a movement?

Here is the doctrine of guilt by association with a vengeance. For almost a hundred and fifty years American law labored under the handicap of being unable to prove guilt by association. The Alien Registration Act of 1940, directed against aliens and enacted under pressure of war, for the first time wrote that odious doctrine into American law. Now, apparently, it is here to stay. Guilt is no longer to be personal, no longer to depend upon overt acts. It is an infectious thing, to be achieved by mere "sympathetic association" with others presumed to be guilty, or even with "movements" presumed to be subversive.

Nor is consolation to be found in the designation of the Attorney General as the person to classify organizations and movements as subversive. An intelligent Attorney General, an open-minded and tolerant one, would doubtless use this broad power with discretion. But how would it be used by a Stanton, who double-crossed his President; how would it be used by a Richard Olney, who smashed the Pullman strike; how would it be used by an A. Mitchell Palmer, who rounded up the "reds"; how would it be used by a Daugherty, who broke the railway strike of 1922? What guaranty is there that J. Edgar Hoover may not some day be Attorney General, Hoover who recently asserted that "so-called progressives and phony liberals" are little better than Communists?

The same pervasive and pernicious looseness of phrasing

characterizes another of the standards set up in this section. For one of the tests of loyalty is "performing or attempting to perform his duties, or otherwise acting, so as to serve the interests of another government in preference to the interests of the United States." What is "otherwise acting" so as to serve the interests of some government other than the United States—and who is to decide? It is worth noting, in passing, that much this same test was enacted once before, in the Logan Act of 1798, and failed. Did Walter Hines Page act so as to serve the interests of Britain rather than the United States? Many contemporaries and some later historians have thought so, and we may well believe that the right kind of Attorney General—Henry Cabot Lodge, let us say—might have agreed with them. If this principle were applied to Congress, as it might logically be, would it result in wholesale decapitations? Anyone who reads faithfully the *Congressional Record* knows how many Congressmen plead the cause of Lithuania, or of the former Polish government in London, or of Eire—at the cost of a good many thousand dollars to the American taxpayer. What government's interests are being served when Mr. de Valera's St. Patrick's Day address is reprinted in the *Congressional Record?*

But let us turn to some of the possible applications of this extraordinary order. What organizations, associations, movements, or groups, after all, may be said to be embraced in the esoteric phrases of Part V? "Communist" and "fascist" are, perhaps, obvious enough, though "totalitarian" takes a bit of defining. But what of others that "advocate or approve" the commission of acts of force to deny persons their rights under the Constitution or to alter the form of government? The Ku Klux Klan is obviously one of these, and we may confidently expect that it will be so designated by the Attorney General and that all its members in government service will be promptly charged with disloyalty.

What shall we say, what may we expect, for other organizations? Is membership in the Democratic party, or "sympathetic association" with it, an indication of disloyalty? Assuredly, that party countenances the use of force to deprive Southern Negroes of their rights under the Constitution. What of membership in labor unions? Several of them have, notoriously, denied to non-members or to the public their constitutional rights. What shall we say of membership in or association with the Brotherhood of Locomotive Firemen and Engineers, which—we follow the Supreme Court here—denied Negro firemen their constitutional rights? Nor should we forget that numerous Congressmen have again and again asserted that various unions were Communist-dominated. Clearly they must know what they are talking about, and clearly all who associate with or sympathize with these unions are guilty through association.

A number of organizations, membership in which must create at least a suspicion of disloyalty, come to mind: whether these organizations are subversive or not will depend upon the interpretation given that slippery word "force," and force, it must be remembered, does not necessarily require violence. Does the American Bar Association come under the Presidential ban? Its committee counseled disobedience to the National Labor Relations Act. Does the American Medical Association come under the ban? It was found guilty of denying members of the Medical Society of the District of Columbia their constitutional rights. Will association with the Associated Press be evidence of disloyalty? According to *Associated Press v. U. S.*, it too was guilty of denying to outsiders rights which they could exercise under the Constitution. What of "sympathetic association" with railroad corporations which persist in denying to Negroes the constitutional right not to be segregated? May stockholders be presumed to be "sympathetic" associates, or is there a presumption of non-sympathy? Or, to turn to government employees, is service with the FBI to be an indication of disloyalty if that agency attempts, as it clearly wishes, to deny Communists their constitutional right of freedom of speech and of assembly?

Fortunately for those who tremble for the safety of the Republic, the dragnet is to be spread widely enough to catch even those whose sympathetic association with subversive groups or movements is not clear. For all those who seek "to alter the form of government of the United States by unconstitutional means" are equally subject to the Attorney General's disapproval. What are "unconstitutional means"? It is a bit difficult to know what may be considered unconstitutional in the future, but perhaps recourse to the past will clarify the issue. Clearly, all those who carried out the Congressional mandate, in 1862, to abolish slavery in the territories were guilty of this crime, for under the Dred Scott decision the act of 1862 was unconstitutional. Even more clearly, all officers who executed the First Reconstruction Act, and its amendments, were equally guilty, for these acts were palpably unconstitutional, and, no less palpably, they altered the American form of government.

An application of Mr. Truman's executive order to the past would, indeed, greatly have simplified our history. An order of this kind would have disposed of that dangerous radical Andrew Jackson, who not once but twice flouted the Supreme Court, and of Jackson's Attorney General, Taney, later Chief Justice, who aided and abetted him, and of his Postmaster General who unlawfully withheld funds which Congress and the Court said must be paid. It would have embarrassed that subversive executive Abraham Lincoln, who illegally, according to Chief Justice Taney, suspended the writ of habeas corpus, thus denying to John Merryman rights guaranteed to him by the Constitution. It might have put that dangerous agitator Theodore Roosevelt in his place—Roosevelt who, according to President Taft, illegally withdrew public lands from entry, thus denying persons their constitutional right to homesteads. And, whatever we may think of more recent situations, such an order—had it but been effective in time—would inevitably have disposed of Mr. Truman's trouble-making predecessor, Thomas Jefferson. For Jefferson "sympathetically associated" with Jacobin clubs, Jefferson "sympathetically" joined combinations to nullify Congressional acts, Jefferson was affiliated with a party which worked a "revolution" in 1800, and—worst of all—Jefferson openly announced that "the tree of liberty must be refreshed from time to time with the blood of patriots and martyrs."

1947

Red-Baiting in the Colleges

Communism and Academic Freedom[1] is the formal record of the University of Washington tenure cases that have attracted nation-wide attention. It is not, of course, the full record: some four thousand pages of testimony remain to be examined by the American Association of University Professors Committee on Academic Freedom. What this little volume provides are the charges against the six suspect professors, the majority, concurring, and minority opinions of the Committee on Tenure and Academic Freedom, and the statement and recommendations of President Raymond B. Allen.

It is important first to make clear the facts about these tenure cases. In 1947 the legislature of Washington enacted a law that no salary should be paid to any state employee who is a member of an organization that advocates the overthrow of the government of the United States by force or violence. The Communist party was not specifically named in this act, nor is that party outlawed by the law of the state. That same year the Washington legislature set up a committee on un-American activities, charged it to inquire into the subversive activities of individuals and organizations in the state, and instructed it to give special attention to Communist party activities that might affect the functioning of any state agency or educational institution. In accordance with these in-

[1] Communism and Academic Freedom. The Record of the Tenure Cases at the University of Washington, including the Findings of the Committee on Tenure and Academic Freedom and the President's Recommendations (The University of Washington Press).

structions the so-called Canwell Committee held hearings on communism in the state university. Following these hearings, complaints were filed by the Dean of the College of Arts and Sciences against six members of the university faculty—three of them alleged to be present, and three past, members of the Communist party.

The Faculty Committee on Tenure and Academic Freedom —a committee whose authority seems to be a bit vague—held its own hearings on these complaints and made a series of reports and recommendations. A majority of the faculty committee advised against dismissal or other disciplinary measures in five of the six cases. President Allen did not feel himself bound in any way by the findings or recommendations of this committee. He recommended the dismissal of three members of his faculty and the probation of three others. The regents of the state university accepted the recommendations of President Allen.

It is proper to say, before we turn to a more particular examination of the findings of the faculty committee and the action of the president, that the university authorities appear to have observed the most scrupulous regard for the rights of the accused teachers. They were given an opportunity to appear, to testify on their own behalf, to confront witnesses, to bring in their own witnesses at the university's expense. Both the faculty committee and the president limited their inquiry to the single question of the relation of present or past membership in the Communist party to competence in teaching and in scholarship. And though President Allen repudiated the recommendations of his committee, he appears to have made an effort to be fair and impartial, to protect the welfare of the university and—by his own lights—academic freedom.

Space does not permit a detailed analysis of the various documents we have here, illuminating as that might be. Nor does it permit an extended consideration of the larger issues involved in this whole question of communism and academic tenure. The issue, as presented and debated, is a fairly simple one.

First, it is clear that, legally, the state can establish its own criteria of appointment and tenure for state-supported institutions. This may be foolish, but a state has the right to act foolishly. In all probability government violates constitutional guarantees of due process if it brands an individual as subversive or disloyal without giving him a fair trial; the procedures adopted by the regents and the president of the University of Washington appear to have satisfied the requirements of due process, and are, from that point of view, unexceptionable.

Second, it is clear that nothing in the law of the state, or in the tenure provisions of the university, makes either past or present membership in the Communist party an offense. Nor did the president or the regents contend that such membership was a violation of law or of regulation. What they did contend was, rather, that membership in the Communist party is in itself evidence of unfitness and incompetence, and that concealment of such membership makes the original offense doubly heinous. Thus President Allen reported of the three members recommended for dismissal that "it has been adequately proved . . . that they are incompetent . . . intellectually dishonest, and . . . have neglected their duties as members of the faculty."

With respect to concealment of membership—an offense charged against the three dismissed professors—it is appropriate to note the position of the AAUP Committee: "Lying and subterfuge with reference to political affiliation are in themselves evidence of unfitness for the academic profession." This position is persuasive enough. Yet it raises an awkward question, or perhaps a series of questions. If mere membership in the Communist party is justification for dismissal, there is a premium on concealment. And there is a further question, relevant as long as the Communist party is a legal one. Could state or university authorities require teachers to reveal membership in the Democratic or Republican parties, or punish with dismissal the failure to reveal such membership?

It was primarily on the grounds of subterfuge and refusal to cooperate that a majority of the faculty committee recommended the dismissal of Professor Gundlach. Those considerations were not prominent in the cases of Professors Butterworth and Phillips. The committee recommended that no action be taken against these two men; the president recommended their dismissal on the ground of incompetence, as proved by membership in the Communist party. Here, then, we have a clear-cut issue.

The faculty committee said, first, that while membership in the Communist party was regrettable, it was not in itself cause for dismissal as long as the party itself was a legal one and neither the state nor the university administration had specifically made such membership cause for dismissal from a teaching post. It said, second, that there was no independent evidence that Professors Phillips and Butterworth were incompetent, or had neglected their academic duties, or that their political views had improperly colored their teaching. Of Professor Phillips, who taught philosophy, the committee observed:

> Although he does have occasion to discuss Marxian philosophy in his teaching, it appears that his practice is to warn his students of his bias and to request that they evaluate his lectures in light of that fact.

Three members of the faculty committee dissented from these findings of the majority. Two of them said that

> active membership in the C.P. is an overt act of such reckless, uncritical and intemperate partisanship as to be inimical to and incompatible with the highest traditions of academic freedom and responsible scholarship.

A third filed a separate opinion chiefly remarkable for its invitation to extreme governmental controls. Public education institutions, writes Professor Williams,

> are instruments created by legislation at the behest of the public on the assumption that they will perform their public functions in terms of the spirit, philosophy, and under the general climate of ideas acceptable to the government of the people who create, patronize, and support them.

This doctrine, of course, would justify Catholic control of the school systems in Massachusetts, Mormon control in Utah, and Fundamentalist control in Alabama.

President Allen's forthright position is that on account of membership in the Communist party, Professors Butterworth and Phillips each

> brought contumely and disrepute upon the University of Washington; his behavior has been bad; he has neglected his duty; he has been dishonest and incompetent; he

cannot render efficient and competent service; and he has demonstrated his professional unfitness to remain as a member of the University faculty.

Now what is the difference between the view of the faculty committee and of President Allen? It is a difference of method that involves, or symbolizes, a difference of philosophy. The committee subscribes to the inductive and pragmatic method; President Allen to the deductive and the *a priori*. The committee looks to the facts, the president looks to the theory. The committee is unwilling to deduce unfitness from the generalization of membership in the Communist party; the president first establishes his premise that membership in the Communist party is *a priori* evidence of unfitness, and then concludes that all members of that party are, of necessity, unfit. The committee's method is that of the doctrinaire. It is not wholly facetious to add that the committee's method is one we have come to think of characteristically American, the president's as un-American.

We may readily grant that membership in the Communist party is presumptive evidence of a lack of critical acumen; we may go further and concede that such membership, logically, disqualifies a teacher as an impartial student of some subjects. The same can be said for membership in, let us say, the Roman Catholic Church. But American law rejects the doctrine of guilt by association and the equally dangerous doctrine of guilt by intention, and experience confirms the legal position. If membership in the Communist party—or in any other organization—does paralyze the critical sense or produce bad teaching or worthless scholarship, it should not be difficult to prove this. But neither the dean who filed the charges nor the president who sustained them submits such evidence.

"Hard cases," Justice Holmes once wrote, "make bad law." It is in a sense unfortunate that general principles must be invoked in connection with specific cases, for our judgment tends to be clouded by the specific case. This problem arises whenever censorship is invoked against a worthless book or the third degree is used on some prisoner who is palpably guilty. The issue here is not, we must remember, the jobs of Professors Butterworth and Phillips. It is not even that question now commonly put: Do

Communists have a right to teach in our colleges, or to work in our laboratories, at public expense? Concentration on the particular case of the two Washington professors will distract us. Concentration on the broader question—do Communists have a right to teach?—will mislead us.

The real question is this: Is it wise or expedient or advantageous to investigate subversive activities in colleges and universities and laboratories? What are the advantages, what the costs, of such investigations? What does society stand to gain by tracking down and driving out a few "subversives" in colleges and universities; what price does it pay for this gain?

In every college faculty, in every church, in every labor organization, in every large corporation, there will be a certain number of incompetents. There will be a small number who are intellectually dishonest. There will be some who have violated laws or who are still violating laws. There may, perhaps, be a very small number of Communists, fellow travelers, and Fascists. The numbers involved in this final group are, apparently, negligible: the most careful investigation at the University of Washington turned up three Communists out of a faculty of some seven hundred!

With an appropriate expenditure of time, energy, and money, society can ferret out these undesirables and dismiss them. This may be a gain. It is not nearly so great a gain as is commonly supposed. No instance has yet been produced where a Communist on a university faculty actually did harm to students or to scientific truth. The assumption that a Communist will fatally mislead students is based on the quite unexplored assumption that college students are such nincompoops that they are unable to distinguish between truth and falsehood, between impartial teaching and propaganda, and on the further misconception that they invariably believe all that their teachers tell them.

But we can cheerfully grant that Communists are not desirable as teachers in colleges and universities. It by no means follows that it pays us to hunt them down and drive them out. We do not yet know what advantage follows from an investigation such as that which we are here considering. It is very much to be hoped that, in the interests of scholarship and public welfare, the University of Washington will investigate this matter for us in a year or two. Will it then appear that competent scholars are more eager to join its faculty than they have been in the past? Will parents breathe more easily, now that they know that the faculty has been purged? Will students come to the campus more gladly, and will their learning and morals show an improvement? Will the faculty be in a better position to do its job of teaching and research?

What, on the other hand, is the cost of such an investigation as that at the University of Washington? What is the actual cost in time taken from the proper business of teaching and study and research and administration? What is the cost in time devoted by President Allen and Dean Lauer, by the regents and by the faculty committee? What is the effect on the faculty and on the student body? Will professors be as free in the future as they have been in the past to explore dangerous ideas, to embark upon original research, to associate with nonconformists? Will students be as free as in the past to discuss whatever interests them, to join whatever organizations appeal to them, to test their intellectual muscles on controversial issues?

It is impossible to exaggerate the importance of the most complete and extreme freedom of inquiry in our universities. That freedom may be abused, but it is so important that society should cheerfully put up with the abuse. Freedom of inquiry may lead some scholars down labyrinthine ways; the alternative is conformity, and conformity makes, inevitably, for mediocrity. It was Whitelaw Reid—surely no radical—speaking back in the eighteen-eighties, who said:

> As for the scholar, the laws of his intellectual development may be trusted to fix his place. Free thought is necessarily aggressive and critical. The scholar, like the healthy, red-blooded young man, is an inherent, an organic, an inevitable radical. It is his business to reverse the epigram of Emerson, and put the best men and the best causes together. And so we may set down, as a . . . function of the American scholar in politics, an intellectual leadership of the radicals.

Nothing, in our own day, is more impressive, or more sobering than the widespread fear of false ideas—chiefly Communist ideas—that has gripped the American people. It is, we must conclude, evidence of deep-seated insecurity. It is evidence of lack of faith in the intelligence and integrity of the American people, lack of confidence in the validity of the American political and economic system. Surely those who are confident of the superiority of their own way of life should not fear competition, in the realm of ideas, from other systems or philosophies.

At this juncture in our history, when freedom of inquiry and freedom of expression are assailed from every side, it is well to recall the familiar but never hackneyed observation of the late Justice Holmes:

> Every idea is an incitement. It offers itself for belief, and, if believed, it is acted on unless some other idea outweighs it. . . . The only difference between the expression of an opinion and an incitement . . . is the speaker's enthusiasm for the result. Eloquence may set fire to reason. . . . If, in the long run, the beliefs expressed in proletarian dictatorship are destined to be accepted by the dominant forces of the community, the only meaning of free speech is that they should be given their chance and have their way.

1949

What Ideas Are Safe?

It is the cardinal failing of much of the current discussion of loyalty and of human rights that it addresses itself to the narrow question of right—almost of legal right. Does the legislature have a *right* to require loyalty oaths? Do school boards have a *right* to purge faculties of Communists or subversives, or to purge books from libraries? Do Congressional committees have a *right* to require witnesses to testify about their political affiliations? Do FBI investigators have the *right* to inquire broadly into the character and activities of government employees? Has the Attorney General a *right* to compile lists of subversive organizations? Or, conversely, do men have a *right* to government employment or teachers to academic immunity, or publicists to speak their mind on all subjects?

Most of these debates have ended in sterility, as they are bound to end. For men will differ, sincerely, over this question of right, and there are no conclusive answers.

What is wrong here? What is it that makes for our confusion?

That confusion is a basic one. It is, if you will, a philosophic confusion. We are confused because we are not asking the essential questions.

And what are the essential questions? They are questions that the pragmatists require us to answer. They are questions that look not to abstract rights, but to actual consequences. "The pragmatic method," William James wrote, "starts from the postulate that there is no difference of truth that doesn't make a difference of fact somewhere; and it seeks to determine the meaning of all differences of opinion by making the discussion hinge as soon as possible upon some practical or particular issue."

What, then, are the practical consequences of the attack

upon independence of thought, nonconformity, heterodoxy, radicalism, which is now under way? What kind of society will it create? What climate of opinion will it encourage? What will happen to our science, our scholarship, our political thought and conduct, even our morals, if this program continues and succeeds?

The first and most obvious consequence is that we will arrive sooner or later—and I think sooner—at an official standard of conformity, orthodoxy, and loyalty. If one is going to silence or punish men for disloyalty one must first determine what is loyalty. If one is going to apply Mr. J. Edgar Hoover's "easy test" of a subversive organization: "Does it have a consistent record of support of the American viewpoint?" one must determine officially what is the American viewpoint. If one is going to dismiss men for membership in subversive organizations, one must establish what are nonsubversive activities and organizations. If one is going to discourage or silence dangerous ideas, one must establish what are safe ideas.

That was the position that President Lowell took, during World War I, when he refused to interfere with the teaching of members of the Harvard faculty: If we pronounce certain ideas disloyal, he said, we in effect stand behind all the ideas we do not pronounce disloyal. It is the position Mr. Conant has taken in a recent situation where super-patriots tried to force him to discipline members of his faculty.

Their position is a logical one; it is indeed the only logical one; and it illuminates our whole problem. Eventually we shall have to establish some official standards of orthodoxy in thought and conduct. Who is to set the standards? Who is to determine what is orthodox, what is loyal? In short, if we drive out those ideas we think dangerous—even those, in the words of Oliver Wendell Holmes, that we loathe and think fraught with death—we must make clear to all what ideas are safe.

Now the fact is that no ideas are safe: that is a consideration that many otherwise intelligent men overlook. "Every idea is an incitement," said Holmes, and John Dewey has written:

> Let us admit the case of the conservative; if we once start thinking, no one can guarantee where we shall come out, except that many objects, ends, and institutions are surely

doomed. Every thinker puts some portion of an apparently stable world in peril, and no one can wholly predict what will emerge in its place.

If we establish a standard of safe thinking, we will end up with no thinking at all. That is the only "safe" way, and that is, needless to say, the most precarious, dangerous, of all ways.

The second consequence is a very practical one, and it is one whose effects are already being felt in many quarters. It is this, that first-rate men cannot and will not work under the conditions set by those who tremble at original ideas. Scholars who have to run the gantlet of legislative investigations of their thoughts, their teaching, their writing, and their associations, will look elsewhere for the exercise of their talents: it will be interesting to see, ten years from now, whether those colleges and universities that have purged their faculties have in fact attracted stronger men to their institutions or a better student body. Young men and women of independent mind, contemplating a career, will hesitate before exposing themselves to the kind of examinations required for entrance into the public-school system. The scholars who are competent to write textbooks will not submit to the straitjackets imposed by school boards, and the texts will be left to incompetents willing to conform. The government service, too, will suffer—as it has already suffered. The distinguished chairman of the Atomic Energy Commission, David Lilienthal, has warned us that

> The conditions of work in the Federal Government are not attractive. They are becoming increasingly less attractive to many of the very men of managerial and technical skills upon whom our world atomic leadership depends . . . for deep-seated reasons. The difficulties are . . . fundamental. They consist in the growing evidence that a tendency toward detailed Congressional supervision of this and other essential technical undertakings make the doing of a creditable job quite impossible. . . . When the public task undertaken is made impossible of accomplishment by the increased worsening of the conditions surrounding Government service, and men and organizations find their efforts quite futile, they then will leave that service, or decline to enter.

In short, if we persist in setting vexatious and impossible standards of conformity of thought, we will lose our leadership in atomic research—and in other fields of research just as crucial.

The third consequence of persistence in our present course grows out of the first two. It is the gradual development in the United States of the kind of society in which freedom of inquiry will not flourish, in which originality will not flourish, in which criticism will not flourish. This is no alarmist prophecy. It is a development already under way. Already civil servants fear to read certain books and magazines. Already teachers fear to discuss certain subjects in the classroom. Already most men hesitate to join good causes, to sign petitions which they otherwise approve, for there is always the suspicion that they might catch the infection of guilt by association. Mr. Raymond Fosdick has described what is happening:

> If you sign a petition to admit colored people to public-housing developments, if you favor fair employment practices or are concerned about civil liberties, if you fight for the protection of the rights of the foreign-born, if you oppose religious prejudice or Jim Crowism, if you sanction cultural exchange with foreign countries . . . if you take any point of view which involves the implementation of the Declaration of Independence . . . you are apt to be suspected in some circles as a knowing participant in the Communist front or at the very least a witless dupe of Moscow's hypnotic influences.

We cannot have a society half slave and half free; nor can we have thought half slave and half free. If we create an atmosphere in which men fear to think independently, inquire fearlessly, express themselves freely, we will in the end create the kind of society in which men no longer care to think independently or to inquire fearlessly. If we put a premium on conformity we will, in the end, get conformity. It will not be a process of some heavy-handed Gestapo striking down independent scholars and scientists. It is more subtle than that. It will be a process that begins in every home, in every schoolroom, in every editorial office, in every pulpit. It will be a process that develops slowly and almost intangibly, until we have created a community where men simply don't make the effort that is required of the nonconformist, where nonconformists are not rewarded as heretofore they have been rewarded in our country, where inertia and apathy take the place of energy and independence.

Such a society is doomed to destruction. We have had, in our time, examples of what happens when governments insist on conformity. We have had examples of what happens when science and scholarship and governmental service are all required to follow a predetermined line. There are many reasons why the Nazis lost the war, but all who are familiar with the internal history of Germany in the last twenty years know that one crucially important reason was that the Hitler regime drove out or silenced its ablest scientists and scholars, and that it crushed that spirit of inquiry, criticism, and dissent so important in time of war. General Halder has recently written a little book—it is a best-seller in Germany now—in which he points out all the failings of Hitler as war leader: how Hitler and his henchmen interfered in the conduct of war on every level, how they diverted scientific research from essentials to pet schemes, how they intimidated the military brains of the nation to the point where none dared dissent. He should know. He is one of the exhibits.

A nation which, in the name of loyalty or of patriotism or of any sincere and high-sounding ideal, discourages criticism and dissent, and puts a premium on acquiescence and conformity, is headed for disaster.

And this is why it is so perilous to suppose some conflict between loyalty and freedom. Freedom is the basic foundation of true loyalty. Loyalty in turn enhances freedom. The case against the conscription of thought is not primarily the case of the individual right, or of the abstract right to speak or inquire, to assemble or associate. It is rather the case of the welfare of society as a whole. It is the commonwealth we must cherish, and the commonwealth can prosper only where the human mind and spirit are left free.

It is later than we think, and if we allow our intellectual and emotional energies to be drained off into frivolous channels, we will find that we have lost the main channel. That is the channel that leads to truth. It is well to keep in mind that even the Biblical injunction to seek truth emphasizes the consequences of that search. The truth shall make you free.

1949

Is Freedom Really Necessary?

I sometimes think that when folks talk about things they've begun to lose them already," says Stark Young's Hugh McGehee to his son after an evening of Southern rodomontade. It would be an exaggeration to say that we have begun to lose liberty in America, but it is sobering that there should be so much talk about it, just as it is sobering that there should be so much talk about Americanism and about loyalty. It was a happier time when these things could be taken for granted instead of being soiled and worn by every sunshine patriot eager for cheap applause. Nor is much of the talk itself reassuring. Liberty is enlisted in strange armies, pressed into service for curious causes, and as we listen to some of the arguments for censorship or exclusion or suppression, all in the name of liberty, we are reminded irresistibly of Madame Roland's cry on the scaffold, "Liberty, what crimes are done in thy name."

Nor is the difficulty wholly with those who, in a sort of vindication of Orwell's 1984, invoke liberty for oppression. Some of the difficulty comes from well-intentioned idealists who are content with familiar formulas, or who would interpret liberty as wholly a personal and individual affair—a matter of abstract principle rather than of conduct, of private rights rather than of general social responsibilities.

When we consider civil and political liberties we must avoid the pleasant illusions of abstractions and get down to cases. We must look to the meaning of our freedoms in their present-day context, and in their operation. And when we do this we must remember what Harold Laski so insistently urged upon us (in

"Reflections on the Revolution of Our Time"), that rights and liberties do not mean the same thing to all of us:

> The rule of law is a principle with a fairly long history behind it. And if the burden of that history has one outstanding lesson it is that, over the social process as a whole, the rule of law is only equally applied as between persons . . . whose claim on the state power is broadly recognized as equal. The rule of law is not an automatic principle of action which operates indifferently as to time and place and the persons to whom, as judges, its application is entrusted. It is very likely to be one thing for a Negro in Georgia and another thing for a white man in Georgia.

The function of freedom—let us say of the guarantee of due process or of the right to vote—for the Negro and the white in the South is one very obvious example of why we have to look to the operation of the principle rather than to its mere formulation. Others occur readily enough: the difference in guarantees of freedom to white and to Oriental during World War II, for example, or the different treatment of the vagrant and the respectable citizen, or that difference in the attitude toward corporate crime and individual crime which Professor Sutherland has explored in his study of *White Collar Crime*.

We must recognize, too, at the outset that there are two very broad categories of violations of liberty: the political and the nonpolitical, or perhaps we should say the official and the unofficial. Only the first has received adequate attention—invasion of personal rights by Federal or state governments or by some administrative body. These are the impairments of liberty that are dramatized in the press and challenged in the courts—a flag salute law, a segregation law, a white primary law, the censorship of a film, or the administrative seizure of an industry. Yet the second category of invasion and impairment, the unofficial, is more widespread and more effective than the first. It is invasion by social or community pressure, by the pressure of public opinion or of public customs and habits—the kind of invasions that Tocqueville described and warned against over a century ago. It is very difficult to get at this by law. Fair Employment Practice Acts may prevent a Negro or a Jew from getting fired for racial reasons, but they will not go far toward getting him a job in the first place. A teacher who has been guilty of dangerous thoughts can take a broken contract to court, but she cannot deal with community pressure that makes it advisable for her to move on, nor can she force other school boards to give her a job. We have only to read Norman Cousins' description (*Saturday Review,* 3 May 1952) of the interplay of social and economic pressures in Peoria, Illinois, to realize how enormously effective these are and how difficult it is to do anything about them. As John Stuart Mill observed a century ago, "The immense mass of mankind are, in regard to their usages, in a state of social slavery; each man being bound under heavy penalties to conform to the standard of life common to his own class."

Our basic freedoms, in short, are not as basic as we like to think, just as our passion for individualism is not as passionate as we suppose. If we content ourselves with abstractions we may go seriously astray; as Professor Denis Brogan has remarked in his recent book on revolutions, the American claim to—and hope for—a special place in the affections of Asian peoples is frustrated by the elementary fact that of all the powers of the world "America is the most color conscious." We may believe that our words, that is, our principles, represent us more truly even than our actions, but to outsiders it is the actions that are more eloquent than the words.

Now it will be granted at once that our traditional liberties are not absolute—not in a mathematical sense, anyway. All of them are qualified by the rights of society, or of the state. There are limits on liberty, as there are limits on authority. The broad principle of those limits is generally recognized and accepted; no liberties may be exercised so as to injure others, or injure the community.

Needless to say, this does not get us very far. That liberty is not absolute is one of those truisms that is almost always brought out and put to work whenever somebody wants to censor a book or a film that he doesn't like, or to throw a teacher or a librarian or a radio performer out of his job. Actually it is worth stating only as an introduction to the real problems. How do we determine the limits on liberty and the rights and interests of the community? And who are the "we" who determine it? It is easy to fall back on the generalization that the freedom of the individual must not be used to injure the community, and easy enough to say that in the last analysis it is society which determines. But these vague answers are of no practical help. To draw the line between the exercise of freedom and the limitations on freedom is one of the most delicate tasks of statesmanship and philosophy. And the power of drawing the line is one of the most complex and sobering exercises of political authority.

It is in the drawing of lines, the setting of boundaries, the fixing of limits, the reconciliation of claims that the problems rise. Look where we will, in our own society we will find that problems of freedom or of rights revolve around this matter of fixing limits and drawing lines. Thus in the conflicting claims of a free press and a responsible press, or of freedom and license in the press. Thus in the conflicting claims of liberty and security in diplomacy, or in science. Thus in the conflicting claims of artistic freedom and of the protection of the morals of the community, or of religious freedom and protection against blasphemy or the stirring up of religious hatreds. Thus in the conflicting claims of the right to public entertainment and the right to privacy. Thus in the conflicting claims of the right to private organization and the interest of society in protecting itself against dangerous organizations. Thus in the conflicting claims of conscience—let us say of conscientious objectors to military service or a flag salute—and of national defense or of patriotism. Thus in the conflicting claims of academic freedom and of the right of democracy to determine what should be taught in its schools, and how.

Now we have been using the word "conflicting" all along. But is not the conflict exaggerated, and have we searched intensively enough for the reconciliation? We must keep ever in mind that the community has a primary interest in the rights of the individual, and the individual a primary interest in the welfare of the community of which he is a part. The community cannot prosper without permitting, nay encouraging, the far-reaching exercise of individual freedom; the individual cannot be safe without permitting, nay supporting, the far-reaching exercise of authority by the state.

There is, in short, too much emphasis on independence and not enough on interdependence; too much emphasis on division and not enough on unity. Actually it is only to the superficial view that there is any genuine conflict between liberty and security, for example, or between academic freedom and social freedom.

For what is clear on closer examination is that we cannot have any one of these alleged goods without the other. There is no real choice between freedom and security. Only those societies that actively encourage freedom—that encourage, for example, scientific and scholarly research, the questioning of scientific and social orthodoxies and the discovery of new truths—only such societies can hope to solve the problems that assail them and preserve their security. The experience of Nazi Germany is all but conclusive on this (we are still required to wait until all the returns are in from Russia, but it is a reasonable prophecy that Russia will fall behind on scientific and social research just as Germany did). A nation that silences or intimidates original minds is left only with unoriginal minds and cannot hope to hold its own in the competition of peace or of war. As John Stuart Mill said in that essay on Liberty to which we cannot too often repair, "A state which dwarfs its men, in order that they may be more docile instruments in its hands . . . will find that with small men no great thing can really be accomplished."

It is probable that other alleged alternatives so vehemently urged upon us are equally fictitious. Take, for example, the matter of the claims of "academic freedom" and of a society concerned with the teaching of truth—as is every sound society. Clearly there is no genuine conflict here. All but the most thoughtless or the most ignorant know that unless education is free the minds of the next generation will be enslaved. Even in American Legion halls it is probably a bust of Socrates that stands in the niche—Socrates who was condemned because he was a corrupter of youth—rather than of those forgotten members of the tribunal who put him to death. We have always known that academic freedom, like other freedoms, was subject to abuse, but we have known too (up to now, in any event) that the abuse was part of the price paid for the use, and that it was not in fact a high price. The simple fact is that the kind of society that cherishes academic freedom is the kind that gets the best teachers and scholars and students, and the kind that tries to control what teachers may teach or students learn is the kind that ends up with mediocre teachers and mediocre students.

So, too, with the problem of freedom of the press as against the right of the community to protect itself against libel or obscenity or sedition or other alleged dangers. Granted that there is no absolute freedom of the press—no right to proclaim blasphemy to church-goers or to distribute obscene literature to children—the alleged conflict is still largely fictitious. The hypothetical dangers linger in the realm of hypothesis; when they emerge from this to reality they can be dealt with by ordinary nuisance or libel or criminal laws, not by censorship laws. The fact is that censorship always defeats its own purpose, for it creates, in the end, the kind of society that is incapable of exercising real discretion, incapable, that is, of doing an honest or intelligent job, and thus guarantees a steady intellectual decline.

We must, then, keep in mind that we are dealing with realities, not abstractions. We must learn to think things, not words; we must fasten our attention on consequences, not on theories. We must keep ever in mind the warning of William James that "there is no difference of truth that doesn't make a difference of fact somewhere," and that meaningful discussion will "hinge as soon as possible upon some practical or particular issue."

The importance of this becomes clear when we realize that almost everyone agrees on the principles that should govern our conduct. At least almost all say and probably think that they agree. It is the application that is different. Southerners who deny Negroes a fair trial purport to be enthusiastic for the Bill of Rights but do not apply it in the same way to whites and Negroes. The legislature of Texas which recently passed a resolution outlawing any party that "entertained any thought or principle" contrary to the Constitution of the United States was doubtless sincere enough, but it did not intend to outlaw the Democratic party because that party "entertains" a thought critical of the Fifteenth Amendment. Senator McCarthy doubtless thinks of himself as a paladin of Constitutional liberties and so does Senator McCarran; Merwin K. Hart and Mr. Zook invoke the Constitution as do the editors of *Counterattack* and of "Red Channels." All this is too obvious for rehearsal. We must get beyond the principles to their application in order to discover where the difficulty is, and to discover how to resolve it.

When we approach the problem this way we can see that the most compelling argument for freedom is not the argument from theory or principle but the argument of necessity. To put the issue as simply as possible, we maintain freedom not in order to indulge error but in order to discover truth, and we know no other way of discovering truth. It is difficult to think of any situation where this principle does not apply.

This does not mean for a moment that the principles are unimportant. They are enormously important. They provide the framework of our thinking. They provide us with a common vocabulary. They crystallize for us the values we cherish. If we did not have a body of principles of freedom, we would not be discussing this matter at all. The principles are important, then, and essential. But it is in the application that we discover their meaning. It is the application that is the test. If we are to solve our problems, it must be by traveling the road of conduct and consequences. Theory may mislead us; experience must be our guide.

Let us note three or four examples. Here, for instance, is perhaps the most important of all at the moment—the conflicting claims of scientific freedom and national security. To talk in abstract terms of the freedom of the scientist does not get us very far, for that is not an abstract freedom; it is a freedom whose effective exercise requires a good deal of cooperation from the community. Nor does it get us very far to talk in abstract terms about national security. Everyone is in favor of national security, but Senators Morse and McCarthy have different notions about how it is to be achieved. The meaningful approach is that of consequences. What happens when you adopt a policy of freedom for research—freedom with common-sense regulations that any sensible man may be expected to observe? What happens when you permit the government or the military to control the research? Fortunately, we need not speculate here; Walter Gellhorn's remarkable study of *Security, Loyalty, and Science* has covered the ground and provided the moral.

> The costs of secrecy are high. When the freedom of scientific exchange is curtailed, an unfavorable re-

action upon further scientific development is inevitable. We pay for secrecy by slowing the rate of our scientific progress, now and in the future. This loss of momentum may conceivably be disastrous, for even from the strictly military point of view "it is just as important for us to have some new secrets to keep as it is for us to hold on to the old ones." If it is unsound to suppress scientific knowledge during the long years of a cold war, the American people may one day discover that they have been crouching behind a protective wall of blueprints and formulas whose impregnability is an utter illusion.

Or let us look to an equally familiar field—the effort to rid our school system of alleged "subversives." Ignore for the moment all questions about the definition of subversive (a term that has not yet been legally defined) or about the rights of teachers. Look solely to the social interest, the community interest, in the matter, and apply the test of consequences. What happens when a state tries to purge its state universities or a community tries to purge its public schools of alleged subversives?

We have a good deal of evidence on this matter by now, for the campaign against subversives has gone on for some time. We can therefore speak here with some assurance. What happens is not that the state or city gets rid of hordes of Communists. Not at all. It very rarely finds any, and it rarely finds any subversives unless it wants to stretch that term to embrace anyone who rejoiced in Russian victories in 1943, or who supported Wallace in 1949, or who favors socialized medicine. What happens is the demoralization and the eventual corruption of the school system. This is not a momentary or even a temporary affair; it is something whose consequences may go on for years. The search for subversives results in the intimidation of the independent-, the original-, the imaginative-, and the experimental-minded. It discourages independence of thought in teachers and students alike. It discourages the joining of organizations that may turn out to be considered subversive. It discourages the reading of books that may excite the suspicion of some investigator, or some Legionnaire. It discourages criticism of educational or of governmental policies. It discourages the discussion of controversial matters in the classroom, for such discussion may be reported, or misreported, and cause trouble. It creates a situation where first-rate minds will not go into teaching or into administration and where students therefore get poor teaching. In the long run it will create a generation incapable of appreciating the difference between independence of thought and subservience. In the long run it will create a generation not only deprived of liberty but incapable of enjoying liberty.

Or we can turn to the impact of the doctrine of guilt by association, the widespread and indiscriminate use of the Attorney General's list of subversive organizations, and of the list of the House Committee on Un-American Activities. The first list now runs to some 150 organizations, the second to almost 700. Let us ignore the question of the legal validity of such lists (the Supreme Court has ruled that they have no validity as such); let us ignore the question of their use by school boards, communities, states, and so forth (the Attorney General originally provided that "no conclusions whatever are to be drawn from membership in any such organization"). Let us ignore the question whether some organizations may or may not be dangerous or wicked or disreputable and look solely to the question of consequences.

What is the interest that society has in preserving and encouraging voluntary organizations and what are the results of the application of the doctrine of guilt by association? If, as would seem clear to any student of our history, the voluntary organization is the chief instrumentality of American democracy, then anything that strikes at it strikes a blow at the effective functioning of democracy.

To discourage the instinct and practice of joining—a practice that has given us all of our political parties, our churches, our labor unions, our professional organizations, our great reform movements, most of our colleges—to discourage such a practice is a serious matter. Whatever may be the results in preventing the citizens of Norwalk, Connecticut, for example, from seeing an art exhibit sponsored by a man who once belonged to the Congress of Arts and Sciences, they add up to very little as against the price we pay for them—the price of depriving the people of Norwalk of an art exhibit, the price of discouraging artists from joining organizations that may come to be considered subversive. The doctrine has not so far seriously interfered with any subversive organization—at least none has been officially banned, a long process. But that it has exercised wide influence in discouraging joining cannot be denied.

Thus, Jahoda and Cook in their study of "Security Measures and Freedom of Thought" conclude that:

> One of the consequences of the loyalty and security programs has been the development of a social atmosphere in which individuals are subject to unfounded suspicion on the basis of certain personal characteristics or group memberships. . . . We asked all Federal employes interviewed in Washington what kinds of people they thought might form the target for unfounded suspicions. . . . Among the list [of answers] one group may be singled out for comment because of the frequency with which it is named by respondents of very different outlooks: by Democrats and by Republicans; by those who regard the consequences of the investigations as entirely beneficial and by those who see harmful consequences; by those who make it quite clear that they do not belong to the group in question, and by those who identify with it; by those who regard it with suspicion and by those who are outraged at the suspicion. . . . The group we have in mind are the people who belong to voluntary organizations with definite social purposes. . . . At present voluntary organizations are not prohibited in this country. Yet our material suggests the possibility that because membership in some organizations can have dire consequences for Federal employes, "a public opinion passes current which tends to cause any association whatsoever to be regarded as a bold and almost illicit enterprise."

Turn where we will to apply the test of consequences, we discover that we must insist on freedom because we cannot do without it, because we cannot afford the price of its denial. Thus the most powerful argument against Senator Cox's program of supervision of foundations ("To determine if they are using their resources for un-American and subversive activities or for purposes not in the interest or tradition of the United States") is that if it is put into effect it will endanger existing foundations and discourage philanthropists from setting up others. The most powerful argument against the censorship of textbooks and the elimination of "un-American" ideas or of anything critical of the "American spirit of private enterprise" is that such censorship will guarantee the elimination of textbooks with any ideas at all. The compelling argument against the purging of libraries is that if the kind of people who believe in purges have their way and work their will, our libraries will cease to be centers of light and learning and become instead instruments of party or church or class. The compelling argument against denying passports or visas on the grounds of unpopular political or economic ideas is that by silencing criticism in those who expect to travel from country to country we deprive ourselves of the value of what foreigners might have to tell us and discourage criticism in our own citizens. The decisive argument against the kind of censorship of radio and motion picture performers that we are now witnessing is that it will leave us, in the end, with programs devoid of ideas and performers devoid of originality or of courage to apply originality where it exists.

In every case it is society that is the loser. Our society can doubtless afford to lose the benefits of ideas or character in any one instance, but the cumulative costs of the intimidation of thoughtful and critical men and women is something no society can afford.

A society that applies doctrinaire notions to social conduct will find itself in the end the prisoner of its own doctrines. A society that takes refuge in shibboleths like "subversive" or "un-American" will find itself unable to recognize reality when it appears—even the reality of danger. A society that discourages experiment will find that without experiment there can be no progress, and that without progress, there is regress. A society that attempts to put education and science and scholarship in straitjackets will find that in straitjackets there can be no movement, and that the result will be intellectual stagnation. A society that repudiates free enterprise in the intellectual arena under the deluded notion that it can flourish in the economic alone, will find that without intellectual enterprise, economic enterprise dries up. A society that encourages state intervention in the realm of ideas will find itself an easy prey to state intervention in other realms as well.

That government which most scrupulously protects and encourages complete freedom of thought, expression, communication, investigation, criticism is the one which has the best chance of achieving security and progress. "They that can give up essential liberty to obtain a little temporary safety deserve neither liberty nor safety," wrote Benjamin Franklin two centuries ago, and what he said is as valid now as it was then. Government and society have a paramount interest in independence, originality, heterodoxy, criticism, nonconformity, because all experience teaches that it is out of these that come new ideas, and because every society needs a continuous re-examination of old ideas and a continuous flow of new ideas. And it is relevant to remember, too, that it is nonconformity that needs encouragement. As William Ellery Channing said over a century ago, "We have conservatives enough."

Three centuries ago John Milton addressed himself to the problem that now confronts us, and what he said in *Areopagitica* is still valid:

> Believe it, Lords and Commons, they who counsel ye to such a suppressing do as good as bid ye suppress yourselves. . . . Ye cannot make us now less capable, less knowing, less eagerly pursuing of the truth, unless ye first make yourselves, that made us so, less the lovers, less the founders of our true liberty.

1953

Tom Paine Talks
Back to Providence

Introductory: *The Mayor of Providence, Rhode Island, has declined, on behalf of his city, a statue of Thomas Paine on the ground that Paine is still "a controversial figure." In the interview below the imaginary chairman of the board reviewing Mr. Paine's credentials asks some stereotyped questions. The replies are quoted from or based on Paine's own words.*

CHAIRMAN: This is an inquiry to determine whether we should authorize a statue to you in the city of Providence, Mr. Paine. It is not a trial, it does not therefore require judicial process. It is merely an effort to discover whether there is anything in your historical file to raise doubts—reasonable doubts—about your complete and exclusive loyalty to the Government of the United States. It is an attempt to find out whether it is clearly consistent with the best interests of Providence and of Rhode Island to erect a statue to you. I think I should make clear at the very outset, Mr. Paine, that no one has a *right* to a statue in Providence. A statue is not a right but a privilege.

PAINE: 'Tis surprising to see how rapidly a panic will sometimes run through a country, but I try always to remember that Those who expect to reap the blessings of freedom must, like men, undergo the fatigue of supporting it.

CHAIRMAN: Now Mr. Paine, your file seems to be an unusually large one; in fact it is bulging with charges of one kind or another. That in itself is pretty suspicious, wouldn't you say?

PAINE: Sir, he who dares not offend cannot be honest.

CHAIRMAN: Yes, yes; but let us get at once to the substance of the charges. Here is the first one that goes to the very heart of the matter. It would appear that you are not an American at all, but English—or perhaps French. It appears that you were born in England and lived there until you were almost forty years old, when you left under a cloud. It is charged that you were dismissed from your job in the customs office as a troublemaker, that you were a bankrupt, and that your wife left you. A bad record, Mr. Paine. Just why did you come over to this country in 1774?

PAINE: The New World hath been the asylum for the persecuted lover of liberty from every part of Europe. And I knew, too, that America was the only spot in the political world where the principle of universal reformation could begin.

CHAIRMAN: Let us get back to this question of your citizenship, Mr. Paine. It appears that you stayed in America only a few years—just long enough to stir up a Revolution—and that you then went back to England where, once again, you stirred up trouble, and that you then fled to France. And it says here that you became a citizen of France—not only a citizen, but actually a member of the Convention that wrote the new Constitution! How do you happen to have so many countries, Mr. Paine?

PAINE: Where liberty is not, there is my country.

CHAIRMAN: Quite. But when you were thrown into jail in France —you seem to have quite an impressive jail record, Mr. Paine— our Minister, Gouverneur Morris, refused to bestir himself in your behalf on the ground that you were either an English citizen, as the French claimed, or a French citizen.

PAINE: True enough, Sir; I shared with Washington, Hamilton, and others honorary citizenship in France. But our Minister, James Monroe, wrote that "I consider you as an American citizen, and you are considered universally in that character by the people of America."

CHAIRMAN: But it appears, Mr. Paine, that not content with citizenship in three countries you tried to become a citizen of the world, whatever that means. There is evidence here that you were heard proposing a toast to "The Republic of the World." And that you wrote on something called "The Republic of Man." Would you say, Mr. Paine, that you were a One-Worlder?

PAINE: Quite right, Sir. My country is the world, and my religion is to do good.

CHAIRMAN: By your own admission, then, you are an internationalist and a One-Worlder. Of course that is your privilege, Mr. Paine, but you will understand that one who willingly serves a foreign nation and who regards himself as a citizen of the world can not claim true loyalty to the United States. Under the terms of our McCarran Act you would be subject to deportation on the ground that you associated with revolutionary organizations after you became an American citizen and that you took an oath of loyalty with mental reservations about other countries, and that you were actually in the service of other countries. But why talk of deportation? With a record like yours we would never let you in at all. You seem to have quite a criminal record, Mr. Paine. You were dismissed from your post in England; you were indicted for criminal libel in the British courts, and it was held that "your writings tended to excite tumult and disorder"—a good description, I gather. Then you were jailed in France as well. How do you explain this propensity for getting in trouble and landing in jail, Mr. Paine?

PAINE: 'Tis the business of little minds to shrink; but he whose heart is firm, and whose conscience approves his conduct, will pursue his principles unto death.

CHAIRMAN: Don't you think it rather odd, Mr. Paine, that any one who purports to be loyal to America should spend most of his life abroad? It would appear that you spent less than twenty years of your whole life in this country, and that even during the period when we needed you most you were busy in England and France.

PAINE: You touch me on a very tender spot. . . . My heart and myself are 3,000 miles apart; and I had rather see my horse Button in his own stable or eating the grass of Bordentown than see all the pomp and show of Europe. A thousand years hence—you must indulge me in a few thoughts—America may be what England now is. The innocence of her character that won the hearts of all nations in her favor may sound like a romance, and her inimitable virtue as if it had never been. The ruins of that liberty which thousands bled for, or suffered to obtain, may just furnish materials for a village tale or extort a sigh from rustic sensibility, while the fashionable of that day deride the principle and deny the fact. When we contemplate the fall of empires and the extinction of nations of the ancient world we see but little to excite our regret in the moldering ruins of pompous palaces, magnificent monuments, lofty pyramids, and walls and towers of the most costly workmanship. But when the empire of America shall fall, the subject for contemplative sorrow will be infinitely greater than crumbling brass or marble can invite. It will not then be said, here stood a temple of vast antiquity, but here, ah painful thought! the noblest work of human wisdom, the grandest scene of human glory, the fair cause of freedom rose and fell. Hear this, and then ask if I forget America. . . .

CHAIRMAN: All very pretty, Mr. Paine, but a bit irrelevant. Perhaps we can get back to some of the material in your file. Let's forget about your chequered career abroad; there's plenty in the domestic file to give us concern. It is alleged, for example, that you are a radical, a revolutionary, an enemy of government, in short a congenital subversive. Would you say that you were hostile to organized government?

PAINE: Society is produced by our wants, and governments by our wickedness. Government, like dress, is the badge of lost innocence.

CHAIRMAN: You do seem to have quite a record for overthrowing government. You helped start a revolution in the American colonies; you went over to England to get a revolution underway there; you flung yourself into the revolution in France. Three revolutions, in three countries; would you say, Mr. Paine, that you have an affinity for revolutions?

PAINE: As I have embarked on the Revolution, I do not like to leave it till it is finished. And, to see it in our power to make a world happy—to teach mankind the art of being so—to exhibit on the theatre of the universe a character hitherto unknown—and to have, as it were, a new creation intrusted to our hands, are honors that can neither be too highly estimated nor too gratefully received.

CHAIRMANS: You are, in short, a professional agitator. I am not surprised when I consider your associations. We have evidence here that you have a peculiar affinity for association with subversives of one kind or another. It is charged that you maintained close sympathetic association with such radicals as Benjamin Franklin, Thomas Jefferson, and Samuel Adams in this country, with men like William Godwin and Joseph Priestley in England and—horrors—with revolutionaries like Danton, Mirabeau, and Condorcet in France. Would you say, Mr. Paine, that birds of a feather flock together, and that a man is known by the company he keeps?

PAINE: When facts are sufficient, arguments are useless.

CHAIRMAN: That is a flippant answer, Mr. Paine, but this is a serious inquiry. I would like your consideration of this charge: that you have been persistently critical of the American system of private enterprise. We have information here that you championed the "welfare state," both here and abroad, and that you proposed to weaken the moral fiber of the American people by providing, out of taxpayers' money, substantial payments to the old, the crippled and infirm, and to every young man and woman who reaches the age of twenty-one. Would you say, Mr. Paine, that you were a precocious, premature New Dealer?

PAINE: It is a position not to be controverted that the earth, in its natural uncultivated state, was, and ever would have continued to be, the common property of the human race. In that state every man would have been born to property. Cultivation . . . has dispossessed more than half the inhabitants of every nation of their natural inheritance, without providing for them, as ought to have been done, an indemnification for that loss, and has thereby created a species of poverty and wretchedness that did not exist before. It is not therefore a charity but a right that I am pleading for.

CHAIRMAN: That seems to me Communist doctrine, Mr. Paine. And I am not surprised, for I find here evidence that no sooner had you come over to our country than you attacked the property and institutions of one-half of our people, accusing them of murder, lewdness, and barbarity because they held property in slaves.

PAINE: Christians are taught to account all men their neighbors; and love their neighbors as themselves; and do to all men as they would be done by; to do good to all men; and man-stealing is ranked with enormous crimes. Is the barbarous enslaving of our inoffensive neighbors, and treating them like wild beasts, reconcilable with all these divine precepts?

CHAIRMAN: I am glad you brought up this matter of divine precepts, Mr. Paine, for it brings us to one of the weightiest charges in your file. We have evidence that you wrote a blasphemous and indecent book called *The Age of Reason*, attacking Christianity and the Church. We do not customarily give the source of these charges, but it may interest you that no other than President Theodore Roosevelt described you as "a filthy little atheist." I pass by the question of your size and your sanitary condition and ask you if it is not a fact that you called Christianity itself a "fable" and the New Testament "a wild and visionary doctrine."

PAINE: Religion is a private affair between every man and his Maker and no third party has a right to interfere between them. I will, however, attempt to answer your charge. I believe in one God and no more; and I hope for happiness beyond this life. I believe in the equality of man, and I believe that religious duties consist in doing justice, loving mercy, and endeavoring to make our fellow-creatures happy. The motive and object in all my publications on religious subjects has been to bring man to a right reason that God has given him; to impress on him the great principles of divine morality, justice, mercy, and a benevolent disposition to all men and to all creatures.

CHAIRMAN: Here, as in so many other things, your methods appear to have been violent and your conduct contumacious. You appear to be a troublemaker not only in politics but in society and religion as well.

PAINE: Tyranny, like hell, is not easily conquered; yet we have this consolation with us, that the harder the conflict, the more glorious the triumph.

CHAIRMAN: There is one matter that puzzles me, Mr. Paine. We may doubt that you are worthy of a statue anywhere, but certainly Providence, Rhode Island, would seem to be the last place that should commemorate you. In the first place it was founded by a devout and pious man, Roger Williams, and founded as a Christian commonwealth, and you have scandalously attacked Christianity. In the second place we have evidence here that you went out of your way to criticize Rhode Island when she exercised her sovereign right of refusing to ratify the proposal for a 5 per cent impost for the Congress in 1782.

PAINE: I have never yet made, and I hope I never shall make it the least point of consideration whether a thing is popular or unpopular, but whether it is right or wrong. Neither is there any Delegate from the State of Rhode Island who can say that I ever sought from any man any place, office, recompense, or reward on any occasion for myself. I have had the happiness of serving mankind, and the honor of doing it freely.

CHAIRMAN: Your answers are very ingenious, Mr. Paine, but plausible as they are they have very little to do with the subject of this inquiry. I think the evidence that I have brought out here, in this examination, makes it inescapably clear that you are a controversial character. And surely even you will agree, Mr. Paine, that a community like ours is much safer and happier when it is free from all turbulence and controversy?

PAINE: There are some Truths so self-evident and obvious that they ought never to be stated in the form of a question for debate, because it is habituating the mind to think doubtfully of what there ought to be no doubt upon. But you will permit me one final observation. In my own lifetime, as you know, I was tried and imprisoned. But *these* are the times that try men's *souls*.

1955

Freedom and the Right to Travel

In his speech to the General Assembly of the United Nations on October 20, 1963, President Kennedy admonished all of us that "new efforts are needed if the Assembly's Declaration of Human Rights is to have full meaning. And new means should be found for promoting the free expression and trade of ideas—through travel and communication, and through increased exchange of people and books and broadcasts. For as the world renounces the competition of weapons, competition in ideas must flourish—and that competition must be as full and as fair as possible."

It was not a new sentiment, nor a new appeal. In 1952 President Truman had asserted that "we shall never be able to remove suspicion and fear as potential causes of war until communication is permitted to flow . . . across international barriers." And four years later, at Geneva, President Eisenhower called on all the nations of the world "to lower the barriers which now impede the opportunities of people to travel anywhere in the world . . . so that all will have a chance to know each other face to face."

Notwithstanding these eloquent appeals, our own State Department has adopted a policy designed to frustrate this principle of freedom of travel and communication, and has instead erected barriers between our people and the peoples of nations whose governments it disapproves. It is an ironic commentary on the plea for free communication that three Presidents have been unable to communicate their ideas of freedom of travel across the barrier that separates the White House from the State Department.

In the fifties we were not supposed to communicate with Russia, and then China. Now the walls are down for Russia, but we have put them up around Cuba instead. A few months ago the State Department officially announced that "travel in Cuba does not meet the established criteria. . . . Passports of United States citizens may be validated for travel in Cuba *only when their travel may be regarded as being in the best interests of the United States.*" Clearly the travel of college students—just the group, one would think, who might be trusted to see for themselves—is not "in the best interests of the United States" and the young men who listened to the President rather than to the Passport Office and defied this edict are now threatened with something resembling a peculiar form of double jeopardy—withdrawal of passports, and examination by the House Un-American Activities Committee!

We need not, perhaps, waste any sympathy on the fifty young men; after all they got to Cuba and—thanks to the blundering of the Un-American Activities Committee—they are in process of getting both publicity and martyrdom. But a moral, and a constitutional, principle is to be asserted when it is challenged, not when we happen to approve of the character or the activities of those who exercise it. To argue that these young men are not sympathetic characters is like arguing that Tom Paine was not a gentleman, or that *The Tropic of Cancer* is not a good book anyway.

What is important is the right of travel. What is important is the claim of the State Department to decide who may and who may not travel; the assertion by the State Department that travel is an instrument of foreign policy; the claim of that Department to decide what is "in the best interests of the United States." These are matters that far transcend the rights or wrongs of fifty youngsters disporting themselves on the international stage.

The passport problem is by now depressingly familiar. There was a time when a passport was merely a card of identification, needed only for admission to a few foreign countries, not for re-entry into the United States. There was a time, too, when the right of Americans to travel and to return to their own country was unquestioned. But beginning in the forties, and feeding on the crises, real and alleged, of the fifties, the State Department took the position that travel was not all that innocent or all that natural; that it was not a right to be exercised at the discretion of the citizen, but a privilege to be exercised at the discretion of the State Department. The Department's behavior has been a curious hybrid of tragedy and farce. Again and again the Department denied a passport to American citizens; again and again it backed down when the Supreme Court told it that its conduct was lawless, until, in the end, the mere threat of legal action was enough to send it scurrying for cover. Forced by the Court to acknowledge that travel was a "natural and a constitutional right," the Department nevertheless persisted in asserting its right to withhold or reclaim passports, and its right to declare which countries on the globe were "out of bounds" for American visitors. And with a stubbornness and arrogance characteristic of the bureaucratic mind it persisted in its argument that travel is an instrument of foreign policy, that travel must be in the best interests of the United States, and that by a happy dispensation of Providence *it* is precisely the body that knew what was in the best interests of the United States.

We can dispose briefly of the constitutional issue. Again and again the highest court has asserted that travel is one of the "liberties" protected by the Fifth Amendment and that, like other liberties and rights, it cannot be denied or impaired except by due process of law. That means that the right to travel is not subject to the caprice of some official in the Passport Office. The State Department can no more tamper with that right than it can tamper with the right of free speech or free press or freedom of association. No mere administrative ruling that "it is not in the best interests of the United States" can silence freedom of speech or press; no official in Washington can legally decide what speech or what associations are in the best interests of the nation.

This does not leave the United States, or the State Department, naked and defenseless. If it has evidence that the travel of some person is in fact dangerous, it can produce that evidence in open court—bring it out from the subterranean files of the Un-American Activities Committee and other equally dubious agencies, and expose it to the light of day. Government by injunction is a thing of the past.

The implications of the position that the State Department asserts are important. First, it arrogates to itself authority to decide what are in fact the best interests of the United States. Yet who has authorized the State Department to make this momentous decision? What criteria does it use; what tests does it apply; how does it validate its judgments? And if the State Department can make this decision within its jurisdiction (which is wide) why should not all other departments make comparable decisions in their jurisdictions? Does the Department of Defense have the authority to decide, by administrative fiat, what are in the best interests of national defense? Suppose it decided that the sale of cigarettes to servicemen was not in the best interest of national defense; would that edict be binding? Does the Treasury Department have the authority to decide that spending money abroad is not in the best interests of the United States and could it make policy by administrative edict? Why should not the Department of the Interior decide on the disposition of public lands and the Department of Agriculture on farm policy by equally easy methods? Or is there a hierarchy of authority in government which permits State to exercise powers not permitted lesser departments?

Second, it arrogates to itself the power to decide what conduct does in fact advance and what conduct does impair the "best interests of the United States." If the State Department really knows what conduct is in our best interests, should it not inform the American people so we can all conduct ourselves properly? May we look forward to Rules of Conduct which we are all to observe, and even to sanctions behind those rules? Alas, we do not even know what are the interests which our travel is supposed to promote. That would be discouraging if it were not for conclusive evidence that the Departments of State and of Defense—and others too—are at loggerheads about the interests which they are supposed to promote in Vietnam, or in Germany.

Third, it should never be overlooked by overly solicitous officials of the State Department that their claim to the right to deny passports is an argument that cuts two ways. For if those whose travel is not in the best interests of the nation are denied passports, it follows with inescapable logic that all those who do receive passports (and almost everyone does) do in fact travel in the interests of the United States. If travel is an "instrument of foreign policy" as Secretary Dulles fatuously observed, then all those who travel are instruments of that policy. We had thought heretofore that the State Department was an instrument of the American people, but it appears now that the people are an instrument of the State Department. Is the State Department really ready to take on this responsibility—the responsibility of placing its stamp of approval on all who travel, of informing the world that they have been cleared as "instruments" of American policy, and that their conduct, however it may astonish the natives of France, Italy, and Spain, is nevertheless "in the best interests of the United States"?

But the Department does not rest its case entirely on the argument that travel should be "in the best interests of the United States." There is another argument, almost a plaintive one, with which it solicits our sympathy. Some travel—to Cuba for example —might "embarrass the conduct of foreign policy." And nothing should be permitted to do that.

Now here if anywhere the State Department might be expected to take its stand on the firm ground of fact. However esoteric the phrase "best interest of the United States" may be, there can be no controversy about what is embarrassing. Surely the Department can submit conclusive evidence that some travel —precisely that which it has attempted to prevent—has in fact embarrassed something.

For the past fifteen years the Department has attempted to deny passports to Americans on the ground that their travel might be embarrassing, only to be forced by the Courts to hand over the passports after all. The accused persons—let us call them Clark Foreman, Paul Robeson, Dr. Kamen, Judge Clark, Arthur Miller, Leonard Boudin, Otto Nathan, Linus Pauling—did in fact travel abroad. Did their conduct abroad injure the United States? Did it embarrass the conduct of foreign relations? Does the empirical evidence bear out the Department's suspicions and charges? Did these men, in the immortal words of the Passport Division's Roderick O'Connor, "capriciously disturb the delicate international situation by breaking restrictions which have been imposed for strong foreign policy reasons"? If so, surely the Department is prepared to prove its case. But so far no single instance of embarrassment or disturbance has been submitted to us. So far the Department has not been able to say "We told you so" in a single case. It comes to us therefore with a record of error in this matter that cannot but excite our admiration—100 per cent.

But there is more to this than the issue of fact. There is the issue of principle as well. For the assumption behind the specious argument of "embarrassment" is that if the conduct of citizens abroad did in fact "embarrass" the conduct of foreign relations, the government would be justified in stopping it. But in our system of government a great many things that citizens do embarrass both foreign and domestic policy. Indeed one might say that the very essence of freedom is the right of the citizen to embarrass his government—by speech, by writing, by petition, by assembly, and by travel too, as long as he does nothing that is unlawful. Totalitarian governments can avoid that embarrassment by easy means, but the habit of embarrassing government by the exercise of constitutional rights is something that democracies have to learn to live with.

Moreover, if government can interfere with travel that might "embarrass" the conduct of foreign policy, why should it not interfere with domestic activities that cause even greater embarrassment? Does Dean Acheson's criticism of Britain embarrass the conduct of foreign policy, or Walter Lippmann's observations on De Gaulle or on the Berlin crisis, or, for that matter, Governor Rockefeller's criticism of our Cuba policy? If so, may the State Department or the Congress silence these men or discipline them on the ground that their speech and their conduct is not in the best interests of the United States? Why not?

But the benign officials of the Passport Office have one further argument with which to confound us. It is really the traveler they are worried about all the time. If he goes to Cuba—or to China—he may be brain-washed. He may be exposed to all sorts of dangerous influences. He may come back with the wrong ideas. He may even get into trouble. We cannot protect him in these countries, nor can we permit him to waive protection. For his own good, therefore, he must stay home.

It is gratifying that the State Department should be so solicitous, but a bit alarming. For if it is to function as guardian and protector and nurse to all travelers it is going to have its hands full. Will it seal off Franco's Spain and Salazar's Portugal to protect young men from the glittering attractions of totalitarianism? Will it seal off Russia and Yugoslavia, as it has sealed off China and Cuba, to protect them against the seductions of communism? And how far does its responsibility go? There are many ways of misleading the unwary and seducing the young. Is it really to our best interests that young men should be exposed to the welfare state in Sweden or to socialized medicine in Denmark? Besides, why stop with foreign travel? Are we to seal off literature and films and broadcasts from these dangerous countries as well, on the ground that they may mislead the innocent and the unsuspecting? That is the way totalitarian countries act; are we prepared to emulate them?

There is of course always a danger that visitors to foreign countries might get into trouble, just as there is always a danger that people who stay at home might get into trouble. Doubtless the fifty young men who went to Cuba were exposed to that danger. It is perhaps sufficient commentary on this argument, however, that they did in fact get home safe and sound, and that their troubles came after they had returned to their own country, and that they came from the State Department and from Congress—and perhaps from the unruliness of refugee groups who are trying to dictate our foreign policy. To blame these troubles on the young men who went to Cuba is like blaming race riots on Negro children who want to go to school. The easiest way to avoid this particular trouble is to deprive the State Department of its authority to declare foreign countries out of bounds, and abolish the House Un-American Activities Committee.

Leaving considerations of law and principle, we may consider the wisdom of our current policy. Even if we were to concede the authority of the State Department to withhold passports (which we should not) it by no means follows that they should do so. A good many things that are legal are unwise. Interfering with travel is one of them.

Is it wise to put up walls around foreign countries?

Is it wise to forget Burke's admonition that we can never indict a whole people?

Is it wise to prevent Americans from finding out for themselves what things are like in foreign countries?

Is it wise to cut ourselves off from whatever information is available to us, or to rely exclusively on official information? Certainly official information about Cuba led us grievously astray some two years back. Are we going to rely on it exclusively in the future?

Is it wise to proclaim to the world that we are afraid of the impact that Cuba—or China—might have on American visitors; that we do not trust our own citizens to resist the wiles of rival systems; that we do not really have confidence in the advantages of our own system?

Is it wise to assert that American citizens are in any circumstances (except of government service in time of war) instruments of foreign policy?

Is it wise to adopt a policy that runs counter to that specific guarantee of the Declaration of Human Rights that "everyone has the right to leave any country, including his own, and to return to his country?"

It is these assumptions and these policies, not the willful gestures of a handful of boys visiting Cuba, that are essentially contrary "to the best interests of the United States."

No one can spell out in detail what those interests are, or what policies serve them best. But surely we must all agree that the interest of the United States is best served by freedom in all its forms and all its manifestations; by confidence in the intelligence and the integrity of our people; by striking down barriers, not by putting them up—the physical barriers of walls, the legal barriers of arbitrary regulations, the intellectual and moral barriers which make for fear and distrust among men.

1964

Federal Centralization
and the Press

The American experience might almost be called an achievement in avoidance. For in historical perspective, the most astonishing thing about the American experience is that we have managed in so extraordinary a fashion to achieve the things that Western nations and societies tried to achieve without paying the price that history or Providence customarily exacted from them. We have achieved nationalism and national unity without what the Germans call *Nationalizmus*. We have achieved colonialism on a very large scale—for everything west of the Appalachians was colony to the thirteen original states—without colonialism, eliminating it so completely that not one out of one hundred Americans realizes that we have been the greatest colonizing power in the nineteenth and twentieth centuries. We have achieved universal education without that vulgarization of learning which was so confidently predicted by the critics of the American experiment. We have separated church and state and embarked upon a policy of no ecclesiastical establishment without that moral depravity which again was predicted as its inevitable consequence. We have achieved majority rule without that despotism over the minority which was expected by Tocqueville and by all those who have echoed Tocqueville's famous chapters on the inevitable tyranny of the majority. We are in process of achieving world power without—so far—that imperialism which made world power more a curse than a blessing in the nineteenth century.

Have we achieved national unity, national centralization,

national strength, without the impairment of local autonomy and without the impairment of the liberty of the individual which so frequently follows the establishment of a powerful central government? In a larger sense, this issue of particularism and nationalism is part of a very ancient issue in politics, one of the oldest, one of the most persistent, and one of the most difficult of all political questions: the question of the reconciliation of liberty and order. It is a problem on which the old British empire was wrecked—it is a problem which the Americans themselves proved unable to solve during the dark days of the Articles of Confederation. It was a crucial issue at the Constitutional Convention—it was solved then at least in principle. But it was not solved in practice; witness the war of 1861 to 1865.

Our history could almost be written in terms of the struggle over the broad and narrow construction, the struggle over nationalism and states' rights. It was this that appeared to divide Jefferson and Hamilton; it was this that created crisis after crisis during the dangerous years from the mid-forties to the Civil War, and that split the nation asunder. It was this that appeared the crucial problem of the war itself. The question of the nature and extent of national authority was by no means settled by victory at Appomattox. It persisted and persists to our own day. Few questions have ruffled the surface and agitated the deeps of American politics in the last half-century as persistently as this one. In one sense, the problem of local autonomy and national authority has been a very real problem and we cannot but stand amazed at the insights of a Jefferson or a Hamilton, both patriots, both statesmen, both nationalists—one putting his faith in the intelligence and virtue of the mass of the people, the other in the power and majesty of the state; one representing what was to be the American tradition, the other what had—and has—been the European tradition. It is a tribute to the understanding and the vision of these Founding Fathers that we are still discussing the problems of state and nation very much in their terms.

Subsequent generations have added little to the analysis or to the clarification of the issues. Quite the contrary—it is not too sweeping a statement to say that subsequent generations, and particularly the last generation, have done much to obfuscate the issues. They have invoked states' rights to rationalize economic interests; to obscure the reality of national unity—the unity of soil and water and forest and resources, of wind and rain and drought, of economy and of society. Certainly it is hard to avoid the conclusion that most of the discussion of national centralization versus states' rights in recent years has been immaterial and irrelevant and designed to confuse the issue.

Perhaps the most urgent observation here is that the problem of governmental power, of the nature and extent and of the limits of that power, is not one that can yield to clichés, nor be disposed of by incantation. We should look to realities, not theories; to functions, not abstractions. We should keep in mind that whenever government exercises authority in America, it is the American people who exercise that authority. Above all this, we should keep in mind that the issue of state and nation is not a moral issue, though it can become one: It is a practical question. In itself, there is nothing either virtuous or wicked about state government and nothing either virtuous or wicked about national government. A highly centralized government like that of Britain is not necessarily a bad one, or even an inefficient one. A decentralized government like that of Germany is not necessarily a good one or even an efficient one. If we look realistically at the issue of the exercise of governmental authority, it will be clear, first, that the process of federal centralization has been steady and persistent from the beginning of our history, and particularly from the eighteen-eighties; second, that the process has been nonpolitical and nonpartisan, furthered by all parties when in power; third, that the process has generally adapted itself to the exigencies of the economy. Centralization, in the political arena, has almost invariably followed, not anticipated, centralization in the economic. Fourth, the process has been enormously stimulated by war and by military considerations generally. The implacable demands of military security make it highly improbable that there will be any diminution of federal centralization in the foreseeable future.

More to the point is the fact that, historically, federal centralization has not appeared to be the most serious threat to the liberties of the citizen. Even in the realm of civil liberties, the states rather than the nation have been most derelict. Whatever the situation today, historically most of the threats, too, and the attacks upon liberties guaranteed in bills of rights have come from states rather than from nation.

Who can doubt that the situation today has changed and is changing? Who can doubt that federal centralization does now pose problems that profoundly affect the liberties of men and the security of the nation (two things that are inextricably tied together, for we cannot have the one without the other)? In recent years, old issues have taken on new form and new dimensions. We can see now that Jefferson's fears were in many ways valid and logical, for Jefferson was not afraid of a strong government—during his presidency, the government did not lack for strength nor did the executive power lack for strength. The real issue, as Jefferson saw it when he advised the addition of the Bill of Rights, when he wrote the memorable Kentucky resolutions against the Alien and Sedition laws, when he prepared his first great Inaugural Address—the real issue was not quantitative, it was qualitative. The real issue was not so much the distinction between state and nation but the distinction between those things that government may do and those things that government may not do. Even this distinction, needless to say, is not mathematically clear. Under our system government may not ordinarily restrict freedom of speech, but may do so in war time; it may not usually restrict freedom of press but may do so in the face of obscenity; it may not demand excessive bail, but what is excessive varies from circumstance to circumstance.

In short, the whole matter is a matter of degree. The emphasis, therefore, should be more on wisdom than on technical or even legal rights. Nevertheless, there is general agreement on those things that government may do and government may not do, should do and should not do. The things government should not do embrace, above all, control of the communication of ideas; control of religion; control of political ideas; control of speech, of the press, and of association. This is one very large category and it is by far the most important single category. There are certain procedural powers government does not have—it may not violate due process but must act in accordance with rules of the Constitution and rules of law; it may not take life or property or liberty arbitrarily but only with due process and under the law.

The reason for the distinction between things government may do and may not do—the reason for setting all matters having to do with the communication of ideas in a special category exempt from governmental control—is as clear as is the reason for giving a preferred position to the First Amendment. It is not a sentimental indulgence to favored or privileged groups as is sometimes supposed. Indeed, the element of privilege does not enter in at all. It is rather a hard-headed recognition that without access to information, without the right to communicate information, without discussion and criticism—in short, without freedom—we cannot make our kind of government work at all. Without freedom, we will fall into error and that error may be irremediable. Freedom is not a luxury but a necessity. It is not an indulgence but a way of avoiding error and discovering truth. It is for that reason that it occupies, and must occupy, a preferred position in our constitutional system. What we have witnessed in the last decade, and especially in the last three or four years, is an ominous development, one that takes us back in a sense to the Jeffersonian struggle against the invasions of liberty by the leviathan state. It is the invasion by government generally—not the national government alone, but all government—of areas heretofore thought immune from government invasion: the areas of the press, religion, education, and association that were specifically exempted from governmental invasion by the bills of rights.

One of the most curious features of this development is that it appears at once so pervasive and in a technical sense so innocent. Nobody apparently wants it this way and nobody in government is prepared to admit that this is in fact what is happening. But almost every department, every branch, every agency of government contributes to the process in one way or another. Everybody calls for decentralization, and the weathering away of the TVA, the return to the states of oil lands and grazing lands goes on apace. But in the realm that really counts—in the realm that will be decisive, in the realm that is far and away the most perilous—it is federal centralization that grows apace, not decentralization.

Let us consider such manifestations of this process as threaten the integrity of our constitutional system and our ability to function as a democracy.

First, education. A very important part of American nationalism has been the absence of statism, and one thing that has contributed to this happy absence of statism is that education has not been the instrument of a powerful national government, but has been very largely a local affair, in this contrasting sharply with the position of education in many Continental nations. Even those who today advocate Federal aid to such things as school building or school lunch programs or scholarship aid would balk at suggesting control over the educational content of schools throughout the country. But in recent years, we have witnessed a series of threats to private and local controls over education through the operation of security legislation and review, through Congressional investigations of one kind or another, and through a variety of other influences that affect the integrity of the educational system. Note that the Jenner Committee, for example, recommended in 1953 a country-wide institution of loyalties programs for all colleges and universities—and that Senator McCarthy, going Jenner one better, urged the withdrawal of tax immunity from any institutions that did not supervise teachers' loyalty to the satisfaction of his committee, or that harbored what he called "Fifth Amendment Communists" on their faculties. Harvard College, you may recall, was a particular target of his criticism.

Other indirect invasions of the realm of education suggest themselves readily enough. In 1953, the Defense Department conditioned granting its contracts to colleges on teachers' getting security clearance. As the Civil Liberties Union observed at the time, this would open the door to a similar action by all other government departments, and through the mere accident of their employment in an institution which desires to sign such a contract the universities might themselves find themselves subject in toto to university clearance.

Similar pressures on education have come from nongovernmental organizations. I have in mind the demands of the American Legion, the Veterans of Foreign Wars, the Minute Women, and similar organizations, for censorship of textbooks and supervision of teaching. Most of the members of these organizations, in their private capacities, are opposed to Big Government and in favor of private enterprise rather than governmental enterprise; but in the one place where enterprise really counts, namely in the mind and spirit of men, they throw their strength to the side of government control over enterprise and, eventually, the smothering of enterprise. This inability of the spokesmen of private organizations to see the inevitable consequences of their demands for censorship over security clearance or for intellectual controls is one of the sobering paradoxes of our time.

What we have here in the realm of education is not merely pressure from the outside, from government or pietistic societies, but from the inside as well. It is one of the tragedies of our day that what Orwell predicted and Koestler described seems to be becoming fact, even in the citadels of freedom—namely, that in many cases the victim cooperates with the process of victimization. Thus Boston University discharged a teacher who refused to answer questions put him by the egregious Jenner Committee. Thus New Jersey has provided that all teachers at Rutgers must answer all questions coming up in legislative inquiries. Just how the constitutionality of some questions is going to be tested, unless someone refuses to answer, is not clear. The files of the American Association of University Professors and of the Civil Liberties Union bulge with complaints from teachers whose institutions have caved in before official demands and who undertake to police —the word itself is an affront—undertake to police their own faculties.

A second broad area into which government is moving increasingly, and with increasing energy, and may in time come to dominate, is science. This has come about in a variety of ways. First there is the elementary fact that science is an essential ingredient of national security and the government itself must have a monopoly on production and control of atomic energy. The claim of the military to establish security safeguards in crucial fields of scientific research is a persuasive one. What was apparent only to far-sighted scientists when it was first advanced—namely that all realms of science are somehow related to security, and that this principle would give government jurisdiction over the entire realm of science—has only gradually come home to the rest of us. What should have been apparent to anyone familiar with the psychology of the administrator—that he would invariably err on the side of caution and put his faith in mechanical regulations—is now becoming crystal clear.

A second factor making for the extension of central government control in the area of science is the power of the purse. In the process of farming out its projects to universities, government naturally indicates what it wants them to investigate. Two things follow: some degree of governmental determination of the kind of research to be undertaken, and some degree of control over those who do the research, and over the findings themselves. What this means is that universities are increasingly committed to projects not of their own choosing, and this often to the neglect of that pure research without which even applied science will become mere engineering. They find themselves permitting governmental supervision over their faculty, their research assistants, and even over the use to which their findings are put. This is the very negation of the function of the university; it is also an enormous accretion to Federal authority precisely in those areas where the government is incompetent to operate effectively. I am not concerned here with the palpable incompetence of government, an incompetence whose monument will ever be the Gray Board report that denied us the services of Robert Oppenheimer. I am concerned rather with the manner in which governmental security procedures create something like a Federal veto power over scientists and scientific projects. The Gray Board cleared Professor Oppenheimer on loyalty grounds and then rejected him on grounds of discretion! Promptly the authorities at the University of Washington withdrew or cancelled an invitation to Professor Oppenheimer to lecture at that institution. Washington may not be ready for Federal supervision over its water-power projects, but it is clearly eager to anticipate Federal suggestions over its intellectual activities. Will universities eager for Federal research money or eager merely to be thought above suspicion start submitting names of prospective professors to the proper security agencies in the Federal bureaus?

A third pressure is in the realm of religion. If there is one thing that in the beginning more sharply distinguished the American experiment than any other, it was the separation of church and state. Ours was the first Western nation to try the experiment of getting along without a state church. Everyone was agreed at the time that government had no business in the field of religion and everyone is, in principle, agreed on that now. Yet by indirection, through such things as the pressures of the Velde Committee and through the operation of the security program, the Federal government is indirectly imposing itself upon religion. The spectacle of the Velde Committee investigating Bishop Oxnam and the sallies of the Jenner Committee into the field of religion are more than straws in the wind. As Bishop Oxnam pointed out, the Committee clearly invaded the field of religion. The book under attack (Jerome Davis' *Behind Soviet Power*) had been sent to Methodist ministers by order of the administrative committee of the Board of Missions of the Methodist church. It was an official action of one of the official agencies of the largest Protestant denomination in America. So far as I know, this is the first time in American history that any committee had presumed to question the right of the church to send such literature to its ministers as it deemed wise.

A fourth area where the Federal government is threatening the field of the control of thought is that of the foundation—that new institution which is one of the most remarkable inventions in social science of modern times. I refer not so much to the puerilities of the Reece Committee as to the reaction to them. The degree to which the champions of the foundations found it necessary to defend their institutions on grounds that Representative Reece chose was an ominous thing. Some of them seemed all too ready to concede that government did, in fact, have a right to pass on the intellectual activities of beneficiaries of foundation grants, and too eager to prove that they had not in fact favored radicals or endowed subversives. No more specious argument than that tax exemption authorizes Congress to pass on the ideas and policies of the foundations was ever advanced. If this is true, it is equally true that tax exemption to churches authorizes governmental agencies to pass on the content of every sermon preached in every church, or on all the doctrines taught in theological seminaries. If it is true, it is equally true that tax exemption authorizes state and local governments to investigate what is actually taught in the classrooms of Minnesota or Harvard or Chicago Universities, a position which Senators Jenner and McCarthy are quite prepared to adopt. If it is true, it is equally true that tax exemption authorizes governmental authorities to inquire into the medical practices of doctors and tax-exempt hospitals. Once establish the principle that tax exemption authorizes supervision, not merely of the finances of any organization but of its intellectual or moral activities, and you have an effective end to freedom for any intellectual and moral activities.

The fifth area where we have witnessed an extraordinary growth of federal centralization is in the realm of literature. Few of us, I fear, appear to realize what is involved in the impudent claims of governmental authority to investigate the principles, ideas, beliefs, the training, background, and character of all persons who write. I have in mind here not only the influence of the Attorney General's list and the list of the Un-American Activities Committee on publishers, librarians, school boards, and private organizations, but the consequences of the principle inherent in the government's position in the Corliss Lamont and O'Connor cases in the Federal courts. Neither Mr. Lamont nor Mr. O'Connor ever served the United States government in any capacity whatsoever. They were, presumably, wholly outside the jurisdiction of governmental committees. On the specious argument that overseas libraries have purchased some of their books, the McCarthy Committee called these gentlemen to testify about their political beliefs and affiliations. Both Mr. Lamont and Mr. O'Connor denied the jurisdiction of the Committee. The district court ruled in favor of Mr. Lamont and the case is now on appeal. In the O'Connor case the decision went the other way!

The principle here is clear. If, through one of its committees, Congress can investigate the beliefs of any author whose books some branch of the government acquires, it can, of course, investigate the beliefs of all authors of books, magazines, and newspaper articles or any other printed word by the simple device of acquiring a copy of the book, magazine, or newspaper for the

Library of Congress or for any other governmental agency. The question is whether the government can investigate any author or any book that it wishes to investigate. If it has this authority, it has the authority to control—that is, to censor, all writers. If it has this authority, it can, in effect, supervise all literature.

It is not clear that this authority differs from the Russian or the Nazi censorship in its ultimate implications or in its potentialities. This is precisely what the concurring opinion of Justice Douglas said in the Supreme Court decision in the Rumley case:

> Once the government can demand of a publisher the names of the purchasers of his publications, the free press as we know it disappears. Then the specter of a government agent will look over the shoulder of everyone who reads. The purchase of a book or a pamphlet today may result in a subpoena tomorrow. Fear of criticism goes with every person into the bookstore; the subtle imponderable pressures of the orthodox lay hold. Some will fear to read what is unpopular, what the powers that be dislike. When the light of publicity may reach any student, any teacher, inquiry will be discouraged. The books and pamphlets critical of administration or that preach an unpopular policy in domestic or foreign affairs, or that are in disrepute in the orthodox school of thought, will be suspect and subject to investigation. The press and its readers will pay a heavy price in harassment. That will be minor in comparison with the menace of the shadow which government will cast over literature that does not follow a dominant party line. Through the harassment of hearings and investigations, reports and subpoena, government will hold a club over speech and over the press. Congress could not do this by law; the power of investigation is also limited.

And as the Court said again in a decision in the Washington *Herald* case,

> a general offensive, inquisitorial, compulsory investigation conducted by commission without any allegation, upon no fixed principles, and governed by no rules of law or of evidence, and no restraints except its own will of caprice, is unknown to our constitution and laws. Let the power once be established, there is no knowing where the practice under it will end.

A sixth area in which we are witnessing one expansion of governmental power is that of security in general and, in particular, governmental distinction between the saved and the damned. What is striking here is not merely the nature and scope of the Federal security program, but the extent to which it has been emulated and adopted by states, local governments, and even private industry. State after state has come up with its own little un-American activities committee, has taken over the lists put out by the Attorney General or the House Committee, and has given to them spurious dignity and legality. Thus state, local, and private associations have identified themselves with the Federal government and allowed the Federal government to lay down controlling principles on matters of security—have made themselves, in effect, law enforcement agencies of the government, or at an even further remove, agencies to punish non-cooperation with a Federal agency, no matter how dubious the authority of the agency or the claims of cooperation. Thus, for example, the New Jersey law providing for the dismissal of those who do not cooperate with Federal investigation by answering questions. Thus, for example, the proposed Illinois Broyle's Act, which provides automatic fine and imprisonment of any persons who remain members of organizations on the Attorney General's list, and this even though the Supreme Court has said that the Attorney General's list has no legal standing! Another example is the pusillanimous retreat of the New York City authorities on the issue of employing the distinguished playwright, Arthur Miller, to write a script on the youth of the city. Mr. Miller was charged with the crime of having belonged to or sympathized with organizations on some governmental blacklist. There was no charge of illegal acts, no charge of disloyalty or subversion. There was no criticism, even, of what he had written, much less of what he proposed to write for the city. But the fact that he was a "controversial" figure was enough to persuade the New York City authorities to withdraw their invitation to him.

The moral is clear. All that is necessary to establish an effective blacklist is to create a "controversy."

Closely connected with, and indeed part of, this activity of government through the application of lists of allegedly subversive organizations is pressure in the field—of radio, television, the movies, and the theater. Wisely or unwisely, Americans decided to confide control of radio and television to private enterprise, not public. One reason for the decision not to adopt the model of the British Broadcasting Corporation was doubtless fear of the state, fear of censorship or of partisanship. Yet we have in considerable part forfeited the advantages and hypothetical benefits of the privately controlled system by instituting private censorship and controls, so that it is probably true to say that there is more freedom today on the B.B.C. than on the American radio—more freedom and less censorship. Certainly the B.B.C. knows nothing of political lists that in effect blackmail potential speakers. Nor does it seek to avoid employment of controversial characters, or even to avoid controversial subjects. On the contrary, it welcomes controversy on the radio. What purpose to deny governmental power to censure ideas if the most powerful media of communications themselves undertake censorship? Government can be challenged in the courts but it is almost impossible to challenge the policies of private corporations judicially. Government can be criticized in halls of Congress but we do not know how to go about effectively criticizing the internal policies of private corporations, privately adopted and privately pursued.

One aspect of this problem has received curiously little attention. That has to do with the rules which appear to guide, if they are indeed rules and if they do indeed guide, the decisions of the Federal Communications Commission. The FCC has authority to license radio stations. That authority is not, or at least should not be an arbitrary one. The FCC should and does fix standards of public service. If it applies standards of political or other orthodoxy, it is guilty not only of grave abuse of power but of seriously frustrating precisely the policy it was set up to defend—namely, making sure that the American public would have a chance to hear competing ideas and that there would be no monopoly of the air by one party, one interest, one faith, or one philosophy. The spectacle of the FCC denying a license to a radio station on the ground that the owner was alleged to have belonged to or contributed to subversive organizations—allegations which later turned out to be false—is one to inspire gravest misgivings in the minds of all who cherish freedom of information. If only those who contribute to the Republican party, or the Methodist Church, or the Red Cross, if only those who are careful enough or dull enough or ignorant enough never to join anything that anybody could possibly disapprove, if only these may be sure of getting government license to the air, then we have precisely that monopoly of the air we seek to avoid. The English, Scandinavians, and others who maintain state-owned and state-controlled radio insist that their radio is in fact freer than ours. Both the radio and the FCC seem determined to prove them right.

An eighth example of Federal invasion of the realm of ideas is supervision over the whole field of foreign travel though passport and visa controls. Time was when passports were not needed at all. Then they came to be used purely as statements of identification and formal requests for admission and for courtesy abroad. The use of the passport and the visa as a mark of approval or disapproval is one fraught with danger, one that must be resisted by all who fear the rise of the leviathan state. There is specious support in law or in administrative rulings to this use, but there is none in wisdom or sound policy. But if travel is to depend on the subjective judgment of anonymous persons in some bureau of the State Department on the imponderable issue of whether travel is or is not "in the best interests of the United States," then there is an end to genuine freedom for any who contemplate travel. The day by day effect of this policy may be negligible: here and there a scientist like Professor Pauling kept at home, here and there a political critic like Louis Boudin denied a passport, here and there an artist like Paul Robeson refused permission to go abroad. But, if persisted in—if supported by the Courts—the long-range consequences will be formidable. The ordinary traveler will not be affected, the average businessman, for example, or those who travel for pleasure. It is the scholar, the journalist, the scientist, the public figure—precisely those upon whom we depend for the criticism necessary for democracy to work—who will be affected. All of them will be tempted to conform or to be silent in order to be sure that when they do come to travel they will not have difficulty getting a passport from the State Department.

Ninth, there is pressure on the civil service through the

loyalty-security program. Who that has read the Yarmolinsky report on civil service security procedures can doubt that the inescapable consequence of investigations and examinations of this kind is to create a civil service made up of conformers and accepters—what are popularly called "yes-men"? Many of us assume thoughtlessly that Federal civil servants, because they work for the Federal government, should inevitably be agents of or spokesmen for that government. But they work, of course, for the American people, and their ultimate responsibility and loyalty is to the people as a whole. One of the most ominous developments in recent years is the emergence of the notion of loyalty to the *administration*. We have long prided ourselves in America that we did not have a national bureaucracy any more than we had a special administrative law. We do not put our civil servants in uniform or give them special privileges or exempt them from the laws that affect other citizens. But there are more ways than one to create a bureaucracy or to create a bureaucratic type of mind, and one of the most effective ways is that which we are now using—to discourage any expression of individuality, to discourage outside interests, activities and loyalties, to discourage criticism of government or policies adopted by political superiors, to induce a general mediocrity, a general acquiescence and a general apathy.

Finally, the pressure on the press itself—pressure which is perhaps tenacious rather than dramatic. That is a growing tendency to internal censorship, the deliberate withholding of information about government from the American people. When Mr. Eisenhower was President of Columbia University he endorsed— as peculiarly fitting for the community of learning—the principle of "man's right to knowledge and the free use thereof." His Presidency of the United States may well be recalled in connection with the principle of the government's right to withhold knowledge and the free use thereof. Other administrations have withheld information; it remained for this administration to elevate that policy into a principle. We may designate it the "Philip Young principle of the inherent nonavailability of information." This principle had, in fact, many inventors. The one who may finally be awarded a patent on it is Secretary of Defense Wilson. On March 30, 1955, the Secretary cut down information forces of the armed services by one-half to one-third and sent a directive to govern the policy of giving out information. That policy was, quite simply, that information was to be "a constructive contribution to the primary mission of the Defense Department." What was constructive, what was a contribution, and, for that matter, what was the primary mission of the Defense Department was not made clear. After a few days came an "experimental balance sheet" for strategic information. According to it, officers were to strike a sensible balance on whether what they said might or might not be harmful to the United States. They were to consider the net effect of what they said on the military and the industrial power of the United States as compared with the power of other countries and whether what they said might help reveal weaknesses or might reveal strength within the United States. Apparently it is dangerous to reveal your weaknesses and equally dangerous to reveal your strength; that pretty well covered the whole ground. Just in case it left some gaps, the directive provided that officers were to invoke other considerations, e.g., "anything else you can think of."

The policy of the control of the flow of information has, as might be suspected, many ramifications. First, as with the security test, it extends from sensitive to non-sensitive and insensitive areas, and from classified areas to various degrees of non-classification. I say various degrees, because the resourcefulness of the American people, or at least of the American administrator, has never been more fully dramatized than by the discovery of between thirty and forty new classifications that are not precisely secret and not precisely non-secret, but something in between. In the second place it has spread from obvious agencies like the Atomic Energy Commission and some parts of the Defense Department to all departments. It is, after all, a sad confession of insignificance not to have anything important enough to conceal! So departments like Agriculture and Commerce and the Civil Service Commission now proudly have their own secrets and their own restrictions on what the public may know. Some of these restrictions are very sweeping indeed. Secretary Weeks, in November of 1954, set up the Office of Strategic Information in the Department of Commerce. His purpose was to prevent unclassified data from being made available to foreign nations which might use it in a manner harmful to the United States. As the National Education Association pointed out:

> If the policy of the Office of Strategic Information were carried out literally, it would bar the teaching of foreign students within the United States, the participation of foreign students and Fulbright scholars, exchange professors and fellows in university seminars, discussions and research programs, correspondence among university members and their opposite numbers abroad, and even fulfillment of contracts for technical assistance to foreign countries sponsored by the foreign operations administration.

The policy has spread through the whole executive department and often into purely domestic matters; witness the withholding of important information about the negotiations of the Dixon-Yates contract.

The invasion of freedom of the press through security regulations and inside censorship is nothing astonishing; it is predictable. The press itself failed to foresee it or to guard against it. But that it is a logical part of a pattern of Federal centralization cannot be denied—the pattern of the invasion by government of the realm of thought and communication. The press as a whole was remiss in not seeing the nature of this problem. It was remiss in failing to make clear the danger to the people—and to their servants, the government. The press is remiss even now in failing to relate the fight for its own freedom to the fight for freedom of the civil servant, the applicant for a passport, the teacher, and the preacher —for failing to relate it to the whole pattern of attack upon the fabric of freedom. It has failed to make clear (has failed even to realize) that freedom is a seamless web.

Those who fear the leviathan state direct their fears and their defenses almost entirely to the political and the economic realm. They fight desperately against the invasion by government, especially by the Federal government, of the realm of labor relations or tidelands or hydroelectric power, or public housing, or public health, or education. They are concerned with the impact of these political developments on private enterprise. But the invasions here are *relatively* unimportant. The only ultimately important area of private enterprise is the intellectual and the spiritual because it is antecedent to all others. Dry up private enterprise in the intellectual or spiritual realm and it will die of itself in the economic realm, a fact that every totalitarian government has known instinctively.

So too with the growth of centralization. Allow the state to invade the areas of thought, of education, of the press, of religion, of association, and we will have statism. It will be too late then to protest invasion of the economic realm. That will be a not very important detail. Those who fear statism, as all who are rooted in American history and tradition fear it, must resolutely oppose it where it is most dangerous, precisely in the realm of the mind and the spirit of men. For if once we get a government strong enough to control men's minds, we will have a government strong enough to control everything.

1955

The Right of Dissent

Your editor's letter[1] referred to the "almost tragic conflict between the need for security and the democratic idea of liberty and justice" and added that the necessity of maintaining military strength along with democracy "sharpens the dilemma." With the implications of all this I disagree strongly. Even to pose the problem in this manner seems to me dangerous, for once assume that our choice is between security and freedom, or that these two are naturally antagonistic, and it is inevitable that many people will choose security, and hope that freedom can somehow be achieved later. But I do not think that there is any conflict at all between these goals, let alone a tragic one, nor do I think that the task of maintaining both security and democracy confronts us with a dilemma. I think, on the contrary, that we cannot have security without justice or lasting military strength without democracy.

Happily we are confronted by no such choice, and no such dilemma. Security and freedom are interdependent, and so are security and democracy. It is, I think, no accident that in the two great World Wars, the nations that practiced democracy and cherished freedom came out on top, and the nations that embraced despotism and flouted freedom went down to defeat; Russia might seem to be an exception here, but without aid from the free nations of the West, Russia would have gone under. It is no accident that the two nations most successful in maintaining independence and prosperity are also the freest and most democratic of the great powers—Britain and the United States.

When we speak of freedom, and of security, we are, needless

[1] In *Current History*, September, 1955.

to say, speaking not of absolutes but of relatives. It is, however, more commonly observed that there is no absolute freedom than that there is no absolute security, and we are still, many of us, bemused by the notion that we can somehow, by taking proper precautions, guarantee ourselves against the consequences of error, wickedness, stupidity, and mischance. There are no guarantees against these things, but if history and experience teach us anything they teach that of all the securities which we attempt to erect, the legal, the mechanical, and the material are the weakest, and the historical, the intellectual, and the moral are the strongest. This was what Francis Bacon said over three centuries ago:

> Walled Townes, Stored Arcenalls and Armouries, Goodly Races of Horse, Chariots of Warre, Elephants, Ordnance, Artillery, and the like: All this is but a Sheep in a Lion's Skin, except the Breed and disposition of the People be stout and warlike. Numbers it selfe in Armies importeth not much, where the people is of Weake Courage.

It is the fundamental error of security-minded zealots that they put their trust in such things as secrecy, or weapons or numbers. But none of these things can be relied on unless the spirit of the people be stout. The prodigious contest between Nazi Germany and Britain should have taught us that it is the free mind and the free spirit that triumphs over all the weapons of secrecy, of hatred, and of fear.

Now when dealing with matters of freedom and security it is well to get away from windy abstractions as quickly as possible, and get down to cases. It is well to get away from generalizations and get down to consequences. For it is one of the crucial weaknesses of our current security program that it does concern itself with theories and abstractions, with ideas and associations, rather than with conduct. And it is, correspondingly, one of the weaknesses of the liberal position that it, in turn, tends to fall back upon natural rights, legal rights, principles and theories, rather than concern itself with conduct and consequences.

There is nothing wrong with the argument from rights and principles except that everyone appears to interpret them differently. To the layman the Bill of Rights seems to be a stone wall against misuse of power. But in the hands of a Congressional committee or, often enough, of a judge, it turns out to be so full of exceptions and qualifications that it might as well be a whole series of arches.

It is essential that we bring any discussion of the claims of security and of freedom down to cases and consequences; that we consider not their theoretical justification but their practical relationship. Let us look at some examples of the restraint of liberty on behalf of security with a view to determining, if we can, the impact of these on both liberty and security.

Look, first, at the impact of the security program on science. That our security—as well as our progress and prosperity—depends on the achievements of our scientists is clear enough, and it is clear, too, that if we lose out in the scientific race we may well lose out elsewhere. True security, therefore, requires that we do everything possible to encourage our scientists—that we provide them with the best possible conditions of work, that we assure them ready access to all information, that we facilitate the recruitment of scientific brains, and the interchange of scientific information and ideas, that we put a premium on boldness, originality, and imagination.

I have not listed secrecy here, for secrecy is of little importance and may be a detriment. There are surely some scientific secrets that need to be guarded, but what American scientists can discover can be discovered by others as well, and it is probable that the machinery of secrecy has done more harm than good to scientific progress in America.

What is evident is that the whole body of security regulations and activities does serious damage to scientific progress. First-rate minds will not and cannot work under constant surveillance. They will not work on projects selected for them by the military and hedged in by security regulations. They cannot work well if their families, their associations, their very thoughts are to be scrutinized by men who understand nothing of science and are themselves bound by arbitrary regulations. The first requisite for effective scientific work is knowledge and the second is freedom. Scientists must have freedom to consult with each other, to select their assistants and co-workers, to travel, to make public their findings except where publicity is premature, or where it involves really secret policies and projects.

Security regulations which end up denying the nation the services of a Dr. Oppenheimer or a Dr. Condon are a self-confessed failure. Security regulations which exclude a substantial number of research workers on public health projects that are wholly divorced from issues of security, are a self-confessed failure. Security regulations—or investigations—that interrupt and demoralize work at Fort Monmouth for a year without producing a single Communist or subversive or (as far as we are informed) a single illegal act, are a self-confessed failure.

Nor are these failures merely occasional and fortuitous, or confined to the particular case involved. They involve the whole of our scientific progress, for they dissuade able men from working for the government, and universities from taking on government contracts, discourage independent and original work on the part of scientists, and put a premium on scientific conformity and mediocrity.

Or look to the alleged claims of security even in the military. Here, if anywhere, a security program would seem to be called for; here, if anywhere, secrecy would seem to be justified. And, of course, there has always been a security system, of a sort, in the military. What is new, however, is the application of tests of associations, relationships, reading, political views, to the military. What is new is the kind of test that results in the denial of a commission to a Lieutenant Radulovich (subsequently reversed, to be sure) or to a Midshipman Landy, or results in the hullabaloo over the honorable discharge given a Dr. Peress; the kind that prevents us from sharing scientific information with our wartime associates; the kind that persuades a Secretary to prohibit a debate on China policy by the two military academies; the kind that produces—even as a passing gesture—the egregious pamphlet "How to Tell a Communist."

Secretary Charles Wilson illuminated this whole problem some time ago in an observation on the Lieutenant Radulovich case. Whenever there is a conflict, he said, between the nation's interest and the individual, the interest of the individual must give way even if some injustice results. There is, of course, some truth here—as the operation of the draft or of martial law illustrates. But for the most part, and almost always when the security program is involved, this conflict is factitious. The nation has, after all, an interest in justice and in truth, and the harm done the national interest by a gross miscarriage of justice is incomparably greater than any harm that might come from an individual who does not meet the somewhat artificial standards of security. There is no genuine conflict between national interest on the one hand and justice to an individual on the other, for the national interest is deeply involved in justice. A nation whose sense of justice and of fairness is blunted is a nation whose strongest weapons and defenses are in danger of being blunted.

What is true in the realms of science and the military is equally true in the realm of diplomacy and foreign affairs. Now that we are a world power and leader of a coalition of nations, the conduct of our foreign affairs has become a task of infinite complexity. To avoid errors that might be catastrophic we need a constant flow of information, criticism, and ideas. We need flexibility and openmindedness to enable us to cope with new situations as they arise; and resourcefulness to enable us to hold, and to deserve, the confidence of our associates. Who would have thought a decade ago that it would be Germany we were making the pivot of our European defense system; who would have thought that we would depend on Japan to defend our Pacific bastions? Suppose then we had said that never, never, never would we do business with Germany or Japan? Who would have thought even a year ago that this administration would be pursuing policies toward Red China that—in milder form—earned Truman and Acheson and Marshall the epithet of treason?

We need, in the State Department, informed, alert, bold, and original minds. Our current security program is not designed to encourage men and women with such minds to enter the foreign service, or to exercise these intellectual qualities if they do. It does not encourage criticism, but discourages it. In effect we say to budding diplomats, or foreign service advisers: If you guess wrong or if you give us unpleasant advice (the only kind we ever really need) we will treat you as we treated such career diplomats as Service and John P. Davies. We say to scholars: If you come to conclusions that we find—at any one moment—unpalatable, we will treat you as we have treated Professor Lattimore. Is this not the path to confusion and insecurity?

The State Department furnishes us with another example of the shortsightedness in its passport policy, now in process of judicial modification. The Courts have ruled that a passport is a right, not a privilege; it is a principle which previous administrations had taken for granted. But it is not merely on legal grounds that the passport policy of the State Department has been misguided, but on very realistic and practical grounds.

For far from strengthening our security, it has weakened our security. It has denied to us the advantage that presumably flows from the interchange of ideas in international conferences, from the visits of distinguished foreigners to this country, and of distinguished Americans to foreign countries. It has denied to us the advantage of criticism from outsiders and has appeared to confess that we are not prepared to expose ourselves to criticism, or to allow our own critics to express themselves abroad.

Far more serious than this have been its indirect consequences. Sooner or later almost every scholar, every scientist, every publicist, wishes to travel abroad. These are the men and women upon whom we would normally rely for that vigilance which, we are told, is the price of liberty. These are the men and women on the whole most competent to point out errors in governmental policy and advise changes. But these are precisely the men and women who are potentially in danger from the policy of the Passport Division; we will never know how many of them refrained from public criticism of current policies because they feared that open criticism might lose them the right to travel. It is improbable that the nation is in any respect more secure because an occasional radical has been denied the right to travel; it is hardly to be denied that it is less secure because it has been deprived of the benefit of much-needed discussion and criticism.

The passport policy of the State Department has operated as a sort of censorship. This is one of the less flagrant manifestations of censorship that is defended in the name of security. Congressional committees draw up lists of dangerous books, and one deluded Congressman has called for the labeling of all the books in the Library of Congress. There is censorship of libraries by local patriotic or veterans' organizations; censorship of overseas libraries at the behest of a McCarthy. Implicit in the Corliss

Lamont indictment—dismissed by the Federal court but now agitated anew by Senator Mundt—is a vast censorship over everything written in the United States. For if, as the Congressional Committee contends, committees have the right to inquire into the political beliefs of any man whose writing has been acquired by and is used by a branch of the government, then the government can inquire into the political philosophy of any writer, for a copy of every book goes to the Library of Congress.

It is not necessary to restate here the familiar argument of the *Areopagitica*, but it is perhaps appropriate to remark that censorship does not and cannot, in any event, strengthen security. I am not speaking now of military censorship in time of war; that is a very special problem. I have in mind rather the kind of censorship practiced, or attempted, against ideas that are supposed to be "dangerous," or persons who are presumed to be "controversial."

Freedom of the press must be maintained not out of indulgence to authors, but because it is the only way we have to discover truth and expose error, and a country that does not do this is not secure. Without a constant flow of criticism, a constant agitation of controversial questions, a constant expression of new and unfamiliar ideas, we are sure to make mistakes. We take this for granted in the realm of medicine or physics, and we should take it equally for granted in the realms of politics and economics. If we do not we will destroy not only liberty but security.

There are two forms of censorship that deserve separate consideration. One of these is what might be called internal, as contrasted with external, censorship—that is, censorship by government departments, bureaus, or agencies, of what the public is allowed to know. Such censorship was almost unknown a generation ago, and rare even a decade ago, but flourishes now, in the name of security. That there is some advantage in not giving information on work in progress will not be denied, but the danger that the plea of security will be used to cover up incompetence is greater than any danger that might flow from premature disclosure. It is probable that if all the data bearing on our China policy were to be conveyed to Peking tomorrow, only confusion would result, not peril. Those governments that take the public into their confidence are stronger and more secure than those that exclude the public, and those that confess their mistakes will remedy them more speedily than those that conceal them.

Another and quite different form of censorship—again in the name of security—operates in the large field of the movies, radio, television and theater; even now a Congressional committee is solemnly investigating past sins of association and membership of entertainers. For years Hollywood has been conducting a sort of pogrom against actors whose sentiments or associations were presumed to be leftist, and in this, needless to say, it has been supported by Congress and by the Passport Division of the State Department. That we are more secure with Charlie Chaplin in Switzerland rather than in California is not wholly certain, especially as we are still allowed to delight in his films. For years, too, some of the radio networks have been maintaining their own blacklist of persons who might have incurred the disapproval of the "Red Networks" or of one of the many state un-American activities committees, and from time to time we hear that this or that entertainer or commentator is no longer permitted to contaminate the air.

No one has yet detected subversive propaganda in what these luckless entertainers or commentators say or sing or act; what is at issue is not their conduct but their beliefs, or their alleged beliefs. Does it in fact strengthen our security to eliminate from the films, or the air, or the theater, individuals who might have supported the Spanish Loyalists or signed petitions against the deportation of Harry Bridges, or joined allegedly left-wing organizations? Obviously it does not, for none of these things can have the faintest effect on our security. Does it impair our security to be confined to films, radio, and theater that carefully avoid controversial subjects or controversial characters, that shift away from ideas because ideas may be dangerous, that require of their participants acts of submission or of penance unbecoming to free men? Just as obviously it does. Perhaps one reason why British and French films seem so much livelier than American, why the B.B.C. programs are so much better than those most Americans are able to hear, is that for a decade now we have been energetically eliminating men and women with ideas from these professions.

Nowhere have the failures of security been more ostentatious than in education. The effort has been prodigious; the results negative. Local, state, and national governments joined hands with filiopietistic and veterans' organizations to root subversives out of schools. The assumption that there were, in fact, subversives in the schools was never subjected to any proper tests, nor the assumption that the transmission to the young of radical ideas was in itself dangerous. A tremendous security apparatus was brought to bear on public schools, colleges, and universities, libraries and scientific institutions and foundations: the apparatus of loyalty oaths; investigations of ideas, associations, and conduct; supervision of curriculum, textbooks, and research projects. Here a Tenney Committee, there a Broyles Committee, here a Feinberg Committee, there a Canwell Committee exhausted themselves and their subjects in an effort to save the young from contamination by dangerous ideas or association with teachers who once harbored such ideas.

That national security depends upon an intelligent, enlightened, openminded and critical electorate is self-evident. That such an electorate can be created only where there is universal education, that is free in the sense that it is uncontrolled and unintimidated, was an article of faith with the Fathers of the Republic. "Error of opinion," said Jefferson, "may be tolerated where reason is left free to combat it." Where reason is not free, error will grow and flourish—as in Nazi Germany, for example, or in South Africa. The first essential of safety and security, and, needless to say, of wisdom and of happiness is freedom of communication. Anything which qualifies that freedom, intimidates the teacher or the scientist, discourages first-rate minds from entering the realms of scholarship, denies to the young the full benefit of the clash of ideas or training in independent thinking, closes off areas of interest or activity from the inquiring mind—anything of this character strikes not only at freedom, but at security itself.

One pervasive example of the concept of security is the claim of security to regulate and supervise the habits of voluntary association. The use of the Attorney General's list as a sort of blacklist has recently come in for some pretty rough handling by the Courts, but it is still widespread. Nor is it the Attorney General alone who has compiled a list of subversive organizations; many states and cities have comparable lists; many private organizations stand ready to supply lists of their own. The purpose of all this is to punish people who belong, or have belonged, to the wrong organizations, and to destroy organizations considered subversive. All this, of course, in the name of security.

Leaving aside the question of the affront to the liberties of individuals, and the rights of groups, what shall we say of the contribution of this vast program to national security? What is really at issue here?

What is at issue is, of course, an institution whose prosperity is of vital importance to our existence as a nation; the private voluntary organization. Our country was, in a sense, founded by private organizations—the London Company of Virginia, which established the Jamestown Colony, and the Pilgrims and Puritans who came over as private congregations or as members of joint-stock companies to Massachusetts Bay. Most of our basic institutions are private voluntary organizations—churches, political parties, labor unions, professional and fraternal societies, and reform organizations. These have been the institutions most effective in creating our democracy and most influential in cementing national unity.

Anything that discourages the habit of joining, or intimidates those who have joined or propose to join, tends to dry up the grass roots of democracy and weaken the bonds of unity. No one has yet made out a convincing case for guilt by association, but the case against impairing the habit of voluntary association is clear to anyone who reads the history of modern dictatorships.

These illustrations of the misapplication of security make it evident, I think, that our real strength lies not in formulae or mechanical devices, in tests or regulations, but in the sense of freedom and justice that animates the people. For it is still as true as it was when Pericles said it twenty-five hundred years ago that "the secret of happiness is freedom and the secret of freedom a brave heart."

1955

PART THREE

Leadership in Eighteenth-Century America and Today

With his customary insight Tocqueville observed back in the eighteen-thirties that leadership was more difficult in a democracy than elsewhere, and more difficult therefore in the New World than in the Old. In the Old World leadership was already given: it was attached to birth, rank, position; in the New World it had to be achieved by trial and error, and as there were no fixed standards, the chances for error were limitless. In the Old World there was no problem at all of formal leadership: it was all arranged by birth and inheritance—the kings, the princes, the aristocracy; in the New World there was no such thing as formal leadership—it had to be won each time, and each time the rules of the contest might change.

Yet who can doubt that in the last quarter of the eighteenth century it was the New World—not democracy by our standards but certainly democracy by European—that provided the most impressive spectacle of leadership, rather than the nations of the Old World? Who can doubt, for example, that in the crisis of 1774–1783, the American colonies and States enjoyed far more competent leadership than the British Empire?

The situation is too familiar to rehearse. In the last quarter of the century the new United States—a nation with a white population of less than three million, without a single major city, and wholly lacking in those institutions of organized society or civilization so familiar in Europe—boasted a galaxy of leaders who were quite literally incomparable: Franklin, Washington, Jefferson, Hamilton, John Adams, Samuel Adams, John Jay, James Wilson, George Mason, Benjamin Rush, James Madison, and a dozen others scarcely less distinguished.

What explains this remarkable outpouring of political leadership, this fertility in the production of statesmen—a fertility unmatched since that day? Was it an historical accident? Was it a peculiar response to the time or the place, or to a combination of the two? Or was it a product of conditions and attitudes that were cultivated and directed to calculated ends, and that can be if not re-created at least paralleled in our time?

There is of course an element of mystery, if not of fortuity, in the outbreak of genius at any time. How, after all, explain the flowering of the little Athens of Pericles and Sophocles and Phidias; the Florence of Michelangelo and Raphael and Machiavelli; the England of Hakluyt and Shakespeare and Francis Bacon; the Copenhagen of Hans Andersen and Thorwaldsen and Kierkegaard; the Vienna of Haydn and Mozart and Beethoven? We do not know with any certainty, yet clearly it would be absurd to ascribe these and comparable outbursts of genius, or of talent, to chance. There must be some principle that explains why the climate of fifth-century Athens was favorable to literature and philosophy; why the climate of fifteenth-century Florence encouraged art and architecture; why the climate of sixteenth-century England encouraged the discovery of new worlds of geography, science, and philosophy; why the climate of eighteenth-century Salzburg and Vienna grew musicians. And there must be some principle that explains why the little frontier colony of Virginia, with a white population less than that of present-day Syracuse or Dayton, without a single city or a major university or a proper school system or a press, produced in one generation Washington, Jefferson, Mason, Wythe, Madison, and Marshall. It is not enough to say that statesmanship was the specialty of Virginia as art was the specialty of Florence and music of Vienna. We want to know why.

The first consideration is elementary and practical. Eighteenth-century America offered extraordinarily few opportunities for the unfolding of talent. Almost the only opportunities it did offer were in the public arena. American society was pastoral and undifferentiated; American economy, rural and parochial; American life, singularly uninstitutionalized. In the Old World the young man of talent—certainly if he belonged to the upper classes—could take his choice, as it were, among the institutions which invited or even competed for his services; nor was he in fact limited to the institutions of his own country but could operate almost anywhere. The New World had few of these institutions, and those which did exist, in a kind of elementary fashion, offered few temptations; and while some colonials—Benjamin West and John Singleton Copley come to mind—could move to the mother country, the overwhelming majority could not. What Henry James later wrote of Hawthorne's America, was far more true of and more pertinent to the America of Thomas Jefferson and John Adams. Like Hawthorne, they looked out upon a "negative spectacle"—how fortunate that they did not know this.

> No State, in the European sense of the word, and indeed barely a national name. No sovereign, no court, no personal loyalty, no aristocracy, no church, no clergy, no army, no diplomatic service, no country houses, nor parsonages, nor thatched cottages; no great Universities, nor public schools . . . no literature, no novels, no museums, no pictures, no political society, no sporting class.[1]*

If these things were left out, said James, everything was left out. Yet the spectacle that greeted a Jefferson or an Adams was even more negative, even more barren, for one might add: no capital, no cities, no manufactures, no newspapers, no journals, no libraries, no professions (except, somewhat feebly, the law and the clergy), no Society. In England, or France, or the Empire, a young man of talent could go into the Church; there was no Church in America, with a capital C, and religion had lost much of its appeal. In the Old World the young man could enter the army or the navy; the new America had neither. He could become a scholar, and attach himself to an ancient university, or a man of letters, or an academician. In America these and similar activities were avocations.

* This note and subsequent notes for this essay appear on pp. 318–320.

Not only did the New World offer few opportunities for the display of talent except in the public arena; it presented few temptations to distract talent from preoccupation with public concerns. There was no quick way to wealth and no likelihood of piling up great riches: nothing is more eloquent of the simplicity of American life than Washington's casting about to borrow a few hundred dollars to take him to the Inauguration, or Secretary of the Treasury Hamilton's requests for a loan of twenty dollars or so. There were no fields for military glory or adventure; the challenge to adventure was there, but with no promise of reward, and soldiers who had served their country well ended their days in penury, while officers who naïvely hoped to enjoy membership in the Society of the Cincinnati were regarded as models of depravity to be compared only with an Alcibiades or a Caligula. Society offered no distractions—indeed there was no Society in the Old World sense of the term, for that was a function of cities, of courts, of a class system. In the Old World young men of talent might become courtiers or adventurers, but it is almost as difficult to imagine a Madame Du Barry, a Lady Hamilton, or a Madame de Staël in eighteenth-century America as a Chesterfield, a Struensee, or a Casanova. It is relevant to recall Jefferson's warning[2] that young men who went abroad to study would surely sink into debauchery, or John Adams's feeling of outrage at the avuncular gallantries of the aged Benjamin Franklin; it is relevant to note that Benjamin Thompson and Aaron Burr, who were adventurers and gallants, found Europe more congenial to their talents than America.

Such talent as there was, then, had no effective outlet except in public channels. But how did it happen that there was so much talent? And how did it happen—it is a question Henry Adams never ceased asking himself—that American society of the eighteenth century was prepared to encourage and use such talent as was available, whereas the America of a century later was not?

Here again, we do well to begin with a practical consideration. Not only were the opportunities for leadership and for distinction almost wholly in the realm of public affairs, but those opportunities were numerous, urgent, and inviting. Has any one generation of less than a million adult men ever been called upon to do more than the generation of Washington and Adams and

Jefferson in these creative years? They had to win independence; set up state governments; write a constitution; win the tramontane West and defend it against Indians and against formidable foreign powers; create a nation and all those institutions, political and cultural, that go into the making of a nation. There is nothing like war for bringing out courage; there is nothing like emergency for bringing out ingenuity; there is nothing like challenge for bringing out character. This is Arnold Toynbee's argument of challenge and response; it is the moral put in simpler form by Lowell's once familiar poem, "The Present Crisis":

> New occasions teach new duties; time makes ancient
> good uncouth,
> They must upward still, and onward, who would keep
> abreast of
> Truth.

In the last quarter of the eighteenth century Americans were exposed to new occasions as well as to new duties. They found themselves not only required to perform heroic deeds, but challenged to do so by the special circumstances of their being. No one can read their public papers or their private correspondence (and how the two are alike!) without realizing that these men saw themselves as characters in history, and that they were weighed down (or perhaps buoyed up) by a special sense of responsibility. A hundred quotations propose themselves, but the best is the most familiar: Washington's moving admonition to the States in his "Circular Letter" of June 1783:

> This is the time of their political probation, this is the moment when the eyes of the whole World are turned upon them, this is the moment to establish or ruin their national Character forever. . . . For according to the system of Policy which the States shall adopt at this moment, they will stand or fall, and by their confirmation or lapse, it is yet to be decided whether the Revolution must ultimately be considered as a blessing or a curse: a blessing or a curse, not to the present age alone, for with our fate will the destiny of unborn Millions be involved.[3]

The Founding Fathers—even the term is not improper— were quite aware that the American people were the first to break away from a mother country, the first to set up as a nation, to try the experiment of self-government, to write constitutions, and to fashion a new colonial system. They thought of themselves not as actors on some provincial stage but as characters in the greatest drama of all history. Thus Jefferson's comment that "Americans undertook to make a communication of grandeur and freedom" to the peoples of the entire world. Thus Tom Paine's conclusion that "we have it in our power to begin the world over again. A situation similar to the present hath not happened since the days of Noah until now. The birthday of a new world is at hand."[4] Thus Ethan Allen's assurance that "it is in our power to make the world happy, to teach mankind the art of being so, to exhibit on the theatre of the universe, a character hitherto unknown . . . to have a new creation entrusted to our hands."

And now we come to the heart of the matter. What was it that impelled so many Americans, from the seacoast of Maine to the frontiers of Georgia, from tidewater Virginia to the backwoods of Pennsylvania, into service to the commonwealth? What was it that made that service on the whole so spontaneous and so harmonious, so that eighteenth-century America presents a spectacle of consensus and cooperation without parallel in modern history? What was it that seemed to give the same character, the same animus, the same style even, to almost every public man—an aristocratic soldier like Washington, a Puritan like John Adams, a Scots immigrant like James Wilson, a West Indian emigrant like Alexander Hamilton, a scholar-statesman like Jefferson or Madison, a scientist like Benjamin Rush, so that their philosophies, their conduct, and even their letters are almost indistinguishable from their public papers? We have greatly busied ourselves with identifying the authorship of the disputed numbers of the *Federalist Papers*; we have not sufficiently remarked how astonishing it is that there should be a dispute—imagine a dispute over the authorship of contributions to a volume by Eisenhower, Stevenson, and Truman!

When we study our history in a vacuum, or in isolation, as we so commonly do, we exaggerate differences and minimize similarities. If we contrast the American Revolution with the English Revolution of the seventeenth century, or the French from 1789 to 1815, or the many revolutions in the states of Latin America, what emerges most sharply is the harmonious quality that pervades the American. We pivot history on the contest between Jefferson and Hamilton, but their similarities are more profound and pervasive than their differences. We have made much of the differences between Jefferson and John Adams, but the two men cherished the same philosophy of history and even of man, worked happily together on the Declaration of Independence and on state constitutions, and in their long and fascinating correspondence rarely wandered off common ground. How much alike, too, are the constitutions of the states and that of the United States; how similar their bills of rights; how almost monotonously familiar are the arguments over the ratification of the Federal Constitution in the various conventions, how superficial the criticisms, how insignificant the proposed amendments; how interchangeable the two factions or parties before and after ratification. Of this whole generation of statesmen and public figures, we can say that the things that divided them were inconsequential, and the things that united them were fundamental.

It is not merely that they were all children of the Enlightenment, consciously or unconsciously: so, for that matter, were Lord Shelburne and Diderot and Casanova. It is more to the point that they were all part of what we may call the American Enlightenment—an Enlightenment that differed strikingly from the French and English versions in that (unlike these) it found support in experience as well as in philosophy, vindicated itself by reference to environment and circumstances, as well as to imagination and logic. That, I suppose, is the underlying reason why John Adams was not really a misanthrope, despite his natural inclinations in that direction; why Washington was not really a Tory, despite his natural predisposition to be so; why Hamilton was such a failure as an aristocrat or an oligarch.

But there were other common denominators for the Americans of this generation besides the ideas of the Enlightenment and the realities of an environment, or a Providence, which "by all its dispensations proves that it delights in the happiness of man here and his greater happiness hereafter";[5] there were other common denominators that operated to encourage service to the commonwealth. There was, for example, the growing secularism, or deism, of society generally and of the upper classes (if we can use such a term for America) in particular. It is suggestive that whereas in the seventeenth century the best brains tended to go into the church, after Jonathan Edwards few first-rate minds were content with theological speculations, and the clergymen who are most familiar to us are remembered for other than contributions to theology: the politically minded Jonathan Mayhew, for example, or the brave John Peter Muhlenberg, or the egregious Manasseh Cutler, or the omniscient William Bentley. But it is not merely that men of talent no longer gravitated instinctively into the ministry; it is rather that deism supplanted piety and that virtue came to be judged by classical rather than Biblical standards. The passion that had earlier gone into the service of God was transferred into service to the commonwealth, and the expectation of personal immortality was transformed into concern for historical immortality and for the welfare of posterity.

The confession of obligation to posterity can, of course, be merely a rhetorical flourish—doubtless it was in Jefferson's grandiose reference to "our descendants to the thousandth and thousandth generation." But no one who immerses himself in the writings of the men of that Revolutionary generation can doubt that it was genuine and pervasive. Remember Tom Paine's plea for independence: " 'Tis not the concern of a day, a year, or an age; posterity are virtually involved in the contest, and will be more or less affected to the end of time." Or John Adams's moving letter to his beloved Abigail when he had signed the Declaration, "Through all the gloom I can see the rays of ravishing light and glory. Posterity will triumph in the day's transaction, even although we should rue it, which I trust in God we shall not."[6] Benjamin Rush recalled that "I was animated constantly by a belief that I was acting for the benefit of the whole world, and of future ages, by assisting in the formation of new means of political order and general happiness."[7]

No one appealed more frequently to posterity than Washington; nowhere is that appeal more moving than in the Newburgh address: "You will, by the dignity of your Conduct, afford occasion for Posterity to say, when speaking of the glorious example you have exhibited to Mankind, 'had this day been wanting the World had never seen the last stage of perfection to which human nature is capable of attaining.' "[8] Were the echoes of this in Churchill's mind when he spoke of "their finest hour"? And here is Washington's friend, Arthur St. Clair, accepting the governorship of the Northwest Territory in 1788: "I am truly sensible of the Importance of the Trust" and aware "how much depends on the due execution of it—to you Gentlemen over whom it is to be immediately exercised, to your Posterity! perhaps to the whole Community of America."[9] Or listen to George Mason's admonition to his children in his will: "If either their own inclinations or the necessity of the times should engage them in public affairs, I charge them . . . never to let the motives of private interest or of ambition induce them to betray nor the fear of danger or of death deter them from asserting the liberty of the country and endeavoring to transmit to their posterity those sacred rights in which they themselves were born."[10] Finally, here is Jefferson on the eve of death—and beyond mere rhetoric—to his friend James Madison, "It has been a great solace to me to believe that you are engaged in vindicating to posterity the course we have pursued, of preserving to them, in all their purity, the blessings of self-government which we had assisted in acquiring for them."[11]

A fourth common denominator of the minds of the late eighteenth-century Americans was education, formal and informal. It is customary now to disparage eighteenth-century education, to equate the colleges of that day with the better high schools of our own day, and to recall how few Americans were exposed to the advantages of formal education. Yet the products of the eighteenth-century educational machinery seemed to think more deeply (certainly in the political realm) than the products of the far more elaborate educational systems of our own time. But again what is most interesting is that almost all the public men of that generation appear to have absorbed the same maxims of conduct, to have studied the same texts, to have subscribed to the same philosophical precepts. All of them knew Plutarch and Thucydides and Tacitus; all knew (at first hand or merely as the common sense of the matter) John Locke and Bolingbroke and Hume and Montesquieu. Almost every one of them might have said, with the

Reverend Jonathan Mayhew, "Having been initiated in youth in the doctrines of civil liberty, as they are taught in such men as Plato, Demosthenes, Cicero, and other persons among the ancients, and such as Sidney and Milton, Locke and Hoadley among the moderns, I liked them; they seemed rational."[12] Almost everyone might have provided in his will, as Josiah Quincy did, that "I leave to my son, when he shall have reached the age of fifteen, the Works of Algernon Sidney, John Locke, Bacon, Gordon's Tacitus and *Cato's Letters*. May the spirit of Liberty rest upon him."[13] How familiar the *Maxims of Civil Conduct*, which the youthful Washington learned; how familiar the long excerpts that went into Jefferson's *Commonplace Book*, or that made up the substance of so much of John Adam's *Defence of the Constitutions*, and *Discourses on Davila*. Adams—as representative a figure as you can find in this generation—took for granted the duty of the academies to inculcate virtue and the love of liberty, and saw to it that the education which he arranged for his son did just that. Thus the youthful "Dissertation on Canon and Feudal Law" concluded with the appeal that

> the colleges join their harmony in the same delightful concert. Let every declamation turn upon the beauty of liberty and virtue, and the deformity and turpitude and malignity of slavery and vice. Let the public disputations become researches into the grounds and nature and ends of government, and the means of preserving the good and demolishing the evil. Let the dialogues and all the exercises become the instruments of impressing on the tender mind . . . the ideas of Right and the sensations of freedom.[14]

It is unnecessary to elaborate on what is so familiar. What is important are the lessons that this generation drew from its study of the classics of Greek and Roman literature and of the literature of English liberty. It learned (the predisposition was there, of course) that the same rules of morality operated at all times, in all places, and in all societies; that the affairs of men were controlled by undeviating "laws of Nature and Nature's God," laws which neither God nor Nature could alter; and that there was, in the words of Washington, "an indissoluble union between virtue and happiness, between duty and advantage, between the genuine maxim of an honest and magnanimous policy and the solid rewards of public prosperity and felicity." And they learned that the first duty of the good citizen was service to the commonwealth. "Every man in a republic," said Benjamin Rush, "is public property. His time and talents, his youth, his manhood, his old age, nay more, life, all, belong to his country." And Elbridge Gerry (something of an expert on the matter of public service) observed that "it is the duty of every citizen though he may have but one day to live, to devote that day to the service of his country."[15]

That was what philosophy admonished; that was what history taught.

History—almost inseparable from literature and philosophy —is a fifth common denominator of the American mind, or character, in this generation, a fifth influence beckoning or persuading men into the public service.

Few aspects of American intellectual history are more astonishing—perhaps we should say puzzling—than the contrast between political and historical writing in the last quarter of the eighteenth century. For the generation that gave us, indisputably, the most eloquent and profound political treatises in our literature —the *Farmer's Letters*, the *Summary View*, the Declaration of Independence, the Virginia Bill of Rights, the Virginia Statue of Religious Freedom, the Constitution, the *Federalist Papers*, Washington's Circular Letter, his Inaugural and Farewell addresses —gave us not a single work of formal history that anyone but an expert can remember or that anyone, even an expert, can read except as an act of duty or of piety. Hutchinson's *Massachusetts Bay* is pedestrian; Gordon's *American Revolution* is plagiarized from the *Annual Register*, and so, too, much of Ramsay's sprightlier *American Revolution*; the Reverend Jeremy Belknap is interesting chiefly to antiquarians and local historians; Ebenezer Hazard was a collector; Noah Webster a dilettante; Mercy Warren lively but unreliable and amateurish; John Marshall's ponderous five volumes on Washington (much of it cribbed from other books) is universally unread. Only the grotesque Parson Weems wrote histories that survive, and everyone agrees that he was not an historian, that he really belongs in the Romantic era, and that his books are fiction anyway.

Yet no other American generation has been so deeply immersed in or preoccupied with history. Indeed, we might say with considerable justice that the Founding Fathers thought history too serious a business to be left to the historians. It was the concern of all, but especially of statesmen—just the view that Winston Churchill took all his life. If we want to read the historical writing of this generation, then, we turn to the writings, public and private, of John Adams, Jefferson, Madison, Franklin, Hamilton, Washington, Rush, Wilson, and others. And the great historical treatises are not the formal histories, but rather such books as the *Defence of the Constitutions*, or "Notes on Virginia," or the *Federalist Papers*, or Wilson's *Lectures on the Constitution*, while commentary and interpretation of history run like a broad stream through the correspondence of most of the leading statesmen.

The evidence here is overwhelming: see, for example, the continuous rain of references to the experience of the ancient world in the debates in the Federal Convention and the state ratifying conventions, and the preoccupation with ancient history —and some more modern—in the *Federalist Papers*. All John Adams's major writings were historical, and so was much of what John Dickinson, James Wilson, and Madison wrote as well.[16]

But the view of history entertained by the philosophers of the Enlightenment was very different from that which had been accepted in the past, or which was to be embraced by the future. It completely repudiated the antiquarianism of the Annalists of the seventeenth century; it would have repudiated, just as convulsively, the narrative and romantic history of the nineteenth century and the scientific history of the nineteenth and twentieth centuries, which addresses itself to what actually happened.

Certainly what happened did not interest the historian-philosophers of the Enlightenment.[17] "Other historians relate facts to inform us of facts," wrote Diderot to Voltaire. "You relate them to excite in our hearts an intense hatred of lying, ignorance, hypocrisy, superstition, tyranny."[18] The tribute to Voltaire was just: "Confound details," that historian had said, and the reason was, clearly enough, that details tended to confound the historian. The same point of view is reflected in the statesmen of the New World when they turned their attention to history. "The sacred rights of mankind are not to be rummaged for among old parchments or musty records," wrote the youthful Hamilton. "They are written as with a sunbeam in the whole volume of human nature by the hand of Divinity itself."[19]

Particular facts, then, were of no interest or importance; only general facts. Details were insignificant and trivial; only general truths commanded attention. When Lessing reviewed Voltaire's *Essay on Manners* (a characteristic eighteenth-century title), he observed that "to know man in particular . . . is to know fools and scoundrels. The case is quite different with the study of man in general. Here he exhibits greatness and his divine origin."[20] That is what the American statesmen-philosophers were interested in, man in general. "When in the course of human events," Jefferson began his great Declaration, and it is a breathtaking phrase. It is "the laws of Nature and Nature's God" that entitle American people to "assume among the powers of the earth an equal station." The truths that justify this claim to equality are "self-evident" and apply to "all men" and to "any form of Government."[21]

So American statesmen, when they turned to the past, drew with equal confidence on the histories of Athens and Sparta, of Carthage and Rome, of the Swiss cantons or the low countries, of Anglo-Saxon England or Stuart England; it was all one. They had in fact no sense of place, as they had no sense of time; they repeated with Samuel Johnson (whom they otherwise detested):

> Let observation with extensive view
> Survey mankind from China to Peru;
> Remark each anxious toil, each eager strife,
> And watch the busy scenes of crowded life.
> —*Vanity of Human Wishes*

The laws of nature were everlastingly the same, and so, too, the laws of history, for the same laws that regulated the movement of the stars in the heavens regulated the movements of politics and economy on earth—the anxious toil, the eager strife, the busy scenes of crowded life.

And just as evolution was unsuspected in the natural order, so it was excluded from the historical. Progress, if it existed, was cyclical, or it was a happy parallel to the movement of the sun from the east to the west: it was as simple as that. The Enlightenment was not really interested in the past at all; in its sight a thousand years were as one, and if the thousand years did not yield a moral lesson, they were as nothing. The historians of the Enlightenment were like Diogenes; they went about the past with a lantern, looking for truth. They knew truth when they saw it, and brought it forth into the light, but they had no interest in what was not truth.

This is one reason they had so little interest in individuals, but only in the individual as a type, and they were always putting contemporaries into some historical niche. Washington was Cincinnatus, and Greene was Fabian, and Burr was Cataline, and Franklin was Solon, and so it went. It is no accident that the American Enlightenment did not produce a single biography of any value: Marshall's *Washington* was not really of any value, and Weem's *Washington* was not a product of the Enlightenment at all.

History, then, in the era of the Enlightenment, in America as in the Old World, addressed itself to great public questions, to broad general issues, to profound moral problems, and left the details to the pedants and the antiquarians. The historians of that day wrote on Man, not men; on the spirit of the laws rather than on specific laws; they gave lectures on the study of history, or commentaries on the Constitution, or provided a *Defence of the Constitutions*, or "Notes on Virginia." When they submitted "facts to a candid world," they did so only as illustrations of a general principle, and it did not so much matter if the facts failed to illustrate the principle, for the principle was valid anyway.[22] The best of histories—the American in any event—were all designed to prove something: "Notes on Virginia" to prove the superiority of the American environment over the European; *Defence of the Constitutions* to prove the superiority of the Massachusetts Constitution to the kind of constitution celebrated by Turgot; the *Federalist Papers* to prove the necessity of revolution in Great Britain, and so forth. Thus, history was utilitarian, but only in a highly moral sense. It took the place of the Bible, and drove home truths which heretofore had depended for authority on the Scriptures.

But if human nature was always the same, and if history was regulated by the laws of nature, what hope was there that man and nature would be different in America? What reason was there to suppose that the New World could escape the fate of the Old? That was a hard nut to crack. In a sense, it was the secular version of the familiar conflict between predestination and free will. Was there any room for the exercise of free will in American history? What a question to ask, in this New World whose very existence was a monument to the exercise of free will, in this new nation which had come into existence through a mighty effort of free will! What a question to ask of a people who were not only prepared to new-make the world, but were actually engaged in doing so!

History was not inexorable, nor was Man's Fate. History, rightly read, presented a spectacle of virtue as of vice, of weal as of woe, of triumph as of failure. The outcome depended on what man did with nature and nature's laws. More specifically, it depended on three things: the natural environment, the political and social institutions, and the character of the men who served—or betrayed—the commonwealth.

Environment was important, far more important in the New World than in the Old, where it had been tamed and brought under control. All Americans were by nature (as they still are) environmentalists, for in America environment triumphed over inheritance. It is the awareness of this that explains the almost convulsive reaction of so many Americans to the Raynal-Buffon theories of degeneracy in the New World. Those theories were not actually extreme, and Raynal at least apologized handsomely enough for his errors, but Jefferson and Franklin and others found them unforgivable.[23] For, to attack nature in America was to destroy the promise of American life. The expectations of future glory so confidently entertained by Washington and Jefferson and Paine and their colleagues were based in considerable part on the American environment. Nor was that environment a simple matter; it operated in two distinct ways to assure both America's escape from the evils that had afflicted the Old World and the promise of future well-being: both can be read luminously in the public papers of Washington and Jefferson. First was the physical bounty of the New World—soil, forests, water, sheer size—"land enough for . . . the thousandth and thousandth generation." Second was isolation from the Old World; as Jefferson put it, we were "*kindly* separated by Nature from the exterminating havoc of one quarter of the globe; too high-minded to endure the depredations of the others." The isolation was not only physical but social, political, and moral as well.

Here, then, was something really new in history: for the first time a numerous and virtuous people were vouchsafed an ideal environment and were freed from the tyrannies, the superstitions, the injustices, the vices, the miseries that had for centuries made a shambles of the history of the Old World. But a rich and spacious environment was not enough. It proved, to be sure, that "by all its dispensations Providence delighted in the happiness of man," but —if we may shift to Washington (and why not, as the Founding Fathers are philosophically interchangeable?)—"there is still an option left to the United States . . . it is in their choice and depends upon their conduct whether they will be respectable and prosperous, or contemptible and miserable as a Nation." In short, everything depended on what Americans did with their environment. Everything depended on the institutions they established, the constitutions they wrote, the laws they enacted. Everything depended on the health and the virtue of society. Everything depended on the integrity and devotion of its leaders. Here is where history, properly read, was really useful. For history was the great school of virtue.

As early as 1749, Benjamin Franklin drew up a series of "Proposals relating to the Education of the Youth of Pennsylvania." History occupied a central position in that scheme of education. Among many other things it would:

> Give occasion to expatiate on the Advantage of Civil Orders and Constitutions; how Men and their Properties are protected by joining in Societies and establishing Government; their Industry encouraged and rewarded; Arts invented, and Life made more comfortable. The Advantages of *Liberty*, Mischiefs of Licentiousness, Benefits arising from good Laws and from a due Execution of Justice, etc. Thus may the first principles of sound Politicks be fix'd in the Minds of Youth.[24]

And Franklin added that in a proper system of education,

> The idea of what is true Merit should also be presented to
> Youth, explained and impressed on their Minds, as con-
> sisting in an Inclination joined with an Ability to serve
> Mankind, one's Country, Friends and Family.

Jefferson, too, thought that history occupied a central position in
any scheme of education, because it taught the young the dangers
of tyranny and the virtues of freedom.

> History, by apprizing them of the past [he wrote], will
> enable them to judge of the future; it will avail them of
> the experience of other times and other nations; it will
> qualify them as judges of the actions and designs of men;
> it will enable them to know ambition under every dis-
> guise it may assume; and knowing it, to defeat its views.[25]

This, after all, was but the common sense of the matter.
Everyone agreed with Bolingbroke that history was philosophy
teaching by example. Everyone read in Hume that,

> History tends to strengthen the Sentiments of Virtue by
> the Variety of Views in which it exhibits the Conduct
> of divine Providence. . . . A regard to divine Providence
> heightens our Satisfaction in reading History, and tends
> to throw an agreeable Light upon the most gloomy and
> disgusting parts of it.[26]

Though the Americans did not know him, they would have agreed
with the fascinating Dr. Zimmermann of Berne and Hanover, who
ransacked ancient history to discover "examples . . . that shine as
patterns to posterity," and that "awaken in every noble mind an
irrefragable sense of the duties we owe to our country; and the
preservation of the history of these examples is nothing more than
the propagation of that national pride founded on real advantages," and who concluded that confidence and self-esteem, based
on familiarity with the historical past, "gives us the power to exalt
ourselves above the weakness of human nature, to exert our talents in praiseworthy enterprises, never to yield to the spirit of
slavery, never to be slaves to vice, to obey the dictates of our
conscience, to smile under misfortune, and to rely upon seeing
better days."[27]

The historical-philosopher with whom Americans were most
familiar (after Bolingbroke, in any event) was the extraordinary

Dr. Priestley, clergyman, scientist, statesman, and historian. All knew his *Lectures on History* (they had gone through many editions before Priestley came to the United States), lectures prefixed by an "Essay on a Course of Liberal Education for Civil Life" and addressed to that lively young Benjamin Vaughan whose later career was a monument to their value. Priestley's American friends could read in these lectures that history serves to amuse the imagination and interest the passions, that it improves the understanding, and that it tends to strengthen the sentiments of virtue.[28]

The chorus was harmonious; too, it was overwhelming; there were no discordant notes—none of any importance. History taught (that was its business) that man was master of his fate, that virtue could triumph over vice and reason over folly, and that the surest road to immortality was service to the commonwealth. The men whom history celebrated (it was the theme of the historians, the poets, the dramatists) were those who devoted their talents to their fellow men. That whole generation drew strength,

> not merely from twice-told arguments—how fair and noble a thing it is to show courage in battle—but from the busy spectacle of our great city's life as we see it before us day by day, falling in love with her as we see her, and remembering that all this greatness she owes to men with the fighter's daring, the wise man's understanding of his duty, and the good man's self-discipline in its performance—to men who, if they failed in any ordeal, disdained to deprive the city of their services, but sacrificed their lives as the best offerings on her behalf.[29]

And they knew, too, that "the whole earth is the sepulchre of famous men; and their story is graven not only on stone over the native earth, but lives on far away, without visible symbol, woven into the stuff of other men's lives."[30]

That was the immortality they sought, and it was the immortality they found; it is impossible to doubt the sincerity of their detestation of the adventurers or soldiers who solaced themselves with private rather than public gain, as it is impossible to doubt their own genuine desire for retirement to their farms or their studies.

These, then, were some of the circumstances, pressures, and considerations that help to explain the phenomenon of public leadership in eighteenth-century America. Talent was to be found everywhere, but in America it was directed, inevitably, into public channels. The zeal for service was to be found everywhere, but in America it could be satisfied on the public stage: who can believe that a Hamilton, a Gallatin, or a Wilson would have found scope for their talents in the countries of their birth? The philosophy of the Enlightenment flourished everywhere in the Western world, but in America it was given a chance to operate in the political and social as well as the moral and cultural realms, and that without the necessity of violence or revolution.

Eighteenth-century Americans assumed that history was philosophy teaching by example, and went far to prove it by modeling themselves on the examples they supposed—sometimes mistakenly—to be history. We no longer subscribe with any confidence to Bolingbroke's dictum, and even if we did we would be unable to agree on the selection or the interpretation of the examples. If we find history in general unusable in a direct or practical way, what of the experience of the Founding Fathers can we use in our search for leadership?

We know that all those who cry "Lord, Lord," shall not enter into the Kingdom of Heaven, and we cannot take refuge in admonitions. Nor can we hope to lift ourselves by our moral bootstraps by an ostentatious search for values: our problem is not to define our values, but to realize them. Let us inquire rather what part of the eighteenth-century experience that provided our country with such distinguished leadership is or can be made relevant to our needs today.

First, we noted that in eighteenth-century America public careers were almost the only careers that were open to great talent. Today openings—indeed invitations—are innumerable, and talent finds more glittering rewards in private than in public enterprise. Can we do anything to tilt the balance back to public enterprise?

Certainly we can, if we will, do something to restore the balance in the purely material realm; in a society where prestige is associated with material status, that is not unimportant. We can and should pay salaries that do not impose too heavy a sacrifice upon those who enter public life. We can use the instrument of taxation to encourage education, literature, the arts and sciences, and to reduce the financial rewards of private enterprise. We have not sufficiently explored these possibilities.

Second, we can and should protect our public servants from some of the more ostentatious penalties that are now associated with public enterprise; we might even give them the same protection and immunity that is enjoyed by those who are engaged in private business. Not only is public service poorly paid: it is exceedingly vulnerable. Horace Greeley observed during the campaign of 1872 that he did not know whether he was running for the Presidency or the penitentiary; a good many politicians, not Presidential candidates alone, must have felt that way during recent campaigns: the "twenty years of treason" campaign comes to mind. The civil servant, even with tenure, is at all times fair game: fair game for demagogues making political capital; for Congressional committees which allow themselves a degree of irresponsibility unparalleled in Britain or Canada; for security investigators whose work—witness the Service and Condon cases—is never done; for journalists who yield nothing to these investigators in their contempt for privacy and for decency. If we are to encourage able men to enter public life, we may have to curb the self-indulgence, vanity, and sadism which now operate to keep so many people out of it.

Third, can we do anything to encourage a livelier awareness of posterity and our responsibility to it? Perhaps the situation here is desperate; after all, a people who were really concerned for posterity would not produce so much of it. Yet here too something might be done by deliberate policy. Remember Pericles' boast in the great Funeral Oration:

> Ours is no work-a-day city only. No other provides so many recreations for the spirit—contests and sacrifices all the year round, and beauty in our public buildings to cheer the heart and delight the eyes day by day.

It is but natural, Pericles added, "that all of us shall work to spend ourselves in her service."

We can, if we will, emulate the Athenians who built so splendidly that their citizens "drew strength from the busy spectacle of our great city's life" and that posterity, too, could delight in its beauty and its glory. We can do this by the deliberate support of those monuments and memorials which are designed at once to remind us of our responsibility to posterity and to remind posterity of its obligation to us. Instead of turning the hearts of our great cities into scabrous parking lots—as Boston is doing even now—we can use public and private money to build parks, squares, fountains, galleries, libraries, theaters, operas—whatever will keep constantly before the eyes of the young of future generations a sense of the greatness of the city and of the spirit of those who built her. A society that wastes its affluence in self-indulgence cannot expect to excite in the young a passion to spend themselves in the service of the commonwealth.

Fourth, what role for education?

Eighteenth-century education with its emphasis on the classics and on history was designed to instill in the young an avid sense of duty and of civic virtue. The Fathers, we remember, were brought up on Plutarch and Cicero, and read Locke and Montesquieu and *Cato's Letters*. They saw history as a morality play whose acts unfolded in ceaseless progression, and themselves as cast in the roles of Solon or Aristides or Brutus or Cincinnatus. Often they consciously displayed the antique virtues which they associated with these Plutarchian characters.

It is an understatement that education and history no longer fulfill these traditional functions. Can they be persuaded to do so?

Certainly not in any calculated way; to "use" history to inculcate particular principles, even good ones, is a dangerous business. But at a time when the history of Greece and Rome and even of England have all but disappeared from the school curricula, and when history itself is giving way to civics, or current affairs, or "world problems," it is relevant to recall that the men who fought the Revolution and wrote the constitutions and the bills of rights were brought up on the histories of Greece and Rome and England. At a time when narrative history has given way to "problems" and when the celebration of heroes is regarded as a vestigial remnant of Victorianism or a subtle attack upon the behavioral sciences, it is relevant to observe that, if we deny young people the wonder and excitement of historical narration and of heroes, we cannot expect them to respond passionately to the moral crises of our own time.

The eighteenth century, which vouchsafed us the most distinguished leadership that any nation has enjoyed in modern times, can, then, furnish us, if not with models and directives, at least with illustrations and guides. Our eighteenth-century experience suggests that leadership is not fortuitous, that both formal policies and informal attitudes influence its appearance and its character, and that considerations of material rewards, prestige, opportunity, philosophy, and education are all involved in the formulation of such policies and attitudes.

1961

Our Declaration Is Still a Rallying Cry

The United States was born of rebellion and grew to greatness through revolution. No other nation, it is safe to say, has a revolutionary history that is so long or so comprehensive, and no other has a record that is so subversive.

Certainly the Declaration of Independence has some claim to be considered the most subversive document of modern history, and members of the Daughters of the American Revolution and the John Birch Society and all the other organizations that mortally fear revolution would do well to work to bar it from schools and public libraries. For, consider how explosive are its principles if they are taken seriously: all men are created equal; all have a right to life, liberty, and the pursuit of happiness; the purpose of government is to secure *these* rights; men have a right to overthrow existing governments and to make new governments!

Americans did not invent these heady doctrines, but they did something far more dangerous; they invented the mechanisms which gave them life and meaning. In the words of John Adams, they "*realized* the doctrines of the wisest writers." Thus, while the philosophers had long argued that men make government, it remained for the Americans to contrive that fundamental democratic institution whereby men can, in fact, create a government, the constitutional convention. Thus, while philosophers had long argued that all power was limited and that no government could exercise unlimited power, it remained for Americans to devise really effective legal limitations on government: written constitutions, checks and balances, dual federalism, judicial review—

devices that for the first time in history really limited government.

The Declaration was just a beginning of the revolution. Thereafter the United States embarked upon a career that was deeply subversive of most things governments and rulers in the Old World believed in and stood for. Just think: no established church, no royalty, no hereditary nobility, no military establishment, no great vested interests, no colonies to exploit. And look at its positive features—self-government, limited government, religious freedom, popular education, and a classless society.

The more we contemplate the American experience, the more we are impressed by its deeply revolutionary character. No wonder that when Tocqueville came to America in the mid-eighteen-thirties he could report, in effect, "I have seen the future, and it works!"—and go home to warn France, and all Europe, to prepare for an inevitable revolution along American lines. "The question here discussed," he said—and he was talking about equality in America—"is interesting not only to the United States, but to the whole world: it concerns not a nation, but all mankind." That was something that thoughtful Americans and Europeans realized from the beginning—that the experience of America concerned not just a nation but all mankind.

Americans were the first people to revolt against a mother country and set up on their own. This established a pattern, first for the nations of Latin America, and eventually for nations and peoples in the Old World and in ancient continents. The revolts against colonialism which have swept Asia and Africa in our time have their historical antecedents or beginnings in the American experience. If any people should sympathize with the impulse to "dissolve the political bands which have connected them with another, and to assume separate and equal station," it is Americans, for in a very real sense they initiated and inspired it.

The United States was the first nation founded squarely on the right of revolution; on the "right to alter or abolish" government. That principle is to be found not only in the Declaration, but in the institution of the constitutional convention. What Madison said shortly after the inauguration of the new government is true today:

If there be a principle that ought not to be questioned within the United States, it is that every nation has a right to abolish an old government and establish a new one. This principle is not only recorded in every public archive, written in every American heart, and sealed with the blood of a host of American martyrs, but is the only lawful tenure by which the United States hold their existence as a nation.

The United States was the first real nation to embark upon the experiment of a broad, popular self-government. Government, said Jefferson, derives its powers from consent of the governed. The government embraced the whole body politic, and consent meant something more than acquiescence; it meant participation. It is fashionable now in some quarters to recall that suffrage was limited in eighteenth-century America, and to quote anguished criticisms of democracy from the rich and the well-born. What is important is that incomparably more people participated in the daily business of government in the American states than anywhere else in the world; that limitations on suffrage evaporated with an ease that astonished envious European liberals; that there would have been no occasion for complaints against democracy if democracy had not been a very real thing; and that, after all, the Federalists did go under in 1800 and the Jeffersonians, with faith in the ability of men to govern themselves, did triumph.

Americans were pioneers in self-government. As Tom Paine wrote, "America made a stand, not for herself only, but for the world, and looked beyond the advantages which she could receive." She undertook to prove to the rest of mankind that self-government could work. All through the nineteenth century, upper-class visitors reported that it did not work, but in that same century some twenty million emigrants from the Old World to the New gave America a resounding vote of confidence.

Americans were the first people deliberately to create a nation: what Lincoln said at Gettysburg was literally true, that our forefathers had "brought forth a new nation." Theretofore nations had not been created; they had grown out of century-long historical processes: thus England, France, Denmark, Spain, and many others. But American nationalism was a creative act, a product of the deliberate application of will and intelligence by statesmen, soldiers, scholars, men of letters, artists, scientists, and others of all ranks to the task of nation-making.

Where in the Old World countries, the foundations of nationalism were laid long before the political superstructure was erected, in the United States the Founding Fathers first built the political structure and thereafter filled in the rest. They contrived the constitutional mechanisms, the political practices, exploited the economic bases, developed the social resources, and added for good measure the historical and the cultural ingredients as well.

With this unprecedented experience with nationalism Americans should have the liveliest sympathy for those peoples throughout the globe who are today striving to create a nation. We were the first to show that it could be done and we should be the first to welcome others when they try to repeat our experience.

The first of the truths which Jefferson announced as "self-evident" was the truth that all men are created equal. We need not inquire, here, just what Jefferson meant by the elusive term; its significance—as with most of the great phrases of history—is not descriptive but prophetic. What the phrase came to mean was never better put than by Lincoln in his Springfield speech of 1857.

The Fathers, he said, meant to set up a standard maxim for free society, which should be familiar to all, and revered by all; constantly approximated, and constantly labored for, even though never perfectly attained, and thereby constantly spreading and deepening its influence and augmenting the happiness and value of life to all people of all colors everywhere. Its authors meant the Declaration to be "a stumbling block to those who in after times might seek to turn a free people back into the hateful paths of despotism."

The concept of equality, first announced as a general principle in the Declaration of Independence, has worked like a ferment in American society, and in the American mind—and not in America alone. Each successive generation of Americans has in its own way felt called on to square reality with the principle of equality.

"Created equal." It applied to the political processes, and struck down limitations on suffrage for men and eventually for women. It applied to the social processes and challenged every manifestation of class—challenged though it could not prevent slavery; challenged though it did not prevent the continuing assertion of white supremacy after slavery was gone; and in the end forced Americans to resolve the pernicious dilemma that had so long frustrated them.

It applied to the economy and helped create an open economic order where material well-being came to be assumed both as a proper foundation to equality, and as a right. It applied to religion and made impossible not only an established church but the association of any one church with social or political power. It applied to education and eventually required an equal chance at education to all comers—a requirement only now in process of realization.

Political equality is now a reality throughout most of the free world. Social equality has been realized in many countries; economic equality has not yet been attained in large parts of the globe. Who can doubt that Tocqueville was right when he predicted that the principles and practices of equality that he found illustrated in America would spread to the Old World, and beyond?

We have two obvious responsibilities here. The first is to put an end to the shameful inequalities that persist in our society. Inequality—as Lincoln said of slavery itself—"deprives our republican example of its just influence in the world; enables the enemies of free institutions with plausibility to taunt us as hypocrites; causes the real friends of freedom to doubt our sincerity; and forces so many good men among ourselves into an open war with the very fundamental principles of civil liberty." The second responsibility is to welcome and support those political practices and economic developments that promise a greater degree of equality in other lands.

Americans were the first people who took for granted and exploited the possibilities of change. Though the eighteenth century did embrace the notion of progress, that progress was, on the whole, an abstraction rather than a reality. It was something that would take place over the centuries, and it was tempered by the conviction that though material circumstances might change, human nature itself would not really change. Americans were the first to prove that, given favorable economic conditions and a favorable political climate, progress would be immensely accelerated, and that human nature itself could be changed in a single generation.

Men could throw off the shackles of the past; they could emancipate themselves from tyranny and ignorance and poverty; they could lift themselves by their own bootstraps. Just give them a chance! Let them enjoy freedom; let them govern themselves; give them an education; provide them with land and jobs; let them worship as they wished—and think as they wished; assure them of equality; give them a chance. Then, not centuries or millennia, but a few years would suffice for progress.

That is what Jefferson said, again and again. That is what the Declaration of Independence said, with its emphasis on equality and on the pursuit of happiness. And that is what Jefferson returned to in his public letter—a letter celebrating the fiftieth anniversary of that Declaration of Independence which he had penned:

> May it be to the world, what I believe it will be, the signal for arousing men to burst the chains under which monkish ignorance and superstition had persuaded them to bind themselves, and to assume the blessings and security of self-government. All eyes are opened, or opening, to the rights of man. The general spread of the light of science has already laid open to every view the palpable truth that the mass of mankind has not been born with saddles on their backs, nor a favored few booted and spurred, ready to ride them legitimately. There are grounds of hope for others.

Of all peoples, then, we should be most ready to sympathize with those who are trying to close the desperate gap between what they are, and what they might be; who are trying to catch up in one generation with the progress of centuries.

The methods of this global revolution, too, are familiar enough. For it is one of the great paradoxes of history that the revolt of Asia and Africa against the West is being carried on with the tools and techniques devised by the West. The political instrument is Western nationalism; the social instrument is Western equality; the economic instrument is Western science and technology.

Now, while the Industrial Revolution had its origins in Europe, nowhere were natural resources, abundant labor, technical and scientific skills more happily combined to lift the general level of well-being than in the United States. Ours, it has been observed, is a business civilization; it would be more accurate to call it a technological civilization. Conservative businessmen who never tire of pointing out the immense achievements of American technology should be the first to sympathize with the impoverished millions of Asia and Africa who have learned the lesson that America taught: that it is possible to lift the level of a society by the application of science and technology.

There is one final consideration that is relevant. The colonies, said Jefferson "are, and of right, ought to be free." That was a phrase which echoed again and again in the speeches, letters, and public papers of the time—"of right, ought to be." If colonies were not represented, they ought to be; if religion was not free, it ought to be; if men were not free, they ought to be. That "ought to be" was a rallying cry, a call to duty and to war. It took for granted that man and Providence would work together to achieve ends that were right and just.

Should we not say today, that men everywhere ought to be free; that they ought to be independent; that they ought to enjoy equality; they ought to share in a higher standard of living and in the pursuit of happiness?

The Declaration of Independence is not merely a museum piece. It is not a parchment to take out once a year, celebrate with ceremonial reverence, and then return to the sterility of a glass case. It is not merely an historical document, something to learn in school as we learn so many things that we promptly forget. It is vital and immediate. It argues a case that is still valid and announces principles that are still true. It still calls upon us to pledge our lives, our fortunes, and our honor to their vindication.

1961

"Yet the Nation Survived"

"These are the times that try men's souls," wrote Tom Paine at a time when Washington was fleeing through the Jerseys and the American cause seemed lost. "The summer soldier and the sunshine patriot will in this crisis shrink from the service of their country; but he that stands by it now, deserves the love and thanks of man and woman." It required faith then to believe, despite all evidence, that the American cause might yet triumph—that cause which Paine himself described as "the best the sun ever shone upon." But Washington and his army survived; despite White Plains and the Brandywine, despite Morristown and Valley Forge, the American cause survived.

In recent years, and especially in campaign years, it has become common to assert that the United States is facing the most dangerous crisis of its history. In the deep sense that all mankind is facing the crisis of atomic warfare and possible extermination, this is true enough. But in the sense in which the statement is made—that is, with reference to the challenge of communism—it is simply not true.

For we are, after all—and in this we do not differ from most other peoples—accustomed to crises: that is one reason we are able to resolve them. Even after independence was won, the success of the new experiment in nationalism was by no means foreordained.

After all, history taught that it was impossible to hold together in a single nation vast and disparate territories. Everywhere in the Old World the particular had triumphed over the general, and this was to be the experience of South America, of Asia and of Africa in the nineteenth century as well. What reason was there to believe that America could reverse the processes of history and make the general triumph over the particular, unity over heterogeneity? As Washington wrote in his moving Circular Letter of 1783:

> It appears to me that there is still an option left to the United States of America—that it is in their choice, and depends upon their conduct, whether they will be respectable and prosperous, or contemptible and miserable as a Nation. This is the time of their political probation . . . this is the moment when the eyes of the whole World are turned upon them, this is the moment to establish or ruin their national character forever. . . . For according to the system of Policy which the States shall adopt . . . they will stand or fall and by their confirmation or lapse, it is yet to be decided whether the Revolution must ultimately be considered as a blessing or a curse.

The States weathered that crisis, and adopted a "system of Policy" which confirmed independence as a blessing not only to Americans but to all mankind. There was no reason to expect that the Americans of 1787—few in numbers and unsophisticated—would create a nation which would grow and flourish while almost every other empire on the globe disintegrated, that they would write a Constitution which would outlast any other, that they would develop a democracy which worked. But they did all these things, and with an ease that confounded experience.

Yet fortunate as was the new nation in its origins, in its leadership, in the principles which it cherished and the institutions which it established, it was not to avoid grave crises. The Washington administration was successful beyond the dreams of the Fathers, but the administrations of Adams, Jefferson, and Madison were years of peril, years in which it was touch and go whether the nation would hold together or disintegrate.

The whole of Europe was involved in a titanic war, and, notwithstanding the almost convulsive efforts of Jefferson to maintain neutrality, the United States was sucked into the war. The War of 1812 all but destroyed the new nation. Although the United States had declared war, she was wholly unprepared to conduct it. Her armies were small, untrained and ill-equipped; her little navy, stout as it was, could not long withstand British might and was soon swept from the seas; her administration was feeble to the point of imbecility, her treasury all but bankrupt. American invasions of Canada were thrown back with heavy loss, and the British invaded Maryland and burned the Capitol. So bitterly did the New England states oppose the war that they withdrew from effective participation in it and threatened to withdraw from the Union itself.

Yet somehow the nation survived—by the courage of sea dogs like Perry and MacDonough, of soldiers like Winfield Scott and Andrew Jackson, of the soldiers and sailors and fighting frontiersmen who refused to acknowledge defeat. And out of the War of 1812 came a new era of national expansion, unity, and greatness.

The gravest danger to the nation came not from without, but from within: there is, after all, no danger like that which we contrive for ourselves. It was the threat to national unity and to freedom and democracy of the slave system. Jefferson had said of slavery that "I tremble for my country when I reflect that God is just; that His justice cannot sleep forever," and at the time of the Missouri Compromise he called the agitation of the issue "the knell of the Union." So it proved to be. The issue came to a head with the election of Lincoln and the secession of eleven Southern states. It seemed like the end of the American experiment, and in far-off Oxford the historian E. A. Freeman composed the title-page of his new book, "A History of Federal Government from the Greek Confederations to the Disruption of the American Union."

It was, unquestionably, the greatest crisis that had yet confronted the American nation, and it remains, in retrospect, the greatest crisis that the nation has ever surmounted. For the Civil War tested not only whether the nation could survive but whether a nation "conceived in liberty and dedicated to the proposition that all men are created equal" could long endure.

Writing of Pearl Harbor, Winston Churchill recalled that many of his countrymen feared that America would succumb to panic, or that it would allow itself to be distracted and confused.

"But," he added, "I had studied the American Civil War, fought out to the last desperate inch. . . . I went to bed and slept the sleep of the saved and the thankful."

It is not only war that has tested the American people but economic and political crises as well. There was the prolonged crisis of Reconstruction; widespread corruption in politics and business; a Congressional assault on the constitutional system which came close to destroying the independence of the executive and judiciary departments; the establishment of military government in the South; the exacerbation of racial relations and of sectional relations. But in a few years moderation supplanted radicalism, and North and South took the road to reunion. There was the deep economic crisis of 1873 and after, a depression marked by the misery and poverty of the working classes and the bankruptcy of many farmers, by bread lines and savage strikes and an appeal to class hatreds, and by the seeming helplessness of government in the face of widespread disaster.

There was the even more widespread crisis of the nineties: farm prices crashing to an all-time low while demagogues like Tom Watson incited class warfare; desperate strikes at the Pullman and Carnegie works and warfare in the mines of Colorado; Coxey's Army of the unemployed marching on Washington in a pitiful "petition on boots"; the banking and currency system exploited by the rich, the government apparently indifferent to the victims of the economic disorder, invoking the injunction against labor unions while giant corporations went their way all but undisturbed. As the Populist leader Ignatius Donnelly put it, "From the same prolific womb of governmental injustice we breed the two great classes—tramps and millionaires."

Again a generation later America was plunged into a depression, deeper, more pervasive, and more prolonged than any that had gone before. The out-of-work reached the staggering total of thirteen or fourteen million, national income sank to one-half its earlier total (and one-tenth its present total); farmers were reduced to tenancy and workers to beggary, and the government seemed paralyzed. Elsewhere—Germany and Italy, for instance— comparable crises had led to the establishment of totalitarian dictatorships.

The nation weathered these economic crises as it had weathered military storms, and this though many Cassandras prophesied nothing but disaster. It survived, too, the greatest of modern crises, the threat from totalitarianism and the World War. Already we are beginning to forget how ominous that danger was, exaggerating our present dangers by contrast. There was danger all through the thirties as Americans failed to appreciate the nature of the totalitarian menace and were content to "build a fortress on a paper pad."

There was danger from 1939 to 1941 when Britain stood almost alone between the Western Hemisphere and a triumphant Hitler. There was the staggering crisis of Pearl Harbor and after when Germany and Japan seemed irresistible, and when it appeared to many observers that democracy and liberty, which had flourished for so short a time in history, were bound to go under before the forces of tyranny and darkness.

If we look back upon all these chapters of our history—the crisis of independence and of nation-making, of the War of 1812, of the slavery struggle and the Civil War, of three major depressions, of two World Wars—we can see that we have survived them without sacrifice of basic institutions or principles. On the contrary, recurrent crises have strengthened our character, toughened our institutions, and confirmed the validity of our principles. And we can discern in these chapters of our history not so much a set of laws as a pattern of conduct, a pattern both coherent and instructive. We have survived and flourished not only because we have been fortunate in our resources and in our isolation, but because we are the kind of people we are; because we respond energetically to challenge and to crisis; because we cling stubbornly to certain practices and principles of conduct.

What are some of those practices and principles?

First, we have dealt with each of our major crises by democratic methods. We have not—as have so many other people—succumbed to the easy solutions of dictatorship or of revolution. We have trusted in the orderly and familiar processes of government. We have maintained, through every crisis, the rule of law and of constitutional government.

Second—and it is perhaps an extension of the first principle

—we have preferred evolutionary to revolutionary solutions. It is a striking consideration that, except for the Civil War, when the slavocracy appealed from the ballot box to arms, a people who are reputedly most lawless and most violent are the only major people except the British who have never had a revolution. With extraordinary skill the Americans have adapted their eighteenth-century institutions to the exigencies of nineteenth- and twentieth-century economy; have made their written Constitution flexible; have discovered a resourcefulness and a liberalism that has made possible change and reform at every critical juncture.

Third, we have never, as a people, given way to panic or fear, not in the darkest days of the Revolution, nor at the time of seeming disintegration in 1813 and 1814, nor when the remnants of a stricken Union Army streamed into Washington, nor when the Japanese wrecked our Pacific fleet and swept out to conquer the Asiatic and the Pacific world.

"The only thing we have to fear is fear itself," said Franklin D. Roosevelt, but—except for the slavocracy in 1860—we have never succumbed to fear. Instead we have based our conduct on confidence and on faith.

Fourth—an outgrowth of the third principle—we have customarily had a positive, not a negative, program of action. We have been for something, rather than merely against something. We have had objectives that could arouse support and excite enthusiasm. Thus out of revolution came an independent nation; out of the misery and confusion of the Civil War a new national consciousness and a growth of democracy; out of the tragic crisis of the Civil War a new birth of freedom, and a reunited nation:

> No poorest in thy borders
> but may now
> Lift to the juster skies a
> man's enfranchised brow,
> O! Beautiful, My Country!
> Ours once more.
> —James Russell Lowell,
> "Harvard Commemoration Ode"

Finally, Americans have exposed every major problem to the processes of freedom—freedom of inquiry, of discussion, of criticism. They have brought all issues to the bar of public opinion, and of reason. They have encouraged the fullest inquiry in order that they might have a firm foundation of knowledge for whatever course they adopted. They have encouraged criticism in order that they might avoid errors. They have not thought to solve problems, to resolve crises, to defeat enemies, by invoking some mumbo-jumbo of verbal patriotism or some ceremonious gestures, but have known that no problems can be solved until they are understood. They have been able to vindicate freedom because they have used the methods and the weapons of freedom.

Our past, then, suggests some obvious morals to the present and the future. Seen in historical perspective there is nothing unprecedented or ominous about the crisis of the present. Never before has the nation been more powerful, more nearly united, more self-confident; never has it commanded more influence abroad or—until the rise of McCarthyism—more respect. And not only is America fortunate in its own strength; it is fortunate in its allies. It is the leader of a great combination of nations who have as a common heritage a devotion to the processes of law and a respect for the dignity of the individual. That position gives it not only immense strength; it gives it immense responsibility.

It is important that we keep in mind these elements of strength, and that we bring them to the support of our present and future policies. It is essential that we apply the lessons and experience of the past; that we approach whatever crises arise with constitutional methods, that we avoid panic and fear, that we repudiate purely negative policies, that we base our conduct on the processes of freedom, on confidence in the intelligence and integrity of our own people and of our allies, on faith in reason and in freedom.

1953

"To Form a Much Less Perfect Union"

Not for more than a century has the doctrine of states' rights been so defiantly proclaimed as now; not since Appomattox has it found such widespread support.

We can dismiss as irrelevant the demagoguery of a Governor Wallace or a Governor Barnett. But we cannot dismiss so easily the formal endorsement by as many as a dozen states of constitutional amendments which embody a states'-rights philosophy and assert "no confidence" in the Constitution and the Government of the United States. Revolutionary as these proposed amendments are, they have received curiously little public attention. Indeed, it is safe to say that the average American is wholly unaware of them or of the changes they would bring about in the American constitutional system.

The first of these proposed amendments is a clumsy effort to repeal the Supreme Court decision, in *Baker vs. Carr*, that Federal courts may take a hand in reapportioning seats in state legislatures; it would deny them any jurisdiction in this area. The second, and most pernicious, would allow state legislatures to bypass the Congress entirely in the amendment process by permitting amendments to the Federal Constitution solely through state action. The third would create a super-Supreme Court to be composed of the chief justices of the fifty states, with power to overrule decisions of the United States Supreme Court in all cases involving state-federal relations. So far, the first of these amendments has been approved by twelve states, the second by eleven, the third by four.

There is perhaps little likelihood that these gestures toward constitutional anarchy will command the support of three-fourths of the states, or that they will be endorsed by the Congress. Yet we should not forget that the Bricker amendment—designed to paralyze Presidential conduct of foreign relations—failed of passage in the Senate by but one vote, and that the Twenty-second Amendment limiting Presidents to two terms—an amendment which President Eisenhower himself called an example of retroactive vindictiveness—slipped through the Congress and the state legislatures almost without notice.

What we are witnessing in these amendments—and in the defiance of the Supreme Court by state governors, in the assault on the constitutional powers of the President to conduct foreign affairs, in the ground swell of revolt against what is vaguely called "federal centralization"—is not merely a recrudescence of states' rights. It is an expression of something deeper—of a philosophy of anti-government and of no-government. Whereas the Constitution was designed "to form a more perfect Union," this is an effort to form a much less perfect Union. It is a philosophy, in fact if not in concept, of constitutional anarchy.

One thing which is clear is that the proponents of these amendments are not genuinely concerned with the powers of the states. They are concerned with non-powers in the nation. They do not want to see state governments invigorated, carrying through broad legislative programs; they want to see the national government frustrated, incompetent to carry through legislative programs. The ambition which animates them is not to strengthen the states, but to paralyze the nation.

Does anyone for a moment suppose that if the apportionment amendment should by some quirk become law, the states would then proceed to reapportion legislative seats on a fair basis? They have had fifty years in which to deal with the problem and have failed to do so; some states have actually defied their own constitutional mandates requiring decennial reapportionment.

Does anyone really suppose that if the amendment permitting the states to bypass the Congress in the amending process became law, the states would proceed to set their domestic houses in order—to end the scandal of racial discrimination themselves, to reform antiquated tax structure, to deal vigorously with the problems of conservation and of public lands, to take care of the needs of public education and public health through a series of constitutional amendments? Clearly, the new authority would be used not to carry through programs of public welfare but to repeal existing programs of public welfare.

Does anyone for a moment suppose that if the fantastic proposal for a super-Supreme Court were to materialize, that court would rule impartially between the claims of state and nation? That amendment would enable twenty-six chief justices representing (and representing unfairly) states with one-sixth the population of the United States, to rewrite constitutional law. In all likelihood, such a court would strip the Supreme Court of that crucial function of harmonizing the federal system which is quintessential to the survival of the nation. As Justice Holmes said half a century ago: "I do not think the United States would come to an end if we lost our power to declare an act of Congress void. I do think the Union would be imperiled if we could not make the declaration as to the laws of the several states. For one in my place sees how often a local policy prevails with those who are not trained to national views."

These amendments, and the forces behind them, are inspired by deep-seated hostility to the national government. They are designed to weaken the whole constitutional structure—not only the positive power of government under the Constitution, but rights guaranteed to persons under the Constitution. They look ultimately to paralyzing the effective operation of the Constitution, which means, of course, paralyzing the nation itself.

There is nothing new about this. Thomas Jefferson invoked the principle of states' rights on behalf of freedom, but he was almost the last statesman who did so. For well over a century now, this pernicious doctrine has been involved for two major purposes, and almost exclusively for those purposes: to weaken government and to endanger freedom.

The most notorious, and historically the most decisive, use of the doctrine of states' rights was, of course, to protect the institution of Negro slavery. States' rights were invoked, too, to delay expansion into the West, to defeat the regulation of trusts and railroads, to frustrate prohibition of child labor, to hold up the grant of suffrage to women, and to oppose social security, the conservation of natural resources, the creation of hydroelectric power for national purposes, the encouragement of public education, and the protection of equality. It is worth adding—it is something Southerners might note—that the doctrine of states' rights was used, too, to disrupt and eventually to destroy the Confederacy itself.

No political doctrine in American history has been more consistently invoked on behalf of privilege; none has had a more egregious record of error and calamity.

What is the explanation of this record, and of the attitude which it reflects?

It is not, I think, to be found in any deep or passionate attachment to the states. There was some of that earlier, and we are still reminded of it on ceremonial occasions. But there is no persuasive evidence that what animated a John Adams, a Jefferson, even a Calhoun, is still a vital force.

The modern champions of states' rights have none of that loyalty to the community which impelled a Jefferson to build the University of Virginia and cherish its integrity; which persuaded a Franklin to lavish his rich talents on his adopted city of Philadelphia; which convinced earlier generations of Bostonians that they had built a Zion upon a hill, and later generations that their city was the Hub of the Solar System ("You couldn't pry that out of a Boston man," said Oliver Wendell Holmes, "if you had the tire of all creation straightened out for a crowbar"). They have not even that generous vanity which compels Texans and Californians to vie with each other in building universities and museums and foundations, and in preserving the natural resources and beauty of their states.

The states'-rights champion of our time displays no real pride in his state, no sense of its past, no feeling for its traditions, no respect for its dignity, no pride in its future. What has he done, what does he do, to preserve its natural resources, to cherish its institutions of learning, to protect its good name? What interest does he show in the richest possession of any state—the welfare of its men and women and children? The mobs invading the university campus at Oxford, the Negro children huddled behind wire fences in Birmingham, and police dogs in the streets—these are the stigmata of states' rights today.

What shall we say of the other side of the shield: that fear of nationalism, that suspicion of the Federal government, which motivates not only the three proposed amendments to the Constitution but the whole crusade against the political effectiveness of the national government?

What an extraordinary spectacle it is, this fear of the United States by its own citizens! The generation of the Founding Fathers worried and bickered over the potential hostility between large states and small, and wrote safeguards against the exploitation of small states into the Constitution. We can see now that these fears were unreal and absurd. But they were neither as unreal nor as absurd as the fear that grips large segments of our population today—the fear of the national government itself.

One might imagine, to hear some of our contemporary nihilists talk, that we were not one people but many, not Americans but Virginians and Mississippians; one might suppose that Jefferson Davis was right when he wrote, long after the Civil War, that "no such political community or corporate unit as one people of the United States existed, has even been organized, or yet exists, and that no political action by the people of the United States in the aggregate has even taken place, or ever can take place, under the Constitution." One might suppose that we had not existed as a nation for 175 years. One might conclude that the attempt at federal union, so hopefully inaugurated in 1787 and so widely copied throughout the globe, had proved a failure, and that we were now called upon to go back to 1787, reject the Constitution, and cleave to the old Articles of Confederation.

Is there any foundation for the misgivings that animate the champions of states' rights; is there any justification for their fears?

Has the national government proved dangerous to the liberties of Americans, or to the rights of the states?

Certainly it would be asking a great deal to ask Negroes to believe that the national government has been the enemy of freedom, and the states the guardians of freedom. It would be asking a great deal to ask labor to subscribe to the doctrine that it should look to the states, not to the nation, for the preservation of its rights.

Opponents of national "centralization" never cease to deplore the invasion of the "rights" of private citizens by the national government, and Governor Wallace played variations on that weary theme in his proclamation. It is fair to ask: What rights have they lost? Freedom of religion, of speech, of the press, of assembly, of petition, of association? Due process of law, the right to a jury trial, immunity from unreasonable search and seizure, from cruel and unusual punishment, from self-incrimination?

To ask these questions is to answer them. As far as the Federal government is concerned (and it is very much concerned) these rights are still unimpaired—or impaired only where considerations of national security have appeared to require qualification. For the past thirty years or so the Federal courts have been engaged not in restricting but in enlarging the scope and meaning of these rights. The same, alas, cannot be said for the states. Who can deny that in the overwhelming majority of instances impairment of the rights and liberties of men has come from the states— and in large measure from precisely those states whose spokesmen are the most vigorous proponents of states' rights? If ever it can be said that advocates do not come into court with clean hands, it can be said of those who today lament the "destruction" of liberties of the states by the national government.

Who, knowing our history, can doubt for a moment that the real source of danger to the freedoms of Americans has been the states themselves? There are some exceptions, to be sure —the episode of the Alien and Sedition Acts of 1798, for example, the repressive legislation of the First World War, the manifestations of McCarthyism in the fifties.

But anyone familiar with the history of freedom in the United States knows that it is the states that interfere most frequently with academic freedom, the states that set up censorship of press and stage and films, the states that threaten freedom of association, the states whose un-American activities committees have chalked up the most shameful records, the states that have most frequently flouted the due process of law and denied equal protection of the laws, and challenged or denied religious freedom.

The vast majority of civil-liberties cases in the Supreme Court come up from the states, and involve local ordinances or state laws.

Do those who now invoke states' rights do so because they want higher standards of freedom, or because they fear the Supreme Court is too active on behalf of freedom?

Has the national government threatened those institutions on whose prosperity our society depends for its social and moral health? Has it threatened the independence of the church? The Federal government started off with complete separation of church and state; it was in the states that discrimination on the basis of religion lingered on. When Madison proposed that the prohibitions of the First Amendment be applied to the states, his proposal was defeated.

Has the national government threatened the integrity of arts and letters and sciences? On the contrary. Since the early years of the nineteenth century, the national government has maintained such institutions as the Library of Congress, the United States Geological Survey, the National Observatory, the Smithsonian Institution and, more recently, the National Archives and the National Gallery of Art. Have these institutions been free? Certainly they have been more free than many state universities. Congress has never interfered with the Library of Congress, for example, as the legislatures of Ohio and Colorado are even now interfering with their state universities.

It is precisely because the national government is so generous to arts and sciences that the proponents of states' rights fear it, for they do not really believe in freedom, nor in those institutions that preserve and prosper freedom: universities, libraries, scientific institutes. All of these foster the open mind and the cosmopolitan spirit. How alien these are to the philosophy of states' rights can be observed in the South of 1860—or of 1960.

Has the national government threatened the general welfare, or failed to promote it? On the contrary. That whole body of welfare legislation that is interwoven with private enterprise to make the fabric of our life today finds it authority and support largely in the national government: Social Security, public health, conservation and, now, education and civil rights.

It is precisely because the Federal government does promote

the general welfare that proponents of states' rights fear it. They proclaim that these enterprises should not be performed by the national government, but by the states. But they are not truly concerned with the general welfare, only with that of members of their own faction. And they have failed egregiously to promote the welfare of even these—to provide schools and housing, for example. All too often, the states have wasted their resources of water and forest and soil, or handed them over to predatory private interests. Ever since the days of Theodore Roosevelt it has been the United States which has stepped in to protect these resources. Has the national government failed to form a more perfect Union, to provide for the general defense, to insure domestic tranquillity? Quite the contrary. There has never been a serious threat to the Union from the national government, or to the domestic tranquillity. There has never been an adventurer, a soldier of fortune, a dictator, or a tyrant in the executive chair.

The only threats to the Union have come from the states. States' rights imperiled the Union in 1803 when New England states flirted at secession because Congress had bought Louisiana. States' rights threatened the disruption of the Union during the War of 1812, when states refused to permit their militias to serve outside state territories. States' rights threatened the integrity of the Union in the eighteen-twenties when Georgia nullified Federal treaties and Supreme Court decisions protecting the Cherokee Indians, and in the eighteen-thirties when South Carolina nullified tariff laws and enforcement laws. States' rights actually broke up the Union in 1861, and precipitated the most tragic war in which the American people have ever been engaged. We cannot say that the doctrine of states' rights threatens the Union today, but clearly it disturbs domestic tranquillity by defying the constitutional mandate of equality and justice.

And what of the states? Have they, in fact, lost any of the rights or powers they originally possessed? They have lost the "right" to secede. That, at least, was settled by Appomattox. They have lost the "right" to deprive persons of life, liberty or property without due process of law, or deny the equal protection of the laws; they have lost the "right" to deprive any person of suffrage on account of race or color. These "rights" they did indeed forfeit, and it was Appomattox which settled them all.

It would be a mistake to imply that the current revival of states' rights has been entirely insincere or misguided. Bigness is dangerous; the welfare state can dry up initiative; power does tend to corrupt, and there is much to be said for fragmentation of political authority; eternal vigilance is the price of liberty.

But a states'-rights philosophy that has its origin in fear of government itself, and is rooted in a deep distrust of majority rule and of the democratic processes, forfeits its claim to respect. A states'-rights philosophy which is never inspired by generosity, never excited by a passion for freedom or for justice, never exalted by magnanimity, but takes refuge in narrowness and selfishness and vindictiveness, exhausts its claim to tolerance.

1963

Television and the Elections

The joint television appearances of Vice President Nixon and Senator Kennedy—really press conferences improperly dignified by the word "debate"—are the distinctive feature of the current Presidential campaign. So heavily has public interest focused upon them that Mr. Arthur Krock of *The New York Times* has concluded that "the public will demand these joint appearances in all future Presidential campaigns."

Let us hope not. These televised press conferences are a misfortune in this campaign, and in future campaigns they could be a disaster.

They are not debates. They are not even discussions. They do not fulfill the most elementary political purpose of permitting the candidates to explore and clarify the vital issues before the American people. They are not designed to enlighten or to instruct the public on the nature of those issues. They submit the greatest elective office in the world to the chances of arbitrary and miscellaneous questions put not to elicit information or to illuminate problems, but to provide sensations. When journalists or commentators are assigned the role of inquisitors, there is no assurance that they will be concerned with real issues, and there is already substantial evidence that they are not. There is every likelihood that there will always be at least one interviewer who will be more interested in asking questions guaranteed to produce headlines, or in making journalistic capital, than in probing the issues or enlightening the public.

The formula of tense and concentrated confrontation, even at its best, is not designed to discover in candidates those qualities really needed for the conduct of the Presidential office—the qualities of patience, prudence, humility, sagacity, judiciousness, magnanimity. But these qualities—or many of them—are a positive handicap in a tense television interview. These televised question hours put a premium on glibness and fluency—qualities not of great value in a President.

It is sobering to speculate on how former statesmen would have survived the ordeal of such televised inquisitions as we have witnessed—a speculation not wholly fanciful. Washington, it is safe to say, would not have come out very well. We have the testimony of Jefferson, who knew him well, that, as far as he saw, no judgment was ever sounder.

> It was slow in operation, being little aided by invention or imagination, but sure in conclusion. . . . If deranged during the course of the action . . . he was slow in readjustment. . . . Perhaps the strongest feature in his character was prudence, never acting until every circumstance, every consideration, was maturely weighed.

Jefferson himself, for all his erudition and his literary gracefulness, was not happy in public conversation, and studiously avoided public confrontation, sending his messages to Congress to be read instead of giving them himself. In a public contest between Jefferson and Aaron Burr, who can doubt the brilliant and facile New Yorker would have come off victor? Henry Clay might have performed well—he was a natural actor—but not Andrew Jackson, who would probably have lost his temper with consequences that would give anguish to our modern nice Nellies.

Lincoln was apt with stories—often longish stories that required more than the sacred two minutes of TV in the telling—but he was not quick in the give and take of politics. Patience, judiciousness, and humility were his outstanding qualities.

Nor can we be confident that President Wilson, for all his immense literary gifts, would have responded well before the klieg lights. He, too, wanted time to think, to formulate his opinions in appropriate words, to analyze, to qualify, to elaborate. And he, too, had a hot temper—not always under control—which did not suffer fools gladly or tolerate journalistic impudence. Indeed, of our major Presidents probably only Franklin D. Roosevelt had the wit, the resourcefulness, the self-assurance, to do well in televised press interviews.

In short, televised interviews of the kind that we have seen in this campaign put a premium on qualities useful for membership on a college debating team or even in a legislative chamber, but not on the qualities that have marked our really great Presidents.

There are even graver reasons why this process is not only misguided but pernicious—why it is not only tactically bad but strategically dangerous. It encourages the American public to believe that there are no questions—no issues before us—that are so difficult that they cannot be disposed of in two or three minutes of off-the-cuff comment. It submits the great and complex controversies of our time to the kind of test that President Jackson established for the civil service of his day: if any ordinary man could not fill any public job, there was something wrong with the job.

So we are seduced to believe that our candidates ought to know, offhand, what to do about inflation, about Berlin, about Cuba, about the Pescadores islands, about civil rights, about our relations with Russia. Worse yet, this television technique creates a situation where it is politically awkward, if not impossible, for a candidate to say, "I don't know." "If all earthly power were given me," said Lincoln, "I should not know what to do about slavery." That is what sensible candidates should say about a great many of the issues that now confront us, and it is doubtless what they very much want to say—about the Congo, or the recognition of Red China, or conflicting educational programs. What we very much need in public life today is men who do not think they know all the answers.

All of us realize, in our private capacities, that there are no "answers" to the really important questions, and that if any problem can be solved by a two-minute comment it is not a serious problem.

Suppose we were put on the witness stand, with our fate depending on what we said, and required to answer questions about our wives and children, our professional objectives and ambitions, our philosophy of life; suppose we were called upon to answer questions about these matters not only for ourselves but for our families, our friends, and neighbors. Any man who presumes to have answers for questions of this nature is justly distrusted.

But, it will be objected, our candidates do in fact manage to answer a great many of the questions put to them. True enough, and the fact is a commentary on the questions. These television performances, with their scattered questions and with answers limited to two or three minutes, encourage the discussion of the irrelevant and the trivial. A Presidential contest is not an exaggerated "Information Please" program, with prizes to the member of the panel who scores the most points. It is a dialogue about great issues of public policy.

Only a fool would attempt to dispose of great problems of public policy with off-the-cuff answers. The wisest of our commentators on public affairs, the most profound, the most judicious, the most resourceful—I mean of course Walter Lippmann—does not undertake to deal with more than two or three issues in the course of a week, and to the consideration of these issues he devotes the whole of his incomparable talents. Yet we call on Presidential candidates to dispose of a dozen major questions in the course of half an hour and this in the midst of a campaign which makes merciless demands on their mental and physical energies.

One of the tests of character and ability in which the public is vitally interested is the choice of subjects which a candidate himself makes—the things he thinks it essential to discuss. These matters should not be the sport of chance, as the "debate" over Quemoy and Matsu is the sport of a chance question. What we want in a President is the ability to think deeply about a few matters of great importance; what television questions encourage is the trick of talking glibly about a great many matters of no particular importance.

The physical circumstances of these television performances, too, put a premium on qualities not otherwise valuable; ability to withstand the glare of lights, to tolerate heat, to withstand tensions, to conceal nervousness, and preserve good humor. And the notion that everything should be extemporaneous—everything but the questions, anyway—is one worthy of a college debate, but one that has no relevance to the great office of the Presidency.

One might suppose that the qualities most desired in a President were a good memory, physical hardihood, and an equable temper; not judgment, character, and courage.

Finally, one of the almost inevitable by-products of interviews of this dramatic character is that they tend to pre-empt the field. So great, and so intense, is public concentration on this game of wits that people are reluctant to listen to slower, longer, and more serious discussions of great public questions. Here a Gresham's Law of politics will almost certainly operate—the glib, the evasive, the dogmatic, the melodramatic, the meretricious will drive out the sincere, the serious, the judicious, the sober, the honest in political discussion.

But it is not the instrument of television itself that is at fault; it is our abuse of it. It would be imbecility not to take full advantage of television in this and future campaigns. The trouble is that we are not taking advantage of it at all, but permitting it to take advantage of us.

The present formula of TV "debate" is designed to corrupt the public judgment, and, eventually, the whole political process. The American Presidency is too great an office to be subjected to the indignity of this technique.

What we need is deep discussion and clarification—the searching out of the meaning of great public issues and the full revelation of the minds and characters of the candidates. Lincoln and Douglas, be it remembered, devoted seven long debates to the discussion of slavery in the territories, and even without benefit of television they succeeded in educating not only the voters of Illinois, but posterity as well.

Nor were they in any way cramped by the limitations of this single subject; by the time they were through they had inevitably made clear their minds and characters, their philosophies of government and of morality.

Let us return to debate in the grand manner—in the press and on the air. On TV each candidate should have the opportunity to talk about any major issue as long as he has something to say about it, without outsiders putting time limits on him. Let us move the questioning newsmen out of the picture and allow the debaters themselves to carry on the argument. Let us have discussions that will produce thorough and concentrated consideration of the great issues that face our generation.

1960

Presidential Age—
and Youth

This fall [1960], for the first time in our history, we are certain to elect a President who is under fifty years of age. There have been Presidential candidates younger than either Mr. Nixon or Mr. Kennedy—Bryan was thirty-six when he first ran for the Presidency. There have been Presidents younger than either of our present candidates—Theodore Roosevelt was only forty-two when he succeeded to the Presidency on the death of McKinley. But never before, in all the forty-three elections, have both major candidates been under fifty years of age.

This is astonishing, and what is most astonishing about it is not the comparative youthfulness of the two current candidates, but the failure to nominate younger candidates in the past.

After all, the wise and, on the whole, conservative men who drew up our Constitution fixed the minimum age for the Presidency at thirty-five. Curiously enough, there was no discussion whatsoever of this matter; the decision went, as it were, by default. The age limitation did not even appear in the proposed Constitution until August 22—some three months after the Convention had got under way—and thereafter, as far as the record goes, no one thought it important enough to mention. What this appears to mean is that it commanded general assent, that to the Framers it seemed the common sense of the matter.

Why did thirty-five seem a sensible minimum age for the Presidency? Because to the generation that won independence and wrote the Constitution, thirty-five was middle-aged. There is an interesting—almost an authoritative—statement of this principle in Judge Joseph Story's magisterial *Commentaries on the Constitution*. The *Commentaries* appeared in 1833, but Story himself had been born in 1779, and had known many of the Founding Fathers. He wrote:

> Considering the nature of the duties, the extent of the information, and the solid wisdom and experience required in the executive department, no one can reasonably doubt the propriety of some qualification of age. That which has been selected is the middle age of life, by which period the character and talents of individuals are generally known and fully developed; and opportunities have usually been afforded for public service, and for experience in the public councils. The faculties of the mind, if they have not then attained to their highest maturity, are in full vigor, and hastening toward their ripest state. The judgment, acting upon large materials, has, by that time, attained a solid cast; and the principles which form the character, and the integrity which gives lustre to the virtues of life, must then, if ever, have acquired public confidence and approbation.

It is perhaps relevant to recall that Story himself was appointed a justice of the Supreme Court at the ripe age of thirty-two.

Clearly, this was the eighteenth-century view of the matter. That was, by our standards, a young man's world. Nine of the fifty-five Framers were thirty-five or younger, and among them were Hamilton, who was thirty—or maybe thirty-two; Charles Pinckney, who was thirty; and Rufus King, who was thirty-two, while the sober Madison, justly remembered as "The Father of the Constitution," was only thirty-six. All of these men had been active in state and national affairs for years before the Convention.

If we look outside the Convention we note that Jefferson wrote the Declaration at thirty-three, that John Jay was thirty-one when he drafted the Constitution of New York, that Albert Gallatin went to the Senate at thirty-two and John Quincy Adams was appointed Minister to the Netherlands at twenty-six, and that, though Washington was a veteran of forty-three when he assumed command of the Continental Armies, he was in his early twenties when he led the fateful expedition to the Ohio that set off a chain reaction of international wars.

Nor was all this merely a New World aberration. The class society of England offered even more glittering opportunities to youth, well into the nineteenth century. The elder Pitt was a Member of Parliament in his twenties and his son, William the Younger, was Chancellor of the Exchequer at twenty-three. The brilliant Charles James Fox was Lord of the Admiralty at twenty-two and Lord of the Treasury at twenty-four. Shelburne was active in politics in his early twenties and Secretary at State before he was thirty.

To move into the nineteenth century, Canning was a Member of Parliament at twenty-seven and Foreign Secretary at thirty-seven, Robert Peel a Member of Parliament at twenty-one and in Liverpool's Cabinet at twenty-two, Palmerston was an M.P. at twenty-three and Secretary at War at twenty-five, and Gladstone began his long Parliamentary career at twenty-three and joined the Cabinet at thirty-four.

If we look to the Continent, the eighteenth-century stage there is dominated by actors who seem to us absurdly young for the roles they are to play. Frederick the Great had launched those wars designed to make Prussia a major power before he was thirty. Leopold the First was still in his twenties when he loosed a whirlwind of reform over Tuscany, and Dr. Johan Struensee was dictator of Denmark-Norway and had carried through revolutionary changes in every department of the state before he was thirty-five. Lafayette joined the American army as a major-general at the age of twenty; Robespierre inaugurated the Reign of Terror before he was thirty-five; and Napoleon became First Consul at thirty.

If we regard all this as precocity, we will miss the point. The point is that the eighteenth century did not regard the mid-twenties as a period of "youth" and looked upon the thirties as "the middle age of life." Four considerations illuminate this attitude:

First, life expectancy was much shorter than in our day. Because life was—or might be—short, it behooved men to get on with their work. Boys went to college or university at fourteen or fifteen; were given command of merchant vessels at eighteen; young men entered Parliament at twenty-two; took commissions in the army before they were twenty; concerned themselves with public affairs in their twenties.

Second, professional life was less demanding in the eighteenth or early nineteenth century than it is today. To put it at its simplest, there was far less to learn, in law, medicine, or science. A year or two in a lawyer's office reading Coke on Littleton and copying writs; two years at a university and an apprenticeship with a veteran surgeon; the careful reading of Swan's British Architect or of various versions of Palladio—these things prepared the young for the law, for medicine, for architecture. It was, too, the day of the glorious amateur, when Jefferson could be lawyer, farmer, architect, scientist, and scholar; when Franklin could be a Universal Genius; when Noah Webster could write with equal enthusiasm on language, politics, economics, medicine, and theology.

In the third place, public life was, quantitatively at least, less complex and less demanding. The world of 1789 was easier to grasp than the world of 1960 if for no other reason than that there was so much less of it.

These three considerations are, in a sense, irrelevant to our current situation. After all, we cannot make our world less complex, nor can we hope to simplify or to abbreviate preparation for the professions or for public life. But a fourth consideration is relevant: education.

Today we provide formal education of a somewhat technical character for young men and women in their twenties who think they want careers in the civil service. The eighteenth century provided informal but enormously effective training for young men—indeed, for boys—who were expected to assume responsibilities in public life. In the Old World much of this education was carried on by what we today call The Establishment: the Court, the Aristocracy, the Army, the Navy, the Universities, the Church—all of those institutions whose business it was to mold the young and to fit them for public careers.

Eighteenth-century America had some of these institutions, but they were neither powerful nor influential. Far more important was what might be called the public philosophy of the time. Jefferson, John Adams, Madison, Marshall, Livingston, were exposed to politics in their boyhood. The books they read, the lessons they learned, the conversations they heard, the sermons to which they were subjected, directed their thoughts and their habits to the issues that agitated their society. The very atmosphere they breathed was charged with the electricity of politics and philosophy. They learned early that they were expected to take part in public affairs; they learned early that their responsibilities were to their communities.

This kind of training, or of education, produced statesmen and political philosophers such as we have not known since. Inevitably the question confronts us whether there is any consequential relation between age and maturity, between education and wisdom, between experience and statesmanship.

It is, perhaps, difficult for us to imagine a political scene not dominated by elder statesmen. Churchill, after leading his people to victory in his sixties, returned to the Prime Ministership at seventy-five. Adenauer, who was born when Grant was still in the White House, has dominated the German scene all through his eighties. De Gaulle emerged from retirement at sixty-eight to resume leadership of France, and Eisenhower was sixty-two when he was elected to the Presidency and seventy when he retired. Khrushchev, who acts with such youthfulness, was well in his sixties when he became Premier of the U.S.S.R., and those two permanent fixtures of the European political scene, Franco and Salazar, were, respectively, sixty-eight and seventy-three by the end of the decade.

These examples, drawn from the contemporary scene, prove very little, and the question persists whether either age or experience can give us any guarantee of maturity and judgment in the arena of statesmanship.

History sheds only a flickering light on this vexatious question. Washington had far less experience in politics than his young friend James Madison, but he made an incomparably better President. Buchanan was one of the most experienced of men in public life when he came to the Presidency, and Lincoln was one of the least experienced; but Buchanan made a mess of the Presidency, and Lincoln was one of our greatest Presidents. Theodore Roosevelt was fifteen years younger than McKinley, whom he succeeded in 1901, and far less experienced in politics and international affairs, but—for all of his posturing and his antics—more mature and more judicious.

William Howard Taft was a good deal more experienced than Woodrow Wilson and so, for that matter, was Warren G. Harding, but no one thinks that they did as well in the White House as the schoolmaster who boasted only two years in politics. And, it is not wholly irrelevant to note, many of those who are today most clamorous about the importance of experience, preferred the inexperienced General Eisenhower to the experienced Governor Stevenson back in 1952.

The sobering fact is that there is no formula of age, education, or experience that will guarantee maturity. Maturity itself is not always a simple or coherent thing. Many artists are mature enough in their music, their painting, their poetry, but children in affairs of the heart or of finance—or of politics!

Nor is the most admirable maturity in the conduct of private affairs any assurance of wisdom in public: one recalls that when, in the campaign of 1884, Republicans contrasted Cleveland's moral irregularities with the probity of their own candidate, the Democrats retorted that "we should elect Mr. Cleveland to the public life which he is so admirably qualified to fill, and remand Mr. Blaine to the private life which he is so eminently fitted to adorn."

The test of experience is not quantitative, but qualitative. Casanova was experienced in love, but not mature, and long experience in public life did not mature Aaron Burr. Some men learn by experience, and others learn nothing. Think how the experience of the Civil War matured young Oliver Wendell Holmes, while it had, apparently, no effect on thousands of others who fought in the same battles and endured the same privations. Think how illness matured young Franklin D. Roosevelt, but had no comparable effect on thousands of other victims of polio. Experience is not something that is added on to character; it is something that is absorbed by and transmuted by character.

In the last analysis, then, there is no formula for achieving maturity, for the word itself embraces too many and too complex qualities. What we look for in our statesmen is intelligence, prudence, sagacity, patience, fortitude, imagination, wisdom, and magnanimity. If we get some of these qualities in our chosen leaders we are fortunate.

1960

The Republican Party
Repudiates Its History

In 1913 Woodrow Wilson said that the Republican party had not had a new idea for fifty years. Now it is one hundred years.

Not only has the Republican party been unable to formulate new ideas; it is, and has long been, in the process of repudiating the three great ideas with which it is associated in history.

The first idea, or principle, with which the Republican party is historically connected is the principle of national unity. It was to preserve the Union that the party came into existence in 1854, that it fought the Civil War, and it was to the preservation of the Union that its first and greatest President dedicated himself.

The second great principle is that of freedom—and after 1862, of freedom for the Negro. Lincoln was not only champion of the Union, he was the Great Emancipator; and while the soldiers in blue shouted "the battle cry of freedom" their families back home sang, "As He died to make men holy, let us die to make men free."

The third great principle is historically rooted in union and nationalism; it was that of world responsibility and world power. No sooner had the Civil War ended than the Republican administration ousted the French from Mexico, asserted its interest in the Caribbean, bared its teeth at the Spaniards in Cuba, bought Alaska, and looked westward across the Pacific toward Asia. The next generation saw Republican administrations formulate the policy of Pan-Americanism, reassert the Monroe Doctrine, make the Caribbean an American Mediterranean, dig a canal across the

Isthmus, take over Hawaii, Samoa, and the Philippines, build one of the great navies of the world, and assert its interest in the affairs of Europe, Africa, and Asia.

What happened to these three grand ideas? How has it happened that the party of the Union is now to an astonishing degree the party that fights almost every manifestation of national authority, and flirts with, if it does not yet embrace, states' rights? How does it happen that the party of freedom and emancipation is reluctant to support a bold civil-rights program and that its leading Presidential candidate has been engaged in appeasing the South on the Negro issue? How does it happen that the party historically committed to activism and responsibility in world affairs has for forty years supported or exploited isolationism and even now finds itself deeply divided over policies of global conduct which are in fact no longer open to reconsideration?

The decline of the sentiment of nationalism is perhaps the most difficult to explain. After all, the very purpose of the party was the preservation of the Union, and the triumphant preservation of the Union gave the party its long tenure of office, its dignity, and its power. It was to stitch nationalism into the Constitution that the Republicans enacted the Fourteenth Amendment, which lent itself so wonderfully to both economic and political nationalism. It was as a national party that the Republicans pushed through homestead, railroad, tariff, and fiscal laws.

But increasingly in the years after Reconstruction, the Republican party began to represent not the whole nation but sections of the nation; not the whole people, but elements of the business community. As it became the doughty champion of private enterprise, it lost sight of public enterprise.

Theodore Roosevelt attempted to reverse this trend away from nationalism and the public enterprise—with some temporary success. But Roosevelt, it must be remembered, was an accident of politics—"that damn cowboy," as Mark Hanna called him, was not the choice of the Republican Old Guard. And once the two-term tradition had disposed of him, the Old Guard turned with relief to William Howard Taft. Not since 1908 have the Republicans selected a candidate with the bold nationalist views of a Theodore Roosevelt; the nationalism of Hughes and Willkie was real, but far from bold or imaginative. Since then the Republican standard-bearers have been cast in the mold of McKinley and Taft rather than of TR.

The spectacular victories the Republicans scored in the elections from 1920 to 1928 confirmed the party in its conviction that "the business of America is business"—that the welfare state was a form of creeping socialism—and committed it even more deeply to private enterprise, decentralization and *laissez faire*. After 1929 these doctrines were no longer acceptable or relevant, but the party found itself unable—even unwilling—to extricate itself from them, since the only choice appeared to be "me-too-ism": the acceptance, that is, of the policies of the New Deal and its successors. This specter still haunts the party's councils.

Historically, the second great commitment of the party was to freedom—the campaign slogan of 1856 was "Free land, Free speech, Fremont." To this was added in 1862, "Free men." This great commitment to freedom—like the commitment to nationalism—became confused and almost lost in the years after Reconstruction.

It was not, perhaps, unnatural that the Republican party should have lost a great deal of that idealism associated with the Civil War and the crusade for freedom; such a reaction is familiar enough in the history of American politics. But it is surprising that the party should so readily have abandoned policies which had contributed so much both to its meaning and to its success, and which promised so much for its future prosperity.

The Republican party, to be sure, made some gestures during the Reconstruction years toward assuring the Negro freedom and equality—a Civil Rights Act, the Fourteenth and Fifteenth Amendments—but for all practical purposes it abandoned the whole enterprise in 1876, and in return for the seating of Hayes permitted the white South to settle the Negro problem its own way. As so often happens, this sacrifice of principle for practical ends forfeited the practical ends as well. The Republican party did retain the loyalty and confidence of the Northern Negro—the memory of Lincoln, the Emancipation Proclamation, the Thirteenth Amendment, took care of that—and for two generations it did not occur to Republicans that anything more was necessary. In any event, as long as the Negro was not in the habit of voting—

and the party did little to encourage this habit—his loyalty was not very important. (To be sure, the Democratic party ignored the Negro even more completely.)

The significance of this long neglect of principle, and of practical considerations too, became clear in 1932 when Franklin Roosevelt—and Eleanor—captured the imagination and loyalty of the Northern Negro—captured it and held it. The Republicans awoke with surprise and consternation to the fact that they had somehow lost Negro gratitude and Negro votes. With the passing of years the loyalty of Northern Negroes to the Democrats was strengthened. And when at long last the Southern Negro achieved political self-consciousness, he too gravitated toward the Democratic party.

Had the Republicans been astute they would have attempted to recapture lost ground all through the forties and fifties by making themselves the champions of Negro rights. This they conspicuously failed to do. Even now a small but vociferous element in the party has been seduced once again, as in 1876, by the notion that it might somehow win the white South. This element appears ready to sacrifice the Negro if necessary to its ambition. Bewitched by the rhetoric of states' rights, and by the dream of a two-party South, this element seems ready to trade Northern Negro for Southern white votes. Any statistician would call this a bad trade; any politician, a shortsighted one; any moralist, an immoral one.

The third major principle with which we associate the Republican party is responsibility and leadership in world affairs. It is with this principle that the names of William H. Seward and James G. Blaine, John Hay and Theodore Roosevelt, Elihu Root and Henry L. Stimson are inextricably connected. They were men who thought globally, who saw the interest of the United States in world terms, and the interest of the world related to the United States—precursors of the "large policy" now so familiar to us. Here the Republicans have been carrying on for some time a retreat, now strategic, now merely disorderly.

How did it happen that the party of Blaine and TR and Root became in a single generation the party of the elder Henry Cabot Lodge, Calvin Coolidge, and William E. Borah? How did it happen that the party of Pacific imperialism, Pan-Americanism, the

Open Door, and internationalism became the party of isolation and parochialism?

What happened was, in a sense, bad luck, certainly bad timing. And if it might be said that the GOP was not at fault in this, it was certainly at fault in accepting so readily the role in which fortuity cast it, and in permitting chance or personal animosities to dictate policies. The Republican bad luck was simply that the Democratic party was in power during the First World War and during the peace-making, and that the normal political opposition to the administration in power was magnified into resistance to those great tides of history which had come in with that administration.

The opposition was in fact abnormal. Hostility to Woodrow Wilson himself, a sense of outrage at his unexpected victory in 1916, TR's impassioned hatred of Wilson, the implacable vindictiveness of Henry Cabot Lodge, a massive accumulation of personal, party, and even racial animosities—all these persuaded the Republican party to oppose and to resist, if not the war, then the consequences of the war: to fight the President, the treaty, the League, and the new responsibilities which history had placed upon us.

This new Republican policy was not imposed on the party without a struggle. Older leaders—like Charles Evans Hughes and Henry Stimson—were by no means prepared to retreat into narrow isolationism. But the spectacular victory of Harding in 1920 surrendered the party to this shortsighted and dangerous course. And after two more such victories, it is now surprising that the internationalists were silenced and the isolationists vindicated.

Bad luck and bad timing pursued the Republicans again in the nineteen-thirties. Once again the Democrats were in office at a time when the world burst into flames and the United States was called upon to decide whether it would hold aloof or meet the great challenge. FDR and the Democrats were reluctant enough to make the decision, but in the end they did make it and made the right one. Republicans under the leadership of Robert Taft went into opposition. Thus the party found itself opposing Lend-Lease and the destroyers-for-bases deal and voting almost unanimously to liquidate the American Army—this in 1941.

Pearl Harbor silenced the more ostentatious manifestations

of partisanship. And to its credit the Republican party did not make the same error in 1945 it had made in 1920. Thanks in part to the impetus from Willkie in 1940, thanks to enlightened Republican conservatives like Senator Vandenburg, the party was prepared to accept the responsibilities of world power. In 1948 and 1952 it was the more enlightened wing of the party which triumphed, and if the defeat of Dewey by Truman strengthened the particularist element, the victories of Eisenhower in 1952 and 1956 vindicated the internationalists. Happily, Eisenhower, who had few domestic political convictions, had strong ones about American responsibility in world affairs, and was able to impose his policies on his party.

Yet beneath the surface of agreement were deep rifts. If the old intransigent isolationism of William Borah and Hiram Johnson was a thing of the past, a neo-isolationism emerged in its stead. This neo-isolationism abjured Europe in favor of Asia, accepted the United Nations (though it was quite prepared to undermine it), looked with misgiving on foreign aid, and nursed the deepest suspicions of all those who accepted Wilkie's hope for One World. It is ominous that when hard-core isolationism emerged again, as with the John Birch Society and other extremist groups, it found refuge in the Republican party.

Along with the decline in ideas in the Republican party has gone a decline in leadership. In the early years of this century the Republican party boasted a galaxy of leaders which compared well with any in our history after the generation of the Founding Fathers: Theodore Roosevelt and John Hay, Elihu Root and Speaker Read and Robert La Follette, Gifford Pinchot and Charles Evans Hughes. All these men merit the term statesman; most of them were of Presidential timber. But after 1916 the decline in Republican leadership was precipitous. Henry Adams observed, in his "Education," that the history of the American Presidency from Washington to Grant made Darwin look ridiculous. That was not true, but might it not be said of the history of Republican leadership from Theodore Roosevelt to Harding? May we not conclude that great men are not attracted to a party which is intellectually impoverished and that, as John Stuart Mill reminded us, with small men nothing really great can be achieved?

After 1912 the center of political and intellectual gravity

shifted to the Democratic party. It was the New Freedom and the New Deal which set the stamp on American politics, not Normalcy or the Middle Way. It was Wilson and Franklin Roosevelt and Truman who captured the imagination of the country, set the nation on that course of domestic reform and reconstruction which enabled it to progress through evolution instead of revolution. It was the Democratic party that embraced the responsibilities and burdens of world power; fought two world wars; caught the vision of international order in a League of Nations, a World Court, the United Nations; accepted free-world leadership; invented—and they were great inventions—the Marshall Plan, NATO, the Alliance for Progress.

If, during all these years, the Republican contribution was not wholly negative, it was rarely positive. What great ideas, indeed, do we associate with that party since 1920—what ideas that captured the imagination, stirred the mind or the spirit, that made history?

Republican spokesmen, to be sure, deny that they have run out of ideas. They have, so they solemnly assure us, a new set of ideas and principles. Two of their most prominent Presidential candidates have only recently furnished us with an up-to-date list of these ideas: fiscal integrity, hostility to communism, the dignity of man, devotion to private enterprise, and maintenance of the federal system. But this is like coming out for virtue, chastity, honor, and loyalty: Who is on the other side? These tired phrases do not even rise to the dignity of clichés; they are declarations of intellectual bankruptcy.

Who can deny that the Republican party desperately needs new ideas? It needs new ideas if it is to command the support of reasonable men. It needs new ideas if it is to vindicate the two-party system and fulfill its function as an opposition party. It needs new ideas if it is to be entrusted with the responsibility to govern. It needs new ideas if it is to serve, as it has in the past, the public welfare, the welfare of the nation, and the welfare of all those peoples and nations that look to us for leadership.

1964

PART FOUR

Do We Have a Class Society?

1

When in the eighteen-thirties Alexis de Tocqueville prepared to write that study of America which is still the most penetrating of all interpretations of our country, he hit upon one basic and pervasive theme that gave meaning to the whole: equality. And he entitled his great work *De la Démocratie en Amérique*, which, accurately translated, means "Concerning Equality in America." Equality was the key that unlocked the meaning of America in history and that explained all that was most significant about the strange new nation. Equality made manhood suffrage inevitable; equality demanded universal public education; equality did away with social differences and class distinction; equality banished idiom and imposed uniformity of speech, equality invaded the domestic circle, the law courts, the legislative chamber, the churches, the universities, the literary salons, and the ateliers.

Nor was Tocqueville alone in seizing upon equality as the master-theme of American history and the master-principle of the American character. Even before independence, Benjamin Franklin had observed that in America we never ask of newcomers, Who are you? but only, What can you do? And in his *Letters from an American Farmer*, the remarkable St. John Crèvecoeur noted the same thing—that in America men threw off the burdens of generations and centuries and stood on their own feet. Thereafter a thousand travelers, a thousand commentators, a thousand interpreters composed variations on this theme: the American was a classless society. Family didn't count; inheritance didn't count;

position didn't count; the only thing that counted was ability and character. In America every man was on his own.

This was what every newcomer learned, too, some with consternation, some with delight. In America officers were expected to sit down at table with privates, British prisoners complained; worse yet, they were expected to associate with the help! In America nobody had to take his hat off to the parson, Norwegian peasants wrote home to their incredulous families: here the parson is just like everybody else. In America everybody took his turn—even the Secretary of State had to wait his turn at table, wrote an astonished English visitor. In America there are no officers swaggering down the streets, expecting everyone to get out of their way; in fact, there are no officers at all. In America everyone can speak his mind—you don't need to stand silent while the squire lays down the law, or vote the way you are told. In America everyone goes to school, wrote a Polish girl, the poor and the ragged sit with the rich and the well-clothed. So it went, in a thousand letters, nay a hundred thousand, all with the same theme: there are no classes in America!

But now a host of sociologists have discovered that we do have a class society. American society, they tell us, like the Danish society of the eighteenth century, is divided into nine categories, and if it cannot be said, as was said of the Danish, that the upper three may not speak to the lower six on pain of death, the differences are nevertheless pervasive and ostentatious. We have long been familiar with the divisions of upper, middle, and lower class; now each of these is divided into three sub-categories, and there is no schoolchild so obtuse that he cannot tell you the stigmata that distinguish middle-middle from upper- or lower-middle. Furthermore, the sociologists have traced in relentless detail the manifestations of class membership. Those manifestations, we are assured, pervade the whole body of our social activities. They regulate child training, fix living conditions, determine the schools we attend and the subjects we study, the associations we join, the newspapers and magazines we read, the way we vote, the way we court and make love, our preferences in literature and in art, our speech and our manners, and a hundred other things.

What is more, the sociologists add, we are all class conscious and we are all status seekers. The most important things we do, the most vital decisions we make, are influenced by our yearning for status. We marry above us, if we can; we mortgage our future for a ranch house in the right neighborhood; we stint ourselves to send our children to an "Ivy League" college; we work overtime to join the country club; we conduct ourselves circumspectly so that we will be acceptable to the Right People; we select our friends—or they select us—to provide some kind of social security or to help us climb the social ladder; we choose our religion not to please God but to please Man.

2

Is this an authentic picture of American society?

In one sense what the sociologists have discovered, and the opinion pollsters have recorded, is all true enough.

Americans are conscious of class, and of status, and differences in class and in status are commonly associated with differences in habits and attitudes of mind. But the interpretation which so many sociologists put upon all this is misguided. For concern with status and awareness of class are in fact characteristic of a society where class and status are so fluid and so malleable that they can be changed by almost anyone—who is white—at almost any time, in almost any circumstances.

The whole concept of class is an Old World concept, and when Henry James wanted to dramatize most sharply the differences between the New World and the Old he did it—in his wonderful essay on Hawthorne—in class terms; that is, in terms of all the things that were left out—everything, as Howells remarked, "but life."

The more closely we look at class in the Old World, the more we are impressed with the abiding character of those distinctions that James conjured up. The essential characteristic of class in the Old World is that it is commonly a legal condition and carries with it legal properties. It is a condition associated with kings and queens, lords and ladies, the army and the navy, palaces, cathedrals, privileges, titles, and ceremonies. It is therefore a condition not normally subject to the vagaries of politics or of the economy, or even of individual eccentricity. It is a condition which the individual does not control and which cannot ordinarily be changed. But the term class in the United States has none of these attributes or connotations. It is not legally fixed. It is not inherited. In so far as it exists it is something that is earned. In all this the difference between Old World class and New is one not of degree but of kind.

Equally important, class in the Old World has not only legal character, it has other fixed and almost ineradicable characteristics as well. It is, as Henry James makes clear, institutionalized. In England it is connected with and dependent on great institutions like the Monarchy, the Church, the Army, the Public School, the University. These are the properties—one might almost say the monopolies—of the upper classes, and they are not the property of the other classes. Until recently it was almost impossible for a member of the middle or lower orders to enter Eton or Harrow, Oxford or Cambridge, Dartmouth or Sandhurst. That is no longer true, but it is still true that these are the institutions that assure consideration at the Foreign Office, the Army, and the Navy, that give you a box at Lord's and entry to the leading clubs; and that without them such consideration and such privilege is hard to obtain.

Class in Europe, and in England, is institutionalized in many other ways as well. Its most overt characteristic is perhaps accent. Every Englishman, wrote George Orwell (who was himself an Etonian), is branded on the tongue at birth, and the observation is valid not only for the English but for most Europeans as well. But who, in America, has ever been able to relate class to accent? As early as the seventeen-nineties, Noah Webster was able to assert that Americans generally spoke the best English in the world, and that America presented a pleasant uniformity of speech instead of the Babel of tongues that betrayed class or region with every syllable in most of the Old World. With exceptions—the exceptions imposed upon us chiefly by large-scale immigration—what was true in the seventeen-nineties is still true: that no one in America is branded on the tongue with his class mark.

3

What still persists in the Old World, and what America has almost wholly escaped, is the psychology of class. Almost everyone in America—at least among the whites—thinks of himself as "middle class," which is to say no particular class at all. A few, and among Negroes and Puerto Ricans more than a few, will somewhat bitterly confess that they belong to the "lower class," but practically none, not even millionaires or Ivy Leaguers, are so brazen as to claim membership in an "upper class." Yet even in so democratic a country as England, substantially half the population cheerfully proclaims that it is "working class" or "upper class," and in most Continental countries—the Scandinavian are an exception—the majority of the people know just where they belong on the social scale, and accept their position with equanimity.

Furthermore, whatever the sociologists may conclude, class membership has in fact fewer overt manifestations in America than in Britain or on the European continent. Thus, English newspapers are directed to class audiences: the *Times* and the *Guardian* are read by the elite, and are content with a modest circulation; the *Herald*, the *Express*, and the *News of the World* are read by the "working classes" (and by university dons) and boast a circulation of five million or more; and few papers occupy a middle ground. But in the United States papers like the *Post-Dispatch* or the Washington *Post* or the *Courier-Journal* have the same circulation as their less high-brow rivals. American newspapers are not, on the whole, directed to one class, but to all classes alike. Much the same can be said too of the mass circulation magazines, that they are read by people of all interests and groups and classes.

So, too, with education, at almost every level. What is most distinctive about English schools is how greatly they differ from one another; what is most distinctive about the American is how much they are alike. Manchester Grammar School is as good academically as Eton or Winchester, but the children whose names are in Burke's peerage rarely go there; and whatever the relative intellectual status of Oxbridge and Redbrick Universities, no one is in doubt about their relative social status. But, outside of parts of the Eastern Seaboard, nobody in America thinks private schools important socially, while the notion that the Ivy League carries with it some kind of social éclat is one assiduously nourished by writers for *Esquire* or advertisers in *Playboy* but regarded as absurd west of the Hudson, where the State University is customarily preferred.

In England religion, too, has class connotations. Those who went to Eton or Winchester, Oxford or Cambridge, were automatically Church of England; indeed, if they were not they could not even enter these institutions as recently as the eighteen-seventies. Because in England the Church is established, and its clergy have both political and social privileges, the terms Church and Chapel are social as well as religious terms. This is less true on the Continent, where there is less religious diversity and where "dissenters" are not sufficiently numerous to constitute either a social class or a problem; but even on the Continent some kinds of dissent are better socially than others. But in the United States any connection between religion and social or class position except perhaps, at the extreme fringes, is fortuitous, fluctuating, and local. If it was, at one time, true that a Virginia gentleman would take only the Anglican path to Heaven, it was equally true that in Boston it was the Unitarian Church that had social prestige, in Philadelphia the Quaker, and in Baltimore the Catholic. Today the socioreligious picture can only be described as kaleidoscopic.

The simple fact is that while it is relatively easy to place a man or a woman in his or her proper social class in England or France, Germany or Italy, it is almost impossible to do so in the United States, except where color or some foreign accent is added. Any English shopkeeper can tell instantly—by accent, dress, and manner—whether his customer is a Gentleman or a Lady, but no American shopkeeper can, and few would if they could. Again, in most countries of Europe, the pattern of class characteristics is logical and coherent and the ingredients harmonious: given any one of them, the others can be assumed. Thus, in England, if you hear a "public school" accent you are safe in assuming an Oxbridge education, the Church of England, a preference for cricket and rugger football, a habit of reading the *Guardian* and of listening to the Third Program, a profession, a country estate, and a London club—all of it familiar to us from that best of all social historians, P. G. Wodehouse. Thus, even in democratic Denmark, an "old boy" from Herlufsholm School will ordinarily have a "family" name—not Jensen or Larsen or Andersen but something double-barreled and probably German or French; a manor house on one of the islands with a farm attached; he will take his Lutheranism lightly, speak with an upper-class accent, and read the conservative *Berlingske Tidene* in preference to the equally good but radical *Politiken*.

What explains the absence of clear or abiding class distinctions in the United States? Even the question is a bit misleading. For might we not say that in America it is the classless society that is the norm, and that what needs explanation is even the hint of class divisions or class psychology? Those who settled America, and those who came to it for three centuries, were in a sense refugees from the class system: with few exceptions (and those rooted in religion which had its own leveling logic) members of the upper classes did not leave Old-World security for the insecurity of the New. Nor, when Americans revolted from the mother country and set up on their own, did they propose to duplicate the Old-World class system. Not only was there no legal basis for class in the first American constitutions, but these constitutions swept away even the vestigial remnants of the class system: primogeniture, entail, and the Established Church. And how prophetic that when officers of the Revolutionary army tried to organize a Society of the Cincinnati on an hereditary basis, public opinion reacted as hysterically as if they had proposed to re-establish the Divine Right of Kings.

4

The United States, then, not inherit the formal institutions of a class society and did not re-create them: the Monarchy, the Aristocracy, the Church, the Army, the Navy, the Bench, and the Bar. It started with a clean slate. But how has it escaped the development of class divisions for the past century and three-quarters?

Let us admit, first, that it did not wholly escape them. Slavery and the plantation system furnished the basis for the creation of a planter class in the ante-bellum South, and that class displayed many of the stigmata of the Old-World class system. Members of that class were clearly "ladies" and "gentlemen"; they were very conscious of race and boasted their "Norman blood."

They had a distinctive accent; they belonged, most of them, to the Church of England; they combined membership in the professions (including the military) with "planting," which was more elegant than plain "farming"; they thought of themselves as Cavaliers, and accepted the Code of Honor; they professed contempt for democracy and for majority rule; they indulged in that romanticism which glorified the past rather than the future. All of this—or all but the nostalgia for this—was swept away by the Civil War and Reconstruction.

Outside the South the circumstances of American life were not favorable to the development of a class society.

First, there was the open frontier, and cheap land, which made for a mobility within the American society unparalleled elsewhere in the Western world. Second, there was the continuous impact of immigration—hundreds of thousands, and then millions of newcomers from every country of Europe, all bringing with them an instinct and a passion for the classless society. Third, there was an open society which invited the young—and not the young alone—to strike out on their own, to try their luck with a new job, a new career, a new profession, a new life: after all, everything was possible in the New World! Fourth, the rise of a business economy, which has always been leveling, promised new and glittering economic rewards as a substitute for the old-fashioned rewards of social rank. Fifth, there was religious freedom, and denominationalism, which broke the crust of religious status as physical mobility broke the crust of social status. And finally there was popular education, more nearly universal then elsewhere in the world, and reaching up into the university, which by ending upper-class monopoly on learning ended its monopoly on power as well. This is a process going on even now in Britain, France, and Germany.

All these influences still operate, some of them—like education—more powerfully than ever before. They discourage hardening of the social arteries, they disrupt fixed social patterns, they introduce a new ferment into social conduct. One manifestation of their operation is an increased awareness of the claims of class, an increased concern for class distinctions. After all, a true class society—the French of the eighteenth century or the English of the nineteenth—takes its position and its characteristics for granted; it is only where social relationships are fluid, where not only the prerogatives but even the overt manifestations of class can be quickly and easily acquired, that these things are not taken for granted. If there is a power elite in the United States, perhaps the most interesting thing about it is that anyone with sufficient talent can join. If the "Ivy League" does have social advantages, the most interesting thing about it is that any bright student can enter. If church affiliations or cultural interests are connected with social position, the most relevant observation to be made about them is that they can be changed at will and achieved at will. Even color is no longer a certain index of class, and the rise of the Negro to middle-class status is as inevitable as was the rise of the Irish and Italians of earlier generations. Sociologists will doubtless continue to divide us all into categories, but the categories are not like separate levels in a building; they are like currents in a flowing stream.

1961

Government
and the Arts

In his book on the *Grass Roots of Art*, the distinguished critic Sir Herbert Read made an eloquent plea for the decentralization of the arts. Centralization, he asserted (he means national control), vulgarizes the artist and deflects him from his proper task. The real problem, writes Sir Herbert, is "whether art in general is best fostered by a centralized and metropolitan culture, or whether it grows deeper and stronger roots in a regional soil. Historically the answer is clear—the greatest artists have arisen under conditions we should now consider regional."

All true enough, but the alternative to local or provincial or regional art is not necessarily national. For great art is universal, as well as regional. It has its roots in provincial cultures—as Haydn and Mozart and Beethoven drew upon the folk music of their communities—but is universal (or at least Western) in character. To speak of national art is either to eliminate some two thousand years of art which flourished before the rise of nations, or to describe something relatively new that has conformed, artistically and psychologically, to political and emotional pressures which have very little to do with true art. Certainly the vast body of art which we have agreed to call great has had nothing particularly to do with nationalism: from Greek, Roman, Chinese, Romanesque, and Gothic to Baroque, Rococo, or that amorphous and all-inclusive thing called Modern. Even in the era of nationalism (which is relatively new) art is mostly universal, or strives to be.

The great tradition of art has been cosmopolitan—a term I

prefer to the pretentious and inexact word "universal," a word which casually ignores the Orient. This was certainly true in the centuries which saw the discovery, founding, and political independence of our own country—that is the centuries from the Renaissance to the Enlightenment. Renaissance art was rooted in Tuscany, Venetia, the Low Countries, and Spain. But it was at the same time cosmopolitan. That tradition of cosmopolitanism flourished most luxuriantly in the century that saw the creation of the United States—the eighteenth. It was an age when artists and scholars and scientists and philosophers moved freely from country to country even in time of war. It was an age when Frederick the Great spoke only in French, even when at war with France; when the rediscovery of the ancient world of Italy and Greece was carried through by Germans, French, and English; when Catherine the Great invited all of the artists and philosophers to her court and tried to create an imitation Versailles and Louvre; when Captain Cook could be declared immune from attack during war because "engaged in explorations of benefit to mankind"; when the Professor Heyne could arrange to exempt the university town of Göttingen from the ravages of war because its scholars were so distinguished; when scientists of the whole civilized world looked to a Linnaeus in Upsala, or to a Buffon at the Royal Gardens, and poured their treasures into their receptive hands. It was an age when Jefferson could write, in the midst of war (1778), to his scientist-friend David Rittenhouse:

> Your time for two years past has, I believe, been principally employed in the civil government of your country. Tho' I have been aware of the authority our cause would acquire with the world from its being known that yourself and Doctor Franklin were zealous friends to it, and am myself duly impressed with a sense of the arduousness of government, and the obligation those are under who are able to conduct it, yet I am satisfied there is an order of geniuses above that obligation, and therefore exempted from it. Nobody can conceive that nature ever intended to throw away a Newton upon the occupations of a crown. It would have been a prodigality for which even the conduct of providence might have been arraigned, had he been by birth annexed to what was so far below him. Cooperating with nature in her ordinary economy, we

should dispose of and employ the geniuses of men according to their several orders and degrees. I doubt not there are in your country many persons equal to the task of conducting government; but you should consider that the world has but one Ryttenhouse, and that it never had one before. . . .

American art—indeed almost the whole of American culture —was born in the age of cosmopolitanism, and emerged out of a cosmopolitan background. Because by great good fortune the United States started without a cultural tradition of her own, she was able to levy on the culture of the Old World without obvious psychological difficulties, and to create what she did create without cultural chauvinism. She inherited her language, law, religion, she inherited, too, her literature, her music, and her art, and she could build on that inheritance without feeling either defensive or passionate about it.

By good fortune, too, the men who stamped their imprint on the American mind and character were themselves children of the Enlightenment, Franklin, of course, and Hamilton, and Rumford, and Dr. Rush, and Dr. Rittenhouse. Some of them, like sturdy John Adams, resolutely put art aside because they had more imperative business:

> The science of government is my duty to study, more than all other sciences; the arts of legislation and administration and negotiation ought to take place of, indeed to exclude, in a manner, all other arts. I must study politics and war that my sons may have liberty to study mathematics and philosophy, geography, natural history and naval architecture, navigation, commerce, and agriculture, in order to give their children a right to study painting, poetry, music, architecture, statuary, tapestry, and porcelain. . . .

Others, like Jefferson, saw no conflict between devotion to the artistic and cultural inheritance of the Old World and service to the New.

What an extraordinary figure he was. Assuredly, he was the very model of a statesman for a new republic. More fully than any other statesman in modern history, he understood the place of art and learning in the commonwealth. He was a man of the frontier,

a man of the western waters, his lovely Monticello looking westward across the valley to the mountains and valleys beyond. He
was deeply rooted in Virginia, collected and edited its laws and its
court records, wrote its natural history, planned a school system, a
land system, a governmental system. Thomas Jefferson was a Vir-
ginian; but Thomas Jefferson was cosmopolitan, too. No one was
more cosmopolitan than this man who was equally at home in the
ancient world and the modern, translating Greek and Latin, com-
piling his own version of the Bible, analyzing the English language; immersed in the art and music, the food and wines, of
France and Italy, delighting in them for their own sake, and for
what they might contribute to America as well. He was a lawyer, a
political philosopher, a practical politician, and a statesman; he
was an explorer, on his own and vicariously, an archaeologist and
an ethnologist. He was an inventor and a gadgeteer—inventing
everything from a plow and a dumb-waiter to a political party and
a new system of coinage. He was a book collector—he laid the
foundation for the Library of Congress—a bibliophile, and a
critic. He was one of the leading agricultural scientists and probably the leading gardener of his section of the country. He was
assuredly its foremost architect; he was a musician (music, he
said, was the greatest passion of his life), he was a patron of the
arts. What was he not? He feared government, but he knew that
government was made for man, not man for government, and he
was ready to place all the resources of government at the disposal
of men, for their benefit and—let it never be forgotten—for their
happiness. Certainly no leader of his own day—no leader of one
republic to this day—was more ready to associate government
with the arts.

Look at two panels from the spectacle of our own eighteenth-
century community of culture:

Let us start with young Benjamin West, shipped over to
Rome at twenty-two to learn how to paint. He was the artistic
sensation of the year—remember this was in 1760, and young
West was the first American artist in Rome, the first of that great
stream of artists and writers who were to make Italy their spiritual
and artistic home. They took him at once to the blind Cardinal
Albani—he was the greatest of art collectors and patrons, and it

was for him that the great Winckelmann, who had rediscovered the ancient world, was collecting and editing—Albani felt of the lad and asked whether he was black or white. Off they all went to see the Apollo Belvedere, and West made that famous remark (it is his Scottish biographer, John Galt, who has recalled it for us) "How like a Mohawk Indian!" The Saxon painter Raphael Mengs took the lad under his wing—Mengs down from Dresden, where August III was setting the pace even in an age of patronage—and worked out for him a study tour of all Italy, and West dutifully visited Florence and Parma and Bologna and Venice and learned what he could from the painters of the Renaissance. Then off to England, to see paintings, and, as it proved, to live for the rest of his life. Trouble was brewing between Britain and the Colonies, but no matter. It was Drummond, the Archbishop of York, who took up the young colonial, and commissioned from him a painting of Agrippina with the Ashes of Germanicus (how secular the churches were in that century!) and it was Drummond, too, who persuaded George III to view the picture, thus inaugurating one of the famous friendships in history. So Benjamin West became painter to the King, and guide and counselor as well. Into West's studio flowed a stream of young Americans—all through the years of controversy, all through the war even—Copley and Stuart and Trumbull painted in West's hospitable studio, and under the patronage of George III; imagine Germany during the last war patronizing artists from England and America—for that matter imagine the United States today patronizing the arts and artists of Russia, or Russia patronizing artists from America!

Or consider the creation of our own capital city: was there ever a more cosmopolitan artistic enterprise? Jefferson, again, was the guiding spirit, the one who provided the continuity from the first; Secretary of State, then Vice-President, then President, and even in retirement, actively concerned with the rebuilding of the city after the British had burned it in 1814. The work was originally entrusted to the French artist, Major L'Enfant—he had come over with Lafayette, had lived through Valley Forge, had made himself part of this new world, even while he remained very French. Soon L'Enfant was joined by James Hoban—he had been born in Ireland and trained in Dublin, and came to the United

States only after the war; he was responsible for the President's House. Next Stephen Hallet took over—he too had been born and trained in France and had come in 1789 to set up the academy of arts and letters in Richmond (alas, it never materialized, but some of his Washington plans did). More important, as it turned out, was the wonderfully versatile William Thornton. We remember him as completely American and he did indeed succeed in becoming just that, but he had been born in the Dutch West Indies, and had studied in Scotland—took his M.D., of all things, in Aberdeen, but then that was the age of versatility—and from there he went to Paris to study art and architecture. He migrated to the United States, drew plans for the Federal Capitol when on a honeymoon in the West Indies, and returned to Philadelphia to win out over Hallet in his designs for the Capitol building. How he lingered on, how he saved the Patent Office from destruction at the time of the burning of the capital, how he labored to rebuild the stricken city, is familiar enough to all. Another of the architects who worked with him was George Hadfield of England—he had actually been born in Leghorn, in Italy; he was brother-in-law to that Maria Cosway with whom Jefferson was so enchanted. It was Trumbull, then in England, who recommended him to Jefferson and they made him superintendent of the construction of the Capitol.

Most colorful of all was, doubtless, that curious product of Huguenot France via America and of Moravian Germany via England, Benjamin Latrobe. He had been trained to the ministry, in Germany, but happily turned instead to art and architecture and, except for a bit of speculation here and a bit of engineering there, it was to art and architecture that he remained true through a long life. He practiced briefly in England, then in the troubled nineties he migrated to Virginia where opportunities, and life, were easier. Soon he was in charge of building the national Capitol, soon he was in charge of everything. He brought in Italian artists to decorate the new Capitol: what a host they were! Giuseppi Franzoni and later his brother Carlo Franzoni, and Giovanni Andrei and the sculptor Luigi Persica who did the Peace, the War and the Discovery in the Rotunda, and Enrico Causici of Verona who did the "Liberty" in Statuary Hall, and the two panels of Daniel Boone and the Landing of the Pilgrims —how delightful that a Veronese sculptor would give us Daniel Boone! And there was Antonia Capello, pupil of the great Canova who had almost come over to do a statue of Washington, and the French sculptor Nicholas Gevelot who carved the panel of William Penn making a treaty with the Indians—the same subject that had tempted Benjamin West so many years earlier and had introduced the native and the natural in modern painting. How appropriate that all of these countries, all of these artists, should have contributed to creating the capital for the new republic.

Jefferson knew that because art was not national, but at once provincial and cosmopolitan, it did not at all follow that the national government should ignore it, or that the nation did not have a responsibility for its prosperity—so should we! After all it is difficult to maintain that science is national, or that education and learning are national—these things are by their very nature universal—but who doubts the obligation of government to encourage science and to prosper education and learning? Not even the most extreme opponents of federal centralization—your neighbor in Arizona, for example, or the egregious governor of Alabama who wishes to repeal the Constitution—raise questions about the scientific activities of the Geological Survey or the Department of Agriculture, or about the scholarly function of the Library of Congress. Why should there be any question about the duty of government to art?

From the beginning it was assumed that the purpose of government was to assure the happiness of man. On that there was complete agreement, among the Founding Fathers, as among the whole body of eighteenth-century philosophers. And what would contribute more to happiness than art?

The relation of government to the arts in our own society is old and extensive. The Founding Fathers assumed that government was responsible for education and for science, and deeply involved in art—directly in architecture and indirectly in sculpture and in painting. There was some decline in this interest after the generation of Founding Fathers, and responsibility for education was left pretty largely to the states. But concern for science persisted and for art as well. It found expression, to be sure, in practical rather than in theoretical areas, thus in the long series of expeditions into the West, from the expedition of Lewis and Clark down through the beneficent work of the geological surveys of the late nineteenth century. Thus, too, in many governmental institutions—the National Observatory, the Coast and Geodetic Survey, the Geological Survey, the Weather Bureau, the Agricultural Bureau which became a department and carried on extensive research, and many others. And note how government took art for granted, how casually it sent artists with so many of the great exploring and geological expeditions into the West. Art was a by-product here of interest in flora and fauna, geography and ethnology, but none the less valued for that. Recall too the role of the Smithsonian Institution in concentrating government concern for science and incidentally the arts. But as yet there was no national museum, no national gallery of art—that was to wait more propitious times.

The most impressive development in government of the past three-quarters of a century has been the growth of responsibility for the welfare of the whole of society. The welfare state—the very phrase used to cause eyebrows to rise—began in the nineties, chiefly in the states. Under Theodore Roosevelt, then Wilson, then Franklin Roosevelt and his successors, it has grown and spread as the economy became increasingly national, as society required protection against the vicissitudes of the economy, and as the demands of national security became more exacting. Inevitably, concern for the physical and material welfare has been accompanied by concern for the intellectual and artistic. If the end is security, government is concerned with whatever makes the society more secure; if the end is prosperity, government addresses itself to what has traditionally contributed to the commonwealth. If the end is happiness, government addresses itself to all of those factors which contribute to happiness.

Let us grant at once that governmental intervention in arts, science, and education is fraught with danger.

First, there is danger from short-sighted political interference, the kind of thing that occurred again and again during the McCarthy era, and that is still very much with us. Clearly, however, there is less of this from the national than from the state and

local governments; even here in Texas there is continuous interference with what is taught in the schools, with the books and
magazines that are permitted to circulate in the local libraries,
with art and with artists. And it is relevant to note that it is not the
national government that is intervening in education in Mississippi
and Alabama now, but the state.

Second, there is the danger, more subtle, perhaps, that government will come to regard "art" as an "instrument of national
policy" and encourage it, not for itself, but for ulterior and often
pernicious purposes. In the last decade or so the government has
fallen into the bad habit of regarding a great many things as
"instruments" of policy—even (according to Secretary Dulles)
travel!

Third, there is danger of capricious support from government
—support on which it is difficult for institutions to rely for any
long-range programs. But that is something very old in our history, and in the history of other governments; for that matter it is
something old and familiar in the history of private patronage as
well.

But against these considerations should be balanced counter-
considerations.

Of course governmental intervention is dangerous: government *is* dangerous; life *itself* is dangerous. We all tend to conjure
up hypothetical dangers, instead of considering how to meet practical problems. After all, think how dangerous it is to marry, how
dangerous to have children—no security, here, no guarantees at
all—how dangerous to embark upon a career, especially one of art
or music; how dangerous to live in a world which may be blown
up by atomic fission. It is not worthy of us to frighten ourselves by
imaginary dangers: there are enough real ones about.

Consider too the danger of *not* using all possible resources,
those of government, at all levels, as well as individual resources.
Some things we can do collectively better than individually, and
for a good many collective things we use the instrument of government. It is certainly dangerous to let things go by default.

Consider our long experience with governmental activity in
this and comparable realms. Surely, I need not remind you of the
role of government in education at all levels, going back to the

Ordinances of the seventeen-eighties, or of the contribution of government to higher education through the Morrill Act and the agricultural experiment stations, the vast enterprise of the G.I. Bill, the contributions to scientific research, now running at over one billion dollars a year. Or think of the long record of government contribution to science, through such affluent organizations as the U.S. Coast and Geodetic Survey, the U.S. Geological Survey, the Bureau of Standards, the research work of the Department of Agriculture. (Do you know the Department runs a university with about twelve thousand students and over a million volumes in its library?) Consider the contribution of government to scholarship—the Library of Congress, the National Archives, the Smithsonian Institution, the National Gallery of Art, the Botanical Gardens, and a score of similar enterprises. Over all of these Congress has almost complete control; yet in more than a hundred years there have been few examples of improper interference with their activities, and none as notorious as legislative interference with state universities that is so frequent as to be commonplace—in Colorado, today, or Ohio, for example. Certainly Federal interference with cultural and academic freedom is feeble compared with that pervasive and compulsive private interference with music, art, letters, and science which is so marked a feature of our own time. How odd it is that a society which witnesses the antics of the Birchers, and other extremist organizations, the ceaseless efforts of filiopietistic groups like the American Legion to censor books, art, and education, the annual safaris of the Daughters of the American Revolution against the twentieth century, should be so distressed by dangers of Federal intervention.

A less ostentatious but more familiar danger is that which comes from sheer bigness, from the apparently inevitable red tape of all things that are big, but particularly from government. Most of us are familiar with the complexity of governmental operations —the detailed records of everything, all in triplicate, the harassments and delays. Whatever the necessity of all this may be, we do know that such processes are antithetical to the artist.

The most convenient solution here is to try to channel government aid to art (as now to science) through universities or their equivalents—museums or foundations—who understand the way artists think and work. It is a commonplace that the ways of business are not the ways of the university; it is equally a commonplace that the ways of politics are alien to those of the Academy. The university is not anarchical, but it is loose-jointed and permissive, and it is run by men who know in their bones how scholars and scientists and artists act and think, who understand their need for independence, for privacy, and for freedom from bureaucratic limitations.

One of the most interesting developments of recent years has been precisely in this area. Beginning with the New Deal, government has turned increasingly to the Academy, or the university, to formulate and administer programs in science and in art. Some of you may remember the enlistment of the academic and artistic community in various New Deal projects—the Federal Theater Project, for example, or the Index of American Design. With the war the government turned to universities to formulate and often to administer large scientific and educational programs. That remained the pattern of the postwar years as well, and it is the pattern which has been followed, on a large scale, and on the whole with remarkable success, in the realms of scientific research.

Government itself may not be in a position to sponsor, participate in, or direct, artistic activities. It is, perhaps, too top-heavy, it is certainly too vulnerable; all of us are painfully familiar with examples of its obtuseness, its heavy-handedness, and its political vulnerability, even in such matters as sending art exhibits or orchestras abroad, even in book and library programs.

How much better for government and for the arts themselves to funnel much of this through universities, museums, and similar organizations. There is no institution like a university for removing political and partisan stains; no institution like a university for insisting on intellectual and moral standards. And almost alone of organizations, the universities are powerful enough and independent enough to resist untoward pressures even from government. That has been revealed time and again.

The universities are, understandably, reluctant to act as middlemen, or even as supervisors of far-flung activities which they do not initiate and over which they have only uncertain control. We should develop—I do not say perfect—machinery whereby the university can function more effectively here, as it now functions so effectively in some realms of scientific research, or in far-flung educational programs overseas. This will of course require that the university itself have some authority—at least the authority to accept or reject proposals, and to maintain standards. From the point of view of the arts this will entail unfamiliar controls or supervisions, but these are surely easier to deal with than governmental controls. Accommodation is called for, from both sides; habits and practices must be worked out so that the government, the university, and the creative arts can live and function together, with governmental support, but not control. Ingenuity is required in all this; it is not ingenuity beyond our capacities.

The fact is that we must learn to live with and to manage danger. We must learn to sterilize financial support, whether from local, state, national, or international sources—whether private or foundation or public. This is not a new lesson. We have learned it in the realm of justice—supported, I remind you, by the state. We have learned it in the realm of religion—indirectly supported through tax exemption. We have learned it for the most part in higher education. Our task is not to bewail the dangers from government (which is us, of course) but to educate governments at all levels in their proper operation, and to perfect techniques which will frustrate dangerous or improper intervention.

I say this is the real problem, the only one that rises to the dignity of an intellectual problem. For government intervention is not a prospect, it is not a theory—it is a fact. It is a fact at almost every level and in almost every realm—in the realm of education at the higher as at the lower levels; in the realm of science and public health; somewhat more tentatively in the realm of museums and music. It is with us, and with us to stay. It will in all probability grow quantitatively and spread into new areas. Let us see to it that what it does, it does wisely. That is our job as citizens. That is your job as artists.

Art is by its very nature cosmopolitan or universal. Throughout history it has played the benevolent role of appealing across the boundaries of people, race, nation, faith, and even of time, bringing together in common intellectual and moral experience peoples separated by languages, religions, and ideologies, by centuries and millennia. As such, art takes its place alongside those other affluent institutions that serve to knit mankind together rather than separate and fragment it—science or the community of nature, the university or the community of learning, the church or the community of morality. If it is to perform its historic and benign mission it must be free from pressures to be an instrument for nation, for race, or for ideology; it must be free—even in time of crisis and war—to operate across boundaries of nation and of continent; it must be free to serve both its immediate community and the larger community of man. And all of us, artist and layman alike, must remember that we are not only members of our own community, but of that greater community of arts and learning that flourished long before the rise of nations or states, and that will doubtless continue to flourish long after nations and states as we know them are things of the past. It is to that larger community that we owe allegiance.

It has long been fashionable to say that we in America were the Romans of the modern world. So we are, in a sense, but may it not turn out that it is our fortune to be the Greeks as well, "embellishing with Athenian taste," as Jefferson wrote Latrobe, "the course of a nation looking far beyond Athenian destinies"? May it not be that we are to perform in the twentieth and twenty-first centuries the tasks which Athens and other Greek city-states performed in the ancient world, but on a vastly larger scale? Perhaps it is our task to serve as the powerhouse of ideas for the non-European parts of the world—to furnish the teachers and scholars and scientists and even the artists for distant peoples—to provide not only the tools for material progress but the intellectual weapons in the war on tyranny and injustice, on ignorance and disease.

This is the new commonwealth which is coming into being, and with astonishing rapidity—a commonwealth that encompasses not a single people or nation or faith, but mankind—a commonwealth that embraces not only our own age, but the heritage of the past and the potentialities of the future. We deceive ourselves if we imagine that this commonwealth can be re-created by individuals alone or by private organizations alone. Inevitably government must provide leadership and support; inevitably national governments must work through international organizations. Unless we can discover the ingenuity to combine the work of the individual artist and scientist, the work of affluent groups such as The American Federation of Arts, the resources of national governments and of international organizations, the great community of science and learning and art built up over the centuries will be destroyed. This is no time to bicker over the problem of who does what, or to exclude great agencies of government from this fateful enterprise. We need all of our resources—and all agencies of hope and faith need all of us.

1963

Change in History

W e are in the midst of changes, at home and abroad, as far-reaching in their implications, and in their demands upon us, as any we have experienced in the past. Some of these flow from scientific and technological developments connected with the harnessing of atomic energy, desalinization and the redistribution of water, automation, and so forth; some are the consequences of the new world pattern created by the emergence of Africa and Asia into modernity. Some are created by—or perhaps just required by—the growth of population, cities, and the welfare state.

This is an old story, yet one that is ever new. How extraordinary, we assure each other, the changes that we have experienced, the changes that our society has experienced: from the horse and buggy to the automobile; from the railroad to the jet airplane; from dependence on the vagaries of weather to reliance on oil heating and air-conditioning; from stage shows to television; from old-fashioned guns to atomic missiles. The list is inexhaustible.

A good many of us never get much further in our contemplation of these changes than an expression of astonishment and—usually, though not always—of gratification that it should be our fortune to live in a civilization so mechanized and improved.

Yet these changes, far-reaching as they doubtless are, and fascinating, too, are almost purely quantitative. Certainly since the Industrial Revolution each generation has experienced them—and almost always with comparable excitement. It is a pretty safe prediction that each future generation will continue to experience them. Let us not disparage them. They add immensely to the interest of life; they maintain the economy; they excite the imagination; they give an illusion of progress and in some instances—

medicine, for example—the reality. But they are not in fact, very surprising. If they did *not* materialize, that would be really surprising. Nor are they, in any intellectual sense, deeply interesting, for they are the commonplace of growth and of time.

There is a second category of change that is more interesting and more significant, but, again, not particularly puzzling. I refer to those changes, often basic and far-reaching, which are brought about by shifts in the economy or in the political machinery. These changes are for the most part self-explanatory. Thus, for example, the passing of thrift: a product of inflation and of the welfare state. Thus the changing position of the military: a product of two World Wars, of dependence on the military for survival, and of the shift in the center of gravity of the military itself from the battlefield to the factory and the laboratory. Thus the passing of the myth that rural life was somehow morally superior to urban life: with the population three-fourths urban or suburban, and the countryside itself largely urbanized, and the advantages of urban life so plain, it is inevitable that philosophy should adjust itself to fact. These and similar changes in the mechanics of life do not present any serious challenge to the understanding.

The really interesting changes are not so much in material circumstances, or in the machinery of life, but in habits of thought and conduct, in manners and morals, in sentiment and taste. In the long run these may well be the most important, as well, for they dictate, or at least condition, changes in the economic and material arrangements of society. What is more, they are irresistibly interesting, for they do not lend themselves to easy explanation, but challenge and baffle our understanding.

An obvious example is the growth of humanitarianism. Our great-grandparents, say, a century ago, were at least as virtuous, as religious, as kindly and humane, as we are. Yet they tolerated, nay, took for granted, what we would consider monstrous inhumanity of man to man—and to woman and to child, too. They took for granted that those who were unable to pay their debts should languish in prison for months and sometimes for years. They condemned the feeble-minded to imprisonment in wretched cells, chained them to walls, beat them for their failings, and starved them too: the whole story can be read in Dorothea Dix's famous report of 1842.

They allowed children to work twelve hours a day in factories and mills. They inflicted brutal punishments on prisoners and seamen—flogging, for example—and they assumed, too, that teachers would keep order in schoolrooms by the liberal use of the rod. They condemned immigrants to life in miserable hovels that were breeding places for vice and crime and disease. South of the Mason-Dixon line, Christian men and women not only tolerated the enslavement of Negroes, but counted the "peculiar institution" a positive blessing for all concerned.

All this has changed. Public opinion no longer permits children to work in factories, no longer tolerates mistreatment of prisoners and the feeble-minded, and has done away with flogging in the Navy and the schoolroom. And even the most intransigent of White Citizens Councils would be appalled at the suggestion of reviving Negro slavery.

Or consider the change in the position of women. A century ago it was taken for granted that while women were morally superior to men they were intellectually, and in almost all other ways, inferior. Like children, they were to be seen but not heard. The London meeting of the World Anti-Slavery Convention broke up because the British would not permit lady abolitionists to participate as delegates!

Women were allowed to work long hours in factories, but not to practice law or medicine, or to preach. The Army did not even want them as nurses in the Civil War. Married women had, in effect, no rights that their husbands need respect: no right even to their children. Everywhere the double standard of morality was taken for granted. As for politics, as late as 1912 intelligent men were gravely prophesying the disintegration of society and the collapse of morality if women were so much as allowed to vote.

In less than a century all this changed. The double standard gave way to the single. Women today not only control their own property, but the major part of the wealth of the nation. There is no profession from which they are barred, and few which they do not adorn. And none of the dire consequences of their participation in politics has materialized.

Or look to a quite different, but no less significant, development: the growth of tolerance in the past century or two—a short period, after all, in human history. From time to time we are alarmed, and justly, by manifestations of intolerance in our society—by anti-Semitism or anti-Catholicism, by racism in the South, by McCarthyism, by dangerous pressures for intellectual and social conformity. But if we look back over a period of a few centuries, what is most impressive is the steady growth of tolerance—in religion, above all, but in politics and society as well.

At one time every nation had a state church and, what is more, enforced conformity to it by rope and fire. Nor did governments tolerate dissent in the political realm. In the seventeenth and eighteenth centuries, and even in the nineteenth in some countries, political dissent was silenced as fiercely as religious. Criticism of the king, or of the state, was commonly treated as seditious libel. As late as 1663 William Twyn was drawn and quartered for "imagining" the death of the king, and a few years later Judge Jeffreys sent the noble Algernon Sidney to the gallows for writing an unpublished manuscript advocating republicanism. Persecution persisted through the eighteenth century and into the nineteenth in England: as late as 1850 Catholics could not attend, nor nonconformists teach, at Oxford or Cambridge.

Nor were our own forefathers much more tolerant. The Puritans of Massachusetts Bay drove out Roger Williams and Anne Hutchinson, and persecuted Quakers and "witches" as did the rulers of Virginia. During the Revolution, Congress made it a penal offense to write or publish anything that was designed to bring the President or the Congress "into contempt or disrepute." A generation or so later Southerners zealous to end all discussion of Negro slavery banned magazines and newspapers, burned books, purged libraries, silenced teachers and preachers who agitated the slavery issue. In 1834 a mob in Charlestown, Massachusetts, burned an Ursuline convent; a jury acquitted the mob leaders and the state refused to compensate the Catholic Church for the destruction of its property. In 1837 a mob in Alton, Illinois, killed the abolitionist Elijah Lovejoy and destroyed his press. The following year a Philadelphia mob burned Pennsylvania Hall to the ground because abolitionists held meetings there.

Clearly the climate of opinion has changed. There is no active religious intolerance in England or in the United States now, no suppression of political discussion or even of social nonconformity. Who would have thought, at a time hardly more than a century ago when mobs were burning Catholic convents, that it would ever be possible to elect a Catholic to the Presidency?

The most baffling of all changes are changes in taste—whatever that elusive word may mean. An infallible way to induce gaiety and a comfortable sense of superiority is to show pictures of bathing costumes of the eighteen nineties, or of domestic architecture and interior decoration in the days when the stained-glass window, the rubber plant, and the antimacassar were the epitome of good taste. How does it happen that our grandparents took delight in architecture with turrets and towers and spires and fretwork and stained glass; that our grandmothers filled their parlors with potted palms, hung heavily tasseled velvet draperies between rooms, and put paper fans in the highly decorated black marble fireplaces? Why did they turn away from the simple and dignified architecture of the Federalist period or of the Greek Revival toward the pseudo-Gothic, the pseudo-Italian and the pseudo-Queen Anne?

Will our grandchildren be as repelled by—or amused by—our glass office buildings, our ranch houses, our functional furniture, and our decorative austerity? Beauty, we know, is in the eye of the beholder; why is it that the eyes of each generation reflect such different visions of beauty?

We may look, finally, to a major social change—the change in the attitude toward work and toward play. For three hundred years—that is, almost up to our own time—Americans took work for granted and, what is more, looked upon it as a blessing. Benjamin Franklin's Poor Richard spoke not only to his own generation but to future generations in his many admonitions to be up and doing: "Diligence is the mother of good luck"; "God gives all things to industry, then plough deep while sluggards sleep"; "The used key is always bright"; "Industry pays debts"; "The sleeping fox catches no poultry"; "There will be sleeping enough in the grave"—these and dozens of others were household axioms for two centuries.

Not only in Puritan New England and Quaker Pennsylvania, but everywhere in the country, in the South and along the frontier as well, it was assumed that work was the destiny of man and that it was on the whole a good destiny. Few Americans of the past were disturbed by long hours of labor; few gave thought to vacations; and the cliché "Relax!" had not yet entered the language. Play was well enough for children—though even children were admonished that Satan found mischief for idle hands—but when boys and girls had passed the age of twelve, they were expected to work like their elders.

Only in the last generation has work come to seem the exception rather than the rule, something to be avoided rather than something to be embraced. The ideal of our time is "relaxation." The coffee break and the cocktail hour, the long summer vacation, the ski week-end, the winter trip to the Caribbean, the cult of sports and of games, the evenings devoted to bowling or to television, the rise of the country club to the position of a national institution—all these reflect the American mania for play.

Nor is this merely a response to automation or to labor-saving devices. The rich of earlier generations had their labor-saving devices as well: cheap labor and slave labor; but that did not persuade them to try to make their lives a perpetual vacation, or free them from a sense of responsibility to work to the limit of their capacity.

How may we account for these, and similar, changes in moral habits and manners and taste? We cannot explain them but we can, in a sense, bound them, as we used to bound states or countries in old-fashioned geography.

Change is a phenomenon of a highly civilized society. The American Indian, the Aztec, and the Inca did not change, nor did the Hindu or the Bedouin during the past three or four centuries. It is a phenomenon of the modern world: there was, apparently, very little change, or interest in change, before the Renaissance.

Change appears to be associated with three major modern institutions—the city, the machine, and democracy. Certainly it proceeds more rapidly and more easily in industrialized economies than in agricultural. It is associated with cities; the very climate of city life encourages experimentation, as well as indifference to tradition and to the past. It is related to education because education presumably opens minds to new ideas; and to democracy because democracy enlists the average man in the affairs of his society and thereby encourages discussion.

These characteristics—industrialization, urbanization, education, democracy—are peculiarly prominent in American society. Historically, Americans have been the people most tolerant of, indeed enthusiastic about, change. That process of uprooting and transplanting which was the settlement of America is the obvious and dramatic manifestation of this. But it is in the realm of society, economy, and politics that Americans proved themselves most resourceful, most ready to challenge the traditional and embark upon new enterprises.

They challenged the notion that men were to be governed by kings and nobles and priests, and set up the first large-scale experiment in self-government. They challenged the principle that church and state were two sides of the same shield and that each was essential to the support of the other, and set up a state without a state church. They challenged the age-old notion that society was divided into classes whose position was part of the cosmic system—"untune that string, and hark what chaos follows"—and they inaugurated an experiment in a classless society. They challenged the notion that colonies were always subordinate to a mother country and designed for exploitation, and were the first people to do away with colonialism altogether.

There is no such thing as standing still; to cling to the past, or try to preserve the status quo intact, is to go backward. Change does not necessarily assure progress, but progress implacably requires change. If our society is to flourish and prosper, it should encourage both institutions and practices that facilitate change: above all, the growth of education and of free discussion.

Education is essential to change, for education creates both new wants and the ability to satisfy them. It inspires at once that discontent with existing conditions and that faith in improvement which are essential to progress; and it provides the technical skills that enable us to achieve the goals we set ourselves.

Also, if we are to progress by evolution rather than by revolution, we need to encourage discussion with no quantitative or qualitative limits. Those who fear change instinctively try to suppress the give-and-take of free discussion. They delude themselves that they can achieve security and maintain things as they are by smothering curiosity, blocking inquiry, and silencing criticism. But that policy has never assured either peace or security, unless it is the peace of stagnation or the security of death, and inevitably it drives discontent underground. We have experience of this in our own history. Thus, leaders of the Old South deluded themselves that they could somehow maintain slavery by preventing any discussion of it, thereby imposing on the people of the South a uniform pattern of thought and conduct. Of course, all they did was to drive discussion not so much underground as North, and to force those who hoped to ameliorate the great evil of slavery into drastic and violent measures. They did not save the institution—perhaps they could not—but they made sure that its liquidation would come about through violence; they did not save their society, but brought about its destruction.

There is no assurance that education and freedom will in fact enable us to solve those tremendous problems that loom upon us or assure a peaceful and prosperous future to mankind. But this is certain: that without education and freedom it will be impossible to solve these or any problems.

1961

The Ambiguous
American

Few Old World countries have been preoccupied with the search for national identity. Because they are the products of history, with their own language, culture, and traditions, they can take their character for granted. Americans have never been able to take themselves for granted in this comfortable fashion. They have been conscious—perhaps they are still conscious—that they were a new nation, and one made out of the most miscellaneous materials, their language, their laws, their culture inherited from the Old World.

At the same time they have, from the beginning, been sure that their nation did have a character and a special destiny. Franklin noted distinctly "American traits" even before independence, and most of the Founding Fathers were determined that the new nation should differ profoundly from the nations of the Old World. From St. John Crèvecoeur and Condorcet to Tocqueville and Grattan, from Bryce and Münsterberg to Brogan and Myrdal, foreign observers drew confidently the lineaments of "that new man, the American."

We have then impressive authority for asserting that there are indeed American traits. To enumerate such traits does not in any way imply that they are unique to the Americans; most Western peoples, after all, share a common character. Nor does it imply that all Americans reveal these traits. Americans are a heterogeneous and individualistic people. And it would certainly be an error to suppose that such traits as we may assign to the American are in any sense inherent. They are, rather, the product of environment and experience; both of these have changed and continue to change.

Let us consider some common denominators in the American character.

Perhaps the most common, and the most pervasive, is carelessness. The American is careless in his manners, his dress and his address; he is careless about his house and his garden; careless in social relationships, shuffling off old and taking on new with utmost casualness; careless about observing laws, rules and regulations; careless about his food and his drink, and impatient with ceremony; careless about money.

He tends to be careless about larger things as well: his social relationships, his educational system, and his politics. He has a long tradition of carelessness toward nature. He used up the soil, burned down the forests, polluted the streams; he turns nature into a desert and his cities into junkyards.

The American is, on the whole, openhanded, generous, and hospitable. No other people pours so much money into churches, schools, hospitals and other charities; no other has given so freely to help less fortunate people around the globe. While it is true that a system of tax exemptions makes it easy for Americans to be generous, it is suggestive that American tax laws are designed to encourage giving. The great philanthropic foundation is a distinctly American institution, almost an American invention.

For two centuries visitors from the Old World have paid tribute to American hospitality; the American—as Denis Brogan has observed—was the first to make the term "stranger" a word of welcome. Along with material generosity went magnanimity. It is not without significance that America achieved nationalism without recourse to national enmities; Americans did not nurse enmity toward Britain in the nineteenth century, nor have they harbored enmity toward Germany or Japan in the twentieth.

Though they have won most of their wars, they have never imposed a vengeful peace upon the vanquished. Southerners fancy that the North imposed a "Punic peace" upon them in 1865, but the fact is that when the war was over, no one lost his life because of the rebellion, and Southerners were back in Congress within a year after Appomattox. Compare this with what happened to unsuccessful rebels in Scotland, Ireland, France, Italy, Spain, Cuba, or Russia in modern times.

There are exceptions, to be sure. We were not generous toward the Indian in the nineteenth century, or the Mexican. Though our immigration policy was on the whole hospitable, we were something less than generous in our attitude toward the refugees from totalitarianism in the nineteen-forties and fifties.

Much of American generosity springs from good fortune and abundance. These account, too, for a third American trait: self-indulgence. The American dearly loves comfort and is acquiring a taste for luxury. He pampers himself, his wife, and his children. He rides instead of walking; overheats his house, his office, and even his car; thinks himself entitled to frequent and long vacations, to summers in the North Woods and winters in Florida. He spends enough on tobacco, liquors, and cosmetics to pay off the national debt; drives his children to school instead of letting them walk or ride bicycles; marries young and takes for granted help from his parents.

The Declaration of Independence included the pursuit of happiness as a natural right, and the American is obsessed with this pursuit. He is sure that Providence and nature mean him to be happy and he regards any interference with the attainment of happiness as a violation of natural law. Advertisements proclaim this more blatantly in America than elsewhere. What is achieved by the cigarette, the vacation in Florida, the electric mixer, the new car, is happiness.

That expectation of happiness bespeaks a strong strain of sentimentality and even romanticism. The American is sentimental about many things: children, the little red schoolhouse, the Old South, nature, college, war, and sports. Where else do men and women rise and uncover as they solemnly intone the Alma Mater at some athletic event; where else, for that matter, do they have college songs?

American advertisements ooze sentiment; American movies and television purvey it relentlessly—along with a good deal of quite unsentimental sadism, to be sure. If novels are not so sentimental as they were in the nineteenth century, the stories that trickle through the advertisements in women's magazines still are.

One of the more amiable of American traits if gregarious-ness. It is doubtless a product of New World circumstances, of a society that has been atomized and is anxious to knit new ties of association to take the place of the old; of a frontier environment where men banded together to conquer nature and isolation; of equalitarianism, which looked with suspicion on anyone who held aloof from his fellow men.

Americans like to do things together and they take comfort in numbers. They are the world's most enthusiastic joiners; they do not want to read alone or walk alone, but join clubs so they can do these things in common. They do not prize privacy, but company, and they submit cheerfully to continuous invasions of privacy—music blaring at them in train and plane, commercials shouting at them over radio and television, the badges worn so conspicuously at every convention. The American tends to distrust the man who lives to himself, who prefers reading to conversation on a bus or a plane, who does not join fraternities or clubs and who hesitates to use first names.

On one American trait almost all European critics are agreed: materialism. Is the American in fact more materialistic than his European cousins? Perhaps he is merely more honest. He is intensely conscious of the material world in which he lives, the world of natural abundance, the world of industry and business. He is conscious, too, of size and space. Almost two centuries ago, Crèvecoeur observed that the overwhelming impact of size and environment at once enlarged and elevated the ideas of the American; a hundred miles, he said, were now what a mile had been before. For the United States was, at birth, the largest of Western nations, and for over a century the American imagination was fired by the prospect of "land enough for our descendants to the thousandth and thousandth generation," by vast mountain ranges, limitless prairies, lakes as large as oceans. Nor should it be for-gotten that, if the "land was ours before we were the land's," the process of becoming American was in part one of identification with the natural environment.

History, too, emphasized material considerations; if the new nation was to preserve its independence in a hostile world and realize its democratic potential, it had to grow, and grow fast. No wonder the American has always been fascinated by size and figures. No wonder he takes pride in the largest lakes, the tallest trees, the most rapidly growing cities. It is fair to add that fascination with material growth has not in fact made the American more materialistic than the Frenchman or German. It is reassuring to note that American power and wealth have commonly been made available to other peoples for benevolent purposes.

The American is confident and self-confident; he is, generally, a yes-sayer to life. He thinks that he is on top of the world and that everything is going his way: challenges and disturbances which point to opposite conclusions he generally considers as aberrations, just as he regards defeat (or even a draw) in war or diplomacy contrary to Providence and to nature. He has confidence in himself, in his school, his lodge, his business; confidence, too, in the good will of that Providence, which, in the prophetic words of Jefferson, "by all its dispensations proves that it delights in his happiness here and his greater happiness hereafter." If the American has somewhat less confidence now in Providence, he has perhaps more in himself.

Yet self-confidence melts easily into complacency and this into arrogance, and the American has rather more than his share of both. He believes that his country has reached the pinnacle of civilization and that the "American way of life" is a moral rather than merely a social condition. The American constantly asserts that he enjoys the highest standard of living, though the Scandinavian countries and Canada have a higher one; that his medicine is the best in the world, though his country is eleventh in infant mortality; that his form of government is indubitably the best, though not one of the some fifty new nations has seen fit to copy it.

Complacency also conditions his attitude toward the rest of the world, and permeates the conduct of foreign policy. The American naturally supposes that his standards and principles have universal validity. He assumes that if we choose to blockade Cuba, all rightminded nations will cooperate; if we choose to ignore Red China, it is somehow treason in other countries to recognize her. He is not prepared to impose his policy on other countries, but he does assume that they will adopt it as a matter of course.

This attitude expresses a deeper trait: the habit of supposing that the Americans are a peculiar people; that they are, somehow, exempt from the normal limitations of history. The American congratulates himself on his equalitarianism even while he excludes one-tenth of the people from the benefits of equality. He believes that there is greater liberty here than elsewhere and regards McCarthy or the Birch Society as aberrations. If there are embarrassing chapters in his history, he ignores them. Other nations are imperialistic, but not the American: ousting the Indian, the Spaniard, and the Mexican somehow doesn't count. Other nations are militaristic but not the United States, even though it engaged in half a dozen major wars and, during the nineteenth century, almost continuous Indian wars.

The United States is perhaps the country where the competitive spirit is most cultivated and admired. Cultural anthropologists assure us that American children compete fiercely for parental love, and we do not need anthropologists to remind us of the ardent competition for "dates" that begins even in the elementary school and carries on through college years. Where else do colleges and universities compete so fiercely in athletics; where else does business engage in such cutthroat competition?

Competition is indeed part of that mysterious thing, "the American way of life." The explanation, again, is to be found in large part in our history. In a sense the American has for generations been competing with the rest of the world, competing for population, for culture, for power. In a sense every newcomer—and we have had some forty million of them over the past century and a half—is engaged in proving that he did the right thing, and that life in America is better than life in the Old World.

Equalitarianism, too, imposed competition on its beneficiaries. Where a man's social and economic position was fixed—as it was in the Old World—there was little point in making an effort to improve it. But the New World, where it was possible to go from log cabin to White House, and from rags to riches, and where careers and social position were open to talent, put a premium on competition.

As the American disregarded the artificial barriers of rank and class, so he disregarded what he thought the artificial restrictions of the law. He revered Law with a capital L, he revered the Constitution, from time to time he even revered the Supreme Court, but that was about as far as his reverence went.

His customary attitude toward laws, rules, and regulations was one of indifference or exasperation. The circumstances of life in the New World encouraged this attitude. Colonials saw no reason why they should respect land laws or trade laws or laws regulating Indian affairs that were enacted in London, and thought themselves justified in taking "law" into their own hands.

After independence the same cavalier attitude obtained on successive frontiers. Now it was the government in Washington whose laws affronted the frontiersman, or the land speculator, or the miner, or the trader, and he saw no reason why he should abide by them. The habit persisted and spread. Southerners who thought a victorious North had foisted the Fourteenth and Fifteenth Amendments on them, saw no reason why they should be bound by them, and ignored them, as they still do. The average American is lawless in small matters as in big—thus the universal disregard of parking regulations in our cities; thus the all but universal flouting of traffic laws whose monument is forty thousand deaths every year.

I have left to the last two of the more familiar American traits: equalitarianism and resourcefulness. What Tocqueville argued so perspicaciously in the eighteen-thirties, that equality was the most pervasive of all American traits, still holds for the nineteen-sixties. Notwithstanding the massive denial of equality to the Negro, and to other colored peoples as well, equality is still the greatest common denominator of the American character. Equality obtains in schools and colleges, in business and in politics, in the church and even in the military. There are class distinctions, to be sure, but they are temporary and fluctuating, while the principle of equality is permanent and pervasive.

The real test is not to be found through a statistical analysis of power or prestige; it is to be found rather in the daily and familiar relationships of men and women, in the instinctive and habitual attitude of people toward each other, in the absence not only of titles but of those class categories familiar even in democratic countries like Britain and Sweden.

Thus the American has scholars and scientists, but no intelligentsia; he has ministers and priests, but no ecclesiastical class; he has soldiers and sailors, but no military class. For that matter, America has no aristocracy, no bourgeoisie, no proletariat, and no peasantry: it just has people.

Finally, the American is resourceful. He learned early that he must be, if he were to survive and flourish in a world that was new, strange, and filled with danger. He early proved resourceful in practical matters, in developing the right kind of ax, the right kind of plow, the right kind of steamboat, the right kind of fencing.

Indeed, if there is an American philosophy, it is pragmatism, which looks to conduct, function, processes. The American wants to get on with the job: he wants to know how a machine or an institution or an idea works and he is inclined to define these in terms of their conduct. Even in religion the American is more interested in good works than in theology or dogma. He invented the case system for the study of law and the problem method for the study of almost everything else.

He is infatuated with common sense, and thinks all problems will yield to a common-sense solution. When he invests time or money or sentiment, he wants results, and he likes results that are material and concrete. He has a naïve faith in his ability to achieve his ends through practical and even mechanical means, and thinks that he can become an orator, a musician, an executive, or a perfect lover by excelling in some appropriate course.

No other people has been so fertile in inventions, mechanical, political, and social. For Americans have been resourceful politically as well as mechanically. They invented the written Constitution, the constitutional convention, the federal system. They invented the political party as well, for English "parties" were really factions and cliques. They proved resourceful intellectually: witness the college, the state university, coeducation, and the foundation.

Most important of all they revealed, and still reveal, resourcefulness in their attitude toward experimentation and change. Change is difficult for any society, but less difficult, perhaps, for the American than for others. America, after all, originated in change and the habit of taking change for granted was one he acquired most readily. Though reluctant now to accept constitutional changes, the American shows himself ready enough to accept change in more unyielding realms: the church for example, or class relationships, or higher education.

This habit of taking change for granted augurs well for the ability of Americans to adapt themselves to the new world order now taking shape. Southerners, to be sure, seem reluctant to accept racial equality, but we may with some confidence predict that acquiescence will prove less difficult than most Southerners imagine. The coming of the "welfare state" inspired verbal violence, but no other, and even conservative Americans accepted it with good grace. Americans did not strive for world power, but when it came they assumed world responsibility without convulsive protests, and fulfilled it, too. On all but one occasion in the past Americans have carried through fundamental changes by the process of evolution rather than of revolution. We may with some confidence assume that this deeply engrained habit will persist.

1964

PART FIVE

An Inquiry into "Appeasement"

"We will not engage in appeasement," said President Truman in his survey of our foreign policy in 1951, and again, "appeasement of evil is not the road to peace." Yet, at the same time, he declared the United States ready to "take every honorable step to avoid general war," and "to negotiate differences." To Mr. Truman there appeared to be no incompatibility between these two principles. To many others, however, negotiation in the face of aggression of any kind is the very essence of appeasement.

"A very great part of the mischiefs that vex the world," said Edmund Burke a century and a half ago, "arise from words." What was true in Burke's day is even more true today, when so many words seem to have been emptied of real meaning and have only emotional content. And what is particularly alarming is that confusion in the use of words reflects confusion in thinking. Partly this is a consequence of the influence of advertising which relies more and more on mere suggestibility; partly it is the result of modern techniques of propaganda; partly it is lack of training in logic and rhetoric.

For two decades, now, our ears have been assailed by words from which meaning has been largely drained by constant misuse: bureaucracy, dictatorship, regimentation, rugged individualism, socialism, private enterprise—these in the realm of domestic politics; isolationism, interventionism, Fascist, Communist, subversive, appeasement—these in the realm of foreign relations.

The trouble with these and many other words and phrases is painfully obvious from experience. They are for the most part lacking in clarity, or they have been shorn of any clarity they once possessed by constant abuse; they are used not as terms of description but as epithets; they come to be substitutes for thinking, persuading us that to attach a name to a policy is to understand it, that to characterize a problem is to solve it.

These observations apply with special force to the term "appeasement" as it is now used. It is, in fact, a very old word, dating back at least to the fifteenth century and originally meaning pacification or satisfaction. Only with the Hoare-Laval agreement and Munich did it take on its present opprobrious connotations and these, it must be admitted, are now inseparable from it. Those connotations are familiar enough. They involve not only pacification but concession. For, in these two instances, the Western democracies made concessions that seriously impaired their material and their moral strength. They made concessions that were dictated by timidity, confusion, and bungling rather than by a clear comprehension of the situation, that cost them more than they gained, and that permanently impaired their moral position. It is no wonder that appeasement took on a bad odor.

It does not, however, necessarily follow that all negotiations, all compromises, all concessions, are appeasement. And certainly, whatever may be the wise policy for the United States to adopt toward the many complex and prodigious issues that now confront it, some things are clear. Those issues are not to be solved by calling them names. The term "appeasement" is not a conclusion, it is not even a point of departure. It is an avoidance of thinking. We must not be frightened by words into denying ourselves essential advantages—the advantages of choosing our own ground, selecting our own issues, determining our own time and our own weapons, in so far as we can.

It is worth while, at this juncture when we are called upon to make decisions involving not only ourselves but all of our allies and associates, to review our own experience with negotiation and compromise, and to draw from our own history such lessons as it may afford us. That history, to be sure, furnishes no exact analogies to our present situation, but it does suggest principles of politics and of statecraft that have served us in the past and may serve us in the present and the future.

For, as it happens, there have been a good many instances in our remote—and immediate—past when we have engaged in what present-day name-callers designate appeasement. Like all peoples we have had long experience in compromise, in negotiation, in the balancing of potential gains and losses involved in different policies. Interesting analogies might be found in our Revolutionary history, and again in that troubled period when Jefferson tried to preserve both peace and honor in the face of French and British aggression. But the most illuminating analogy is in the prolonged sectional struggle over slavery, that struggle which ended in the greatest civil war of the century.

For almost a generation—roughly between 1830 and 1860—extremists North and South looked upon the conflict between slavery and democracy as irreconcilable, just as many today look upon the conflict between communism and democracy as irreconcilable. They thought it irreconcilable because they considered it a moral issue and therefore not susceptible to negotiation or compromise. On the issue of slavery they were prepared to sacrifice everything else, even the Union. That was the position of Garrison, who described a Constitution that protected slavery as "a covenant with death and an agreement with hell." That was the position, too, of some Southern extremists who in the end proved ready to give up the Union rather than endanger the "peculiar institution."

The whole issue came to a head in the Compromise of 1850, and particularly in the provisions of the Fugitive Slave Act which was an essential part of that compromise. That act deeply outraged Northern opinion. Yet its enactment was an essential part of the compromise, and therefore essential to the preservation of the Union. It was at this crisis in American history that the aged Webster made his most splendid effort. In the great seventh of March speech he spoke for Union—and for the Compromise. That speech cost him dear. "The word liberty in the mouth of Mr. Webster sounds like the word love in the mouth of a courtesan," wrote Emerson in his journal, and the poet Whittier composed those lines that schoolboys now read:

> Of all we loved and honored, naught
> Save power remains;

> A fallen angel's power of thought
> Still strong in chains.

Webster, in short, was an appeaser. He put the Union before slavery. He realized that to force the issue in 1850 would be fatal: had the South chosen to secede then it might have made good its independence. Then slavery would have been secure. Who can doubt now that Webster was right, and that Whittier and Parker and Garrison and the other extremists, for all their moral fervor, were wrong?

A comparison of the crises of 1850 and 1860 is particularly illuminating. For once again, in 1860, secession threatened, this time over the election of a "black Republican" to the Presidency. And once again there was a possibility of compromise: the extension of the 36:30 dividing line westward to California might have appeased the South. But this time Lincoln refused to entertain compromise. For the situation was different in important respects. In the first place, the North was relatively far stronger in 1860 than it had been in 1850. In the second place, while the Compromise of 1850 did not strengthen slavery in any important way, the proposed Compromise of 1860 would have added greatly to its strength. And, in the third place, the moral issue was, in fact, far clearer than it had been a decade earlier. The rendition of fugitive slaves was, after all, called for in the Constitution. But to permit the extension of slavery into the territories was to compromise fatally the moral position of the Republican party. This time, therefore, the North stood fast. The whole situation, dramatizing as it does the essential difference between compromise and appeasement, is worth study today.

The Wilson administration, too, furnishes us examples of the essential differences between compromise or negotiation on the one hand, and appeasement on the other. The first of these examples concerns our policy toward Mexico. After 1911, Mexico went through a series of revolutions and counter-revolutions that exacted a heavy toll of American lives and property and that appeared to challenge American honor and perhaps American security. The demands for intervention were loud and insistent, but President Wilson adopted a policy of "watchful waiting." Had the term appeasement been used at the time he would have been called an appeaser. For this policy he was denounced as a coward, a poltroon, an enemy of American interests. He refused to be intimidated by these attacks, preferring to work for long-range objectives rather than to win easy popularity.

In a broad way, Wilson was sympathetic to the objectives of the Mexican revolution, a revolution that seemed to many Americans then as wicked as the Chinese revolution seems to many Americans now. He was anxious to reverse policies that Latin Americans had been accustomed to think of as imperialistic, and to win not only Mexican but Latin-American good will. By exercising unparalleled patience, he succeeded in doing this. Who can doubt now that he was right, and that those who clamored for intervention were wrong?

Toward the great European conflict, too, Wilson tried to maintain a policy of watchful waiting. He early announced American neutrality; he tried to hold even the balance between our claims against Germany and against Britain; he refused to be stampeded into war at the time of the Lusitania outrage, but resorted instead to writing notes which won for him the contempt of men like Theodore Roosevelt. Yet he was not unaware of the moral issues involved, or of the threat to American security that would come from a victory of the Central Powers.

He was, however, determined to keep control of the situation as far as he could; to stay out of the war as long as there was any possibility of maintaining peace with honor and safety; to wait until the issues of the war had become clear to the American people; to rally and solidify American opinion. Not until the renewal of the U-boat campaign in 1917, the direct attack upon American shipping and the clear repudiation of international law, did he go to the Congress and ask a declaration of war. He made sure, in short, that when we went to war we would go on issues of our own choosing, at a time of our own choosing.

It was Munich that dramatized "appeasement" and it remains the classic example of appeasement. The story of Munich belongs properly to European rather than to American history, yet it left a scar upon the American consciousness. Nor can Americans wholly escape responsibility for it. The United States had no part in those concessions which abandoned Czechoslovakia to Hitler, but it did have some part in creating the situation which Hitler so skillfully exploited. It had refused to cooperate in creating a system of collective security; it had been instrumental in persuading Britain and France to disarm; it had announced to the dictators that it would have no part in any European war. Munich was the fruit of American policy as well as of British and French weakness.

In what sense could it be said that the decisions at Munich constituted appeasement? In the first place, the democracies surrendered far more than they obtained. They surrendered a powerful ally and the chance—perhaps not very good—of Russian support at this early stage. They did not gain even time, for Germany made greater progress toward rearmament during the next year than did Britain or France. In the second place, they surrendered their moral position, for the sacrifice of Czechoslovakia was an immoral act. And finally—and this is a valid test—they did not even appease. True appeasement rarely does; Munich merely whetted Hitler's appetite.

What shall we say of subsequent policies or programs for which the United States was in part or in whole responsible? Have we "appeased" Franco? Certainly, during the war we followed a policy of pacification and this in the face of strong evidence that Franco was deeply hostile to the democracies and worked for German victory. Yet, we have only to compare our policy toward Spain with Munich to see the difference between concession and appeasement. For our policy toward Spain was strategically sound. At whatever temporary cost, we gained more than we lost.

So, too, with our wartime alliance with Chiang Kai-shek. Here again, the United States and its associates allied themselves with a reactionary, corrupt, and dictatorial regime. They did this for the soundest of reasons, namely, that such an alliance seemed the best way to defeat the Japanese enemy. Support of Chiang Kai-shek did not necessarily imply approval of his regime; it was merely the most sensible policy in the circumstances, the soundest strategic deployment of our forces, diplomatic, military, and political.

It is popular, now to cite Yalta as an example of appeasement and even to characterize it as an American Munich. The characterization is misleading. There was no surrender at Yalta of anything that the Western powers could have withheld, nor was there any substantial weakening of the position of the democracies. The Yalta agreements involved mutual concessions. On paper, the concessions from the West seemed greater than those made by Russia, but in reality the West conceded nothing that Russia could not have taken anyway, while in return it obtained what seemed to be of great importance at the time—quite mistakenly as we now know—a promise to enter the war against Japan.

It should not, after all, be forgotten that when the Yalta agreements were made the Allies had not yet crossed the Rhine, nor had the atom bomb been exploded at Los Alamos: President Roosevelt's military advisers expected that the war with Japan would go on for another year or even two. As it turned out, the atom bomb made Russian entry into the war an embarrassment rather than a help, and Russian membership in the United Nations proved an obstacle rather than an aid to peace. Yet, it is doubtful whether the course of history was changed in any important particulars by Yalta.

What shall we say of other policies which are open to the charge of appeasement? There is, for example, our recognition of the Peron regime in the Argentine and our support of membership for that country in the United Nations. Certainly, Peron had followed an anti-American policy during the early years of the war. Only belatedly in March, 1945, did Argentina declare war on Germany and Japan and even then, as Samuel Flagg Bemis remarks, "Her Government furnished aid and comfort to the enemy." Yet, support to Peron did not mean approval of his regime; only extremists could call it "appeasement"—and extremists did. It was dictated by larger strategic considerations—considerations of Pan-American unity that appeared to take priority over disapproval of this particular regime.

Even more illuminating in this whole matter is a consideration of American relations with Tito since the war. The thing to keep in mind is that Tito is a Communist and Yugoslavia a Communist state. If communism is not only evil but the kind of evil with which it is impossible to compromise, our position is certainly an equivocal one. The second relevant consideration is that our relations with Yugoslavia were subjected to very severe strains during the years immediately after the war. We have not yet forgotten—or have we?—the shooting down of American planes over Yugoslav soil and the military threat to Trieste. Tito's defection from Stalinism is as recent as the summer of 1948. Since that time we have been engaged in what critics might well call "appeasement"; the same Congress that voted aid to Franco's Spain voted aid to Tito's Yugoslavia.

To logicians and doctrinaires, either of the Right or of the Left, who think in black and white and hold that every Communist nation is wicked or every Fascist nation evil, these policies are at once baffling and irreconcilable. On the surface, they look like appeasement and it is easy enough to attach that term to them. But if we characterize particular manifestations of our recent foreign policy as appeasement, it will be difficult to know whom or what we are appeasing. Is it communism? So it might appear from our decision to extend Lend-Lease to Russia, from the Yalta conference, from our policy toward Tito. Is it fascism? So it might appear from our aid to Franco, to Chiang Kai-shek, to Peron. Is our State Department actually so confused and bewildered that it pursues contradictory policies?

These difficulties evaporate if we turn away from abstractions to realities. Great principles of foreign policy are not formulated in response to some syllogism; they are formulated in response to national needs, above all to the needs of collective security. The United States is committed neither to a policy of appeasement nor of nonappeasement. It is committed to two great policies which are, in fact, two sides of the same shield: collective security and the triumph of the principles of freedom over the principles of tyranny.

To achieve these grand ends is a task of incalculable difficulty. It is a task that calls for a firm grip of fundamental principles of national policy, for a profound understanding of global strategy, for a sympathetic consideration of the interests and aspirations of allies and associates; for the subordination of all interests that are local, private, or partisan; for self-restraint, courage, and strength. These ends will not be achieved if we allow our thinking to be confused by shibboleths or our conduct to be dictated by fear rather than by intelligence. They will not be attained if we follow vagrant emotions instead of firm principles.

1951

Yalta Reconsidered

We in America have always been a bit spoiled—largely because we have been isolated, and in part because we have been successful. We assume not only that we can have our way, but that it is right that we should have our way, and that Providence and nature intend that we should have our way. In the last twenty years or so we have added to this moral assumption a practical one: we assume that we are the strongest power in the world and that we ought to be able to order the globe the way we want it. What is more, we even do this retroactively, and undertake to impose our view on reluctant history.

All participants in wars, whether individuals, services, or nations, tend to exaggerate their own role and contributions. We might recall Mr. Dooley on T.R.—"how he armed himself and equipped himself and mounted himself and encouraged himself with a few well chosen words: what I don't understand is why he didn't call the book 'Alone in Cuba.'" (Sometimes I suspect that our histories of World War II may yet be called "Alone in Europe.") How many of us really realize that the major fighting took place on the Eastern, not the Western front and that both Russians and Germans had vastly larger armies in the East than the Allies or the Germans had in the West? How many of us remember that the Russians were within forty-five miles of Berlin before we had even crossed the Rhine; how many of us can sympathize with the Russian view that *they* were the ones who deserve chief credit for winning the war?

Closely connected with this original misconception of the relative positions of Russia and the West is another, which has its roots deep in our national experience and character. We have always known success—at least those of us in the North (Southerners conjured up for themselves a different and not inglorious success). We have always known victory or what we took for victory in war. We have almost always had our way. We have come out well in all of our major diplomatic negotiations, from the Treaty of Paris of 1783, which gave us far more than we had any right to expect, to the Treaty of Paris of 1898, and beyond; the stereotype of the wily Old World diplomat and the innocent American is a figment of the imagination—part of that even larger conception of Old World corruption and New World innocence that haunts our literature. We assume not only that we will win on the battlefield and at the conference table, but that God and morality are on our side. We are "conscious of our own rectitude," we know that our intentions are good, our motives pure, our ideals noble, and we find it hard to understand how others can fail to appreciate all this: opposition to American policy almost always takes on a somewhat sinister mien.

This is one reason why so many of us indulge ourselves in the conspiracy theory of history: after all if God and Nature are on our side, and if we are the strongest of nations, how explain anything that goes wrong, or fails to come up to expectations, but by conspiracy?

How often our understanding has been bedeviled, and our conduct misled, by this conspiracy theory of history. We have used it retroactively: in the interpretation of the Constitution (it was the rich and the reactionary who got together in Philadelphia and wrote a document designed to protect their interests against the welfare of the plain people); in the coming of the Civil War (it was a conspiracy of Northern abolitionists and Black Republicans, so Southerners convinced themselves, that brought on the war); in the writing of the Fourteenth Amendment (it was a clever group of spokesmen for the corporations who insinuated the crucial words into the amendment—no state shall deprive any person of . . . property without due process of law—and thus made it possible for the corporations and the courts to conspire to deprive Americans of their liberties). The Populists convinced themselves that all their economic troubles flowed from a conspiracy between Wall Street and Lombard Street! Worse still, it was a conspiracy of Wall Street bankers and munitions manu-

facturers—and sometimes for good measure British propaganda
—that pushed an innocent America into World War I and thus
associated the United States with the iniquities of that war and of
the Versailles Treaty: so firm and so widespread was this conviction that it helped produce the pernicious neutrality legislation of
the thirties. The habit of seeing conspiracies, and explaining great
events of history by conspiracy, has grown upon us in recent
years: it was the stock in trade of Senator McCarthy, who
explained everything he did not approve by the presence of Communists in the government. It has brushed even President Roosevelt; to read some accounts one might think he himself flew over
Pearl Harbor and dropped those bombs. It was, and is, the basis
for the popular theory that "we lost China"—it was all the fault of
Owen Lattimore, who planned it that way!

The conspiracy interpretation of history is naïve and misguided. It is naïve because it supposes that great forces of history,
the great tides in the affairs of men and of societies, are somehow
the creatures of chance, under the control of an individual or a
group of individuals who can by a flick of the hand—or of the
pen—change everything. It is misleading because it supposes that
everything would be different if only the right word had been said,
if only the right gesture had been made, at the right time; if only
something else had been written down on a piece of paper; it
seduces us to study history from the smokefilled room or the
Communist cell or the Masonic lodge; to imagine that what happened in history is the product of a handful of men planning and
plotting, not of fundamental forces underlying historical development. It distracts our attention from the significant to the insignificant, from the consequential to the trivial; because it leads us to
spend our time and strain our minds with the search for subversion,
the search for the conspiratorial, the disloyal—always somebody
other than ourselves, of course—and to impose on the great and
heaving substance of history and of human conduct low and
sniveling explanations. How degrading this is even in personal and
social life: we all know the student whose failure is inevitably
because some teacher had a down on him; the teacher who is not
promoted because there is a conspiracy against him; the scholar
whose book does not get the prize because the reviewers are all

in conspiracy to do him down; the athlete who would infallibly be the first stringer if the coach did not have it in for him; the inside dopester who explains everything by some event of low cunning or of subversion.

There is a third observation to be made about history and historical interpretation in general before we turn to Yalta in particular: the perils and distractions of history as hindsight. Few things are more misleading than to read back into history everything that we now know. We cannot require men of the past to know the future, to foresee everything that was going to happen and conform themselves to it. Thus in the case of Yalta, one of the arguments brought up again and again by those who criticize what they think unnecessary concessions to Russia in the Far East, is that Russian intervention was not really necessary—the atomic bomb took care of Japan! And for that matter, even without the atomic bomb it was probable that Japan would have been defeated by the destruction of her merchant shipping, thus starving her into submission. But these things were not known at the time, either to FDR or to Churchill, to General Marshall or even to General McArthur—the McArthur who wanted sixty Russian divisions to invade Manchuria; the McArthur who, even after the surrender of Japan, refused to permit a few of his divisions to go to the Chinese mainland to help hold Manchuria from the Communists. Statesmen, like generals, must make decisions on the facts available; if they do everything possible to get the facts, that is perhaps all that can be required of them.

Actually the history of the Yalta controversy belongs more properly in the realm of psychology than of history. Yalta itself, as it turned out, made very little difference. Nothing much was done there that would not have been done anyway; the concessions which the West made were concessions which Russia did not need. The Russians themselves—and according to the Russians the Western powers, too—flouted the Yalta agreements. Ordinarily Yalta would take its place in a long line of conferences and agreements of one kind or another that somehow did not come off: those tiresome seventeenth- and eighteenth-century treaties that were so promptly broken, or those impressive arbitration agreements and cooling-off treaties which Bryan negotiated that nobody seemed to remember. The interesting question is why Yalta looms so large; why there is a voluminous literature on it; why it has figured in Congressional debates and political campaigns. The answer is that Yalta's significance is primarily symbolical rather than historical. Somehow the hopes of Western peoples were bound up in it; somehow the disappointment when these hopes were frustrated was extreme. But more: Yalta got into politics—like the Kansas-Nebraska Act, let us say, or the Dred Scott decision: two events whose importance was a drummed-up affair. Yalta came to mean stratagems and treason; Yalta came to mean conspiracy; Yalta somehow took on the character of a moral Armageddon.

Let us look at Yalta objectively; let us look at it in terms of 1945 rather than of 1962; let us look at it as reality rather than as symbol. Let us consider what was actually agreed upon, not at what conspiracy-minded critics imagine was agreed upon, or what was done in later years.

It is relevant to recall, first, what Yalta was. Sometimes we are almost induced to believe that it was a meeting of enemies rather than of allies; sometimes we are tempted to suppose that it was a battlefield rather than a conference. Actually it was a prolonged and, for the most part, friendly discussion of wartime plans and postwar programs. Roosevelt, Churchill, and Stalin met in an atmosphere of victory and of hope. The destruction of German power was certain; only Japan was still to be conquered.

The Yalta Conference was designed to do two major things: to plan the death blows against Japan, and to lay the groundwork for the organization of free nations after the war. The Conference addressed itself successfully to these two grand subjects.

Now for some of the details of the Conference itself. There was give and take, there were bargains and concessions. This is what one should expect in a diplomatic conference; after all, we were not there to impose unconditional surrender on the Russians. The tendency now is to emphasize the concessions of the West to Russia, to argue that Yalta was a one-sided affair with Stalin emerging triumphant in every contest of wills.

Actually, the give and take was pretty evenly balanced: Stettinius, who was Secretary of State at the time, insists that "the

record shows clearly that the Soviet Union made greater concessions to the United States and Great Britain than were made to the
Soviets"—and that Stalin got in trouble at home as a result of his
excessive amiability! However this may be, Yalta was no one-
sided agreement. We can distinguish three broad categories of
controversy: that in which Stalin made substantial concessions to
the views of Roosevelt and Churchill; that in which concessions
appear to be evenly balanced; that in which the Western Allies
made substantial concessions to Stalin.

To the first category we assign Stalin's agreement to enter the
war against Japan "within two or three months" after the surrender of Germany. It is irrelevant to discuss now whether Russian aid was necessary, or whether it was an embarrassment. The
Chiefs of Staff were convinced that without Russian aid the conquest of Japan might require another one or two years and exact
perhaps a million American casualties; it is worth noting that
General MacArthur, who had previously thought Russian aid unnecessary, did not at the time of Yalta disagree with his military
superiors. Moreover, although Stalin had previously promised to
fight Japan, his terms were vague, and apparently the Joint Chiefs
felt it necessary to spell out a definite agreement in dealing with
such people as the Russians. In connection with this agreement
Stalin promised the Allies air bases in the Maritime Provinces of
Siberia, as well as in the west, promises that were never implemented.

Next—and to Roosevelt it may have been first in importance
—Stalin agreed to help organize and support the United Nations,
and in this connection agreed with Roosevelt's proposal to admit
to the new organization all those who had fought the Axis, including the Latin American states. Granted again that in theory Stalin
stood to gain as much as did any other power from a world
organization, the fact is that he had appeared indifferent to it and
that Russian participation was thought essential to its creation and
effective operation.

Third, Stalin accepted the American proposal to admit
France to membership on the German Control Commission and to
give her a zone of occupation.

Fourth, Stalin accepted the American draft of a Declaration

on Liberated Europe: "To jointly assist the people of any European liberated state . . . to form interim governmental authorities broadly representative of all democratic elements in the population. . . ."

To the second category, that which embraces compromises that appear to be nicely balanced, we must assign (if that is not too strong a word) agreements on reparations, on the voting formula in the U.N., and on Poland.

Russia wanted to include in the agreement a firm reparation figure of 20 billion dollars, of which she was to be entitled to half. Roosevelt and Churchill—familiar with the unhappy reparations story from World War I—opposed this stipulation. Finally the figure was put in but only "as a basis for discussion." The Americans took this phrase at face value, the Russians pretended to believe that it constituted a guarantee of that sum. The provisions for representation in the United Nations Assembly and for voting in the Security Council were likewise compromises, wholly satisfactory to none. Russia withdrew her preposterous demand for sixteen votes in the Assembly and settled for three—a matter, as it turned out, of no importance. As for the more important question of the Security Council, Russia accepted, on the whole, the American formula of the great-power veto on action, but not on discussion.

The agreement on Poland was perhaps the most difficult of all, and it is the one that has given rise to gravest charges of defeat and betrayal. It must be remembered that by the beginning of 1945 the Russian armies had overrun almost the whole of Poland, and that Russia had already recognized the so-called Lublin or Communist Government of Poland while the Anglo-American armies did not cross the Rhine until March. There was really very little room for diplomatic maneuvering, for the real question was not what the Western Allies would permit Russia to do in Poland but what Russia would agree to do. Stalin did accept the Curzon line, with some variations—a line to which Churchill had long been committed. And he agreed—on paper of course—to reorganize the Lublin Government "on a broader democratic basis." This was unsatisfactory, but it is difficult to know just what Roosevelt and Churchill could have done about it.

It is the third category—concessions to the Russians—that the critics of Yalta have in mind when they denounce the agreement as appeasement or betrayal. What were the specific concessions? Mostly they were in the Far East. First, Russia demanded the restoration of all territory lost in the war with Japan in 1904: the southern part of the island of Sakhalin and the Kurile Islands, a lease of Port Arthur, and the internationalization of Dairen. Second, Russia demanded and the West conceded that the "preeminent interests of the Soviet" in Manchuria be safeguarded, and that the status quo in Outer Mongolia—a status quo distinctly favorable to the Russians—be recognized. Roosevelt pledged himself to obtain the consent of Chiang Kai-shek to these arrangements, and it is not irrelevant to note that this consent was forthcoming, not reluctantly but enthusiastically.

Here then are the essential parts of the famous Yalta agreement. What does this examination show? It shows that each side made concessions not only to the other but to reality. This is perhaps the most striking thing about Yalta. Where it was applied it ratified reality; where it did not ratify reality it was not applied.

Aside from such things as the restoration of Russian sovereignty in Sakhalin and the Kuriles, the Western Allies conceded nothing that Russia did not already have or could not have taken. Neither the Polish boundary nor the agreement on the Lublin Government were satisfactory to the West, but Stalin had no intention of giving way on any of these issues, and short of starting a war with Russia—a dubious program while we were still fighting with Germany and Japan—there was nothing effective that the West could do.

So, too, with the situation in the Far East. The Russian armies were there, after all. Mr. Hanson Baldwin has argued that "we" permitted Russia to become a Pacific power. But Russia had been a Pacific power for a century; the vacuum created by the defeat of Japan and the disintegration of China opened the way for the vast extension of that power. Again it is difficult to see what we could have done about it. Now, when pushed to the wall, critics admit all this: how, indeed, can they deny it? But, they say, shifting their ground from the realm of *real-politik* to that of morality (and here I quote the ablest of them all, Chester Wilmot), "The real question was not what Stalin would or could have taken, but what he was given the right to take. This agreement provided Stalin with a moral cloak for his aggressive designs in Asia and, more important, with almost a legal title enforceable at the Peace Conference to the territories and privileges which he demanded."

Now this is a very interesting statement, crowded with assumptions which are wholly unfounded. There is, for example, the primary assumption that Stalin needed or desired a "moral cloak" for his aggressions. Nothing in Stalin's career, either before or after Yalta, supports this. Nor is there any evidence that Stalin was concerned with "legal title." He did not turn to law to justify his attack upon Finland, his absorption of the Baltic countries, or his postwar subjugation of satellite countries. But aside from this the whole argument is irrelevant. Yalta gave moral cloak and legal title only to what it gave, and nothing more. An agreement to recognize Russian interests in Manchuria did not give either moral cloak or legal title to aggression in Korea. An agreement to broaden the base of the Polish Government gave neither moral cloak nor legal title to the destruction of Polish democracy. Nothing in the Yalta agreements gave moral cloak or legal title to aggression in Rumania, or Hungary, or Czechoslovakia.

This brings us to a final observation about Yalta. The difficulty which disturbs so many of the critics of Yalta is not with the Yalta Agreement. Those who talk so glibly about Yalta do well not to cite the document, or even to familiarize themselves with it. The trouble is, of course, with the persistent violation of the Yalta Agreement. Had Russia really lived up to the Yalta Agreement, peace and harmony might have obtained.

The notion that Yalta was a victory for Stalin, that Yalta was an American Munich, that Yalta was a great betrayal, is a notion without foundation in history or in logic. It is a product of the kind of thinking that traces great events to small causes. It is a product of the kind of thinking that sees in the immorality of a king, in the corruption of a minister, in the error of a general, in the blundering of a legislator, the explanation for fateful courses of history. It is a product of the type of mind that subscribes to the

Great Man theory of history, the conspiracy theory of history, the devil theory of history, and the catastrophic theory of history—theories about as valid in the realm of history as their corollaries are in the realm of nature. It is the product of the kind of thinking that led us so woefully astray in our interpretation of the causes of the First World War, that led us through the Nye Committee to the ostrich-like neutrality legislation. It is thinking that creates, in the end, a myth, and we cannot afford to base our foreign policy on myth.

About all one can legitimately say in criticism of Roosevelt and, to a much lesser degree, of Churchill—for let us not overlook what is so commonly ignored, that Churchill signed the agreements, and that whatever theory of error or of conspiracy is applied to Roosevelt and his colleagues must logically be applied to Churchill as well—is that they should have been more cynical, that they should have consulted their suspicions rather than their faith. Yet would we really have it so? Can any lasting international order be built on the foundation of fear and suspicion? Would Franklin Roosevelt have been the leader that he was—the leader of the free world, the architect of the grand coalition, and of victory—if he had been the kind of man who consulted his fears rather than his hopes, if he had been a man made cynical by a study of the past rather than a man inspired by a vision of the future?

1952

PART SIX

The Double Standard
in Political Morality

"Every philosophy," wrote Alfred North White-
head, "is tinged with the coloring of some secret, imaginative
background, which never emerges explicitly in its train of reasoning." True enough—though *never* is a strong word. What is the
secret, or perhaps the inarticulate imaginative background, that
colors American thinking about relations with other peoples and
nations in the past and today? Is it not the once explicit and
openly avowed, but now implicit assumption of American superiority, both material and moral, especially to lesser breeds without
our law? Is it not the assumption that America is somehow outside the workings of history, above the processes of history, exempt from such laws as may govern history?

The origin of this attitude may be traced to the generation
that created the new nation and came to think of that nation as a
people apart. It is rooted in the long-popular notion of New World
innocence and Old World corruption, New World virtue and Old
World vice, a notion that runs like a red thread through the whole
of our literature from Benjamin Franklin to Henry James, and
through our politics and diplomacy as well. It is connected with
the convulsive fact of physical removal—the uprooting and transplanting to new and more fertile soil, with the phenomenon of a
continuous westward emigration from the Old World, while so few
went eastward across the ocean. It is related to the American
priority in independence and in nation-making, with the glowing
achievements of the new nation—religious freedom, for example,
the end to colonialism, the classless society—and over the years it

was strengthened by the argument of special destiny, and by the experience of abundance and freedom from Old World wars, and of growth even beyond the dreams of the Founding Fathers. No wonder the notion of a special Providence and a special destiny caught the American imagination.

Something was to be said for all this in the early years of the Republic, when the American world was not only new but brave. Rather less was to be said for it as the nineteenth century wore on—the century that saw the new nation indulge in so many of the follies of the older nations: slavery, racial and religious intolerance, the disparity between rich and poor, civil war, imperialism, and foreign wars.

But even in the nineteenth century, perhaps especially in the nineteenth century, Americans developed the habit that still characterizes them of brushing aside whatever was embarrassing, the habit of taking for granted a double standard of history and morality. There were, to be sure, awkward things in our history, but somehow they were not to be held against us, somehow they didn't count. The conquest and decimation of the Indian didn't count—after all, the Indians were heathens—and when that argument lost its force, there was the undeniable charge that they got in the way of progress. The students of my own college celebrate Lord Jeffrey Amherst on all ceremonial occasions, but few of them remember that Lord Amherst's solution to the Indian problem was to send the Indians blankets infected with smallpox. How many of us remember what Helen Hunt Jackson called a "Century of Dishonor"? Or there was slavery; it was pervasive and flourishing, and slaveholders defended it as a moral good. Somehow slavery didn't count, either, because it was nature's way of bringing the African to Western civilization, or because it was all so romantic (only recently have we developed a sense of guilt here).

The Industrial Revolution, too, brought in its train most of the evils that afflicted Europe in these same stormy years, but that could all be put down as the price of progress, which is just what Herbert Spencer and his infatuated American followers did. And surely no one could assert that the price was too high. So, too, with what, in other nations, would be called imperialism, but with us was called "westward expansion"—manifest destiny working itself out in some foreordained fashion. The Mexicans do not take quite this view of the matter, but that has not troubled us. Even now we do not inquire quite as closely into the war-guilt question for the Mexican War, or the war with Spain, or the Filipino war, as we do for the Franco-Prussian War or World War I. Poets like William Vaughn Moody raised their voices in vain against the Philippine War:

> Alas, what sounds are these that come
> Sullenly over the Pacific Seas—
> Sounds of ignoble battle, striking dumb
> The season's half awakened ecstasies? . . .
> Was it for this our fathers kept the law?
> This crown shall crown their struggle and their truth?
> Are we the eagle nation Milton saw
> Mewing its mighty youth,
> Soon to possess the mountain winds of Truth
> And be a swift familiar of the sun . . .
> Or have we but the talons and the maw . . . ?

But who now remembers William Vaughn Moody?

We are no longer quite so sure of the New World innocence and Old World corruption as in the past—sometimes we suspect it may be the other way around—but the older notions of American superiority, and of the exemption of America from the familiar processes of history, persist. They were very much in the mind of Woodrow Wilson when he prepared to make the world safe for democracy. But then the world we made did not suit us at all; clearly we had been betrayed by the wicked diplomats of the Old World. We cut our losses and withdrew into isolation and watched the Old World destroy itself with a kind of malign satisfaction, meanwhile congratulating ourselves that we were not involved and that our irresponsibility was really a form of moral superiority.

We were very sure of our own virtue, and we read history to discover that we were a peculiar people. Our history books exalted everything American. They contrasted our Indian policy with the wicked policy of the Spaniards—that was part of the black legend —conveniently overlooking the elementary fact that the Indian survived in Mexico and South America but not in the United States. They painted slavery as a romantic institution, or perhaps as a kind of fortunate accident for the Africans. They even ascribed the exceeding bounty of nature not to Providence or to luck but to our own virtue. In recent years many of our spokesmen commit the vulgar error of identifying an economy based on unrestricted exploitation of natural abundance as "the American way of life," and of scorning less fortunate people for having fewer resources and a different, and obviously inferior, way of life. We forget Reinhold Niebuhr's admonishment that "The more we indulge in uncritical reverence for the supposed wisdom of the American way of life, the more odious we make it in the eyes of the world, and the more we destroy our moral authority. . . ."

During the Great War we responded, generously and unselfishly, to the challenge that confronted us; this was, in a sense, our finest hour, too: Lend-Lease, the alliance with Britain, the acceptance of the Soviet as an ally in the struggle against tyranny, the Atlantic Charter and the United Nations and the farsighted Marshall Plan, the response to the challenge of aggression in Korea. But the rising threat of communism did what the actual attack by Nazi and Fascist powers had been unable to do. The prolonged struggle with communism, which we sometimes call the Cold War, accentuated our innate sense of superiority. To vast numbers of Americans it justified—and apparently still does justify—resort to almost any weapons or conduct. For years now we have heard, and not from extremists alone, that the struggle between democracy and communism is the struggle between Light and Darkness, Good and Evil, and that the moral distinction is an absolute one.

The arguments that were invoked to justify religious persecution in past centuries are invoked now to justify sleepless hostility to communism—even preventive war. Happily, the extremists have not had their way in the conduct of foreign policy, but we know how effective they have been on the domestic scene, how they have denounced as traitors those who do not agree with them and persecuted them with relentless venom, how they have poisoned public life, and private, too, preaching hatred of Russia, hatred of Cuba, hatred of China—hatred directed toward all those who do not agree with them and with their easy remedies. Those hate-mongers, sure of themselves and of their moral superiority, have not hesitated to ignore law and the Constitution or to lie and cheat and betray in what they complacently assumed was a good cause because they espoused it. In 1801 Jefferson warned against suspicion and hatred in public life: "Let us," he said in his first inaugural address:

> . . . restore to social intercourse that harmony and affec-
> tion without which liberty and even life itself are but
> dreary things. And let us reflect that, having banished
> from our land that religious intolerance under which man-
> kind so long bled and suffered, we have yet gained little
> if we countenance a political intolerance as despotic and
> wicked, and capable of as bitter and bloody persecutions.

Not since the decade of the eighteen-fifties has that warning been more relevant than in this generation. Those who cultivate and spread the gospel of hatred throughout our society bear a heavy responsibility. They do not really weaken communism; they weaken democracy and liberty. By their conduct and their phi-losophy they lower the moral standards of the society they pretend to defend. Eager to put down imagined subversion, they are them-selves the most subversive of all the elements in our society, for they subvert "that harmony and affection" without which a society cannot be a commonwealth.

Much of our current foreign policy takes once again the form of indulgence in a double standard of morality. Thus it is contrary to international law to make reconnaissance flights over the ter-ritory of another nation—the Soviet reminded us of that a few years back—but we boast that we make such flights over Cuba and over China. If Cuban planes flew over Florida or Chinese over Hawaii we might take a less amiable view of the matter. We justly condemn Nazi destruction of Rotterdam and Warsaw, cities that were not military objectives, but we conveniently forget that we were chiefly responsible for the senseless destruction of Dresden— not a military objective—within a few weeks of the end of the war, with a loss of 135,000 lives. It is a matter for rejoicing that *we* have the nuclear bomb, but when China detonated her first bomb our President told us that "this is a dark day in history." Perhaps so, though so far we are the only nation that has ever used the bomb—a fact which the Asians remember better than we do. And even now Senator Russell assures us that he would favor using it again if our soldiers in Vietnam faced defeat. Even the present war in Vietnam—the President has now used the word "war" for it, so perhaps we can abandon the hypocritical vocabulary with which we have heretofore bemused ourselves—tempts us constantly to indulge in a double standard. The Vietcong engages in "terror attacks" but our bombings do not presumably hurt anybody. When we use gas it is not really gas but just something our own police use here at home. Our airmen and marines are "observers" but the enemy's soldiers are terrorists. Guerrilla warfare—is it from the North?—justifies bombing at the source: if Castro accepted that theory and bombed those bases in Florida and Guatemala that launched guerrilla attacks on his island, we might take a different view of the matter. When the Russians announced that they would not tolerate an unfriendly government in Hungary, and sent their troops and tanks crashing into that country in 1956, we were rightly outraged, but we think it quite right for us to announce that we will not tolerate an unfriendly regime in Santo Domingo and to send twenty thousand Marines to "restore order" in that island. We complain, and rightly, that other countries do not abide by their international agreements, but we are ready to forgive ourselves for brushing aside international agreements when we face something we regard as an "emergency."

We have always criticized secret diplomacy—but when the CIA operates with such secrecy that even our own government is apparently taken by surprise, that just shows how clever we are. For the Russians or the Chinese to stir up revolution in other lands is subversive of international order, but when we encourage a coup d'etat or a revolution—from Iran to Brazil to Vietnam—it is all in a good cause.

We have not of late heard quite so much as some months back of what must surely be counted the ultimate arrogance—the cry of the "better dead than Red" crusaders. Those highly vocal potential martyrs are so sure that they speak for God that they are quite ready to condemn to extinction not only themselves and their fellow citizens, but the rest of the world and all potential posterity.

It is three-quarters of a century now since Lord Acton made the famous pronouncement that all power tends to corrupt and that absolute power corrupts absolutely. We had thought, and hoped, that we were exempt from this rule, but it is clear that we are not. Power exposes us to the same temptation to ruthlessness, lawlessness, hypocrisy, and vanity to which all great powers were exopsed in the past.

In a simpler day we could survive this threat of corruption without serious damage. We could count on wearing out the brief spell of violence and corruption, or on circumscribing its effects. But now that we are a world power and our conduct affects the fate of every nation on the globe, we can no longer afford this piece of self-indulgence. Now we must square our conduct with principles of law and of morality that will withstand the scrutiny of public opinion everywhere and the tests of history as well.

1965

The Problem of
Dissent: Vietnam

It is barely two months now since Pope Paul VI made his historic plea to the United Nations and to the peoples of the world for an end to war and a restoration of brotherhood. "No more war. War never again," he said, and the whole nation applauded his noble plea. But when young men and women from our colleges and universities take the papal plea in good faith, and demonstrate against the war in Vietnam, they are overwhelmed with a torrent of recrimination and obloquy that is almost hysterical. Even students catch the contagion. "We're sick and tired of peaceniks," shriek the students of the Catholic Manhattan College. Are they sick and tired of Pope Paul, who said, "It is peace that must guide the destinies of mankind"?

Surely it is time to bring a little clarity and common sense to the discussion of this matter of student protests and demonstrations.

First, as Attorney General Katzenbach has reminded us, there is no question about the right of students, or of others, to agitate, to demonstrate, to protest in any nonviolent manner against policies they consider misguided. That is, after all, not only a right but a necessity if our democracy is to function. People who ought to know better—Senator Dodd of Connecticut, for example—have loosely identified agitation with "treason." Treason is the one crime defined in the Constitution, and the Senator would do well to read that document before he flings loose charges of treason about. Students have the same right to agitate and demonstrate against what they think unsound policies—even military policies—as have businessmen to agitate against the TVA or doctors against Medicare. When, back in New Deal days, distinguished lawyers publicly advised corporations to disregard the Wagner Act and the Social Security Act on the ground that they were unconstitutional, when distinguished medical men called for the sabotage of Medicare, no one called them traitors. Businessmen and doctors and lawyers, to be sure, funnel their protests through respectable organizations like chambers of commerce, or the American Medical Association, or the American and state bar associations, or resort to well-paid lobbyists to express their discontent; students have no such effective organizations nor can they support lobbying. To penalize them for their weakness and their poverty is to repeat the error of the Cleveland administration in arresting Coxey's Army for walking on the grass, or of the Hoover administration in sending soldiers to destroy the pitiful Bonus Army. The rich and respectable have always had their ways of making their discontent heard; the poor and the unorganized must resort to protests and marches and demonstrations. Such methods have not customarily been considered un-American.

Second, we are not yet legally at war with Vietnam, though what is going on there has, to be sure, the character of war. Nor are we acting in Vietnam under the authority or the auspices of the United Nations, as we did in the Korean crisis. We are in Vietnam as a result of executive decision and executive action, and it is not yet traitorous or unpatriotic to criticize executive action. In so far as they were consulted on the matter, the American people voted, in 1964, for the candidate who appeared to promise them peace in Vietnam, and against the candidate who advocated war. It was not thought unpatriotic for President Johnson to demonstrate against war in Vietnam in 1964; what has changed in the past year is not the law or the principle, but Presidential policy, and it is not unpatriotic to fail to change when the President changes his policy.

But, it is said, whatever the legal situation, war is a fact. We do have 165,000 men in Vietnam; we do send our bombers out every day to rain destruction on our "enemies" there. The time for discussion, therefore, has passed; we must close ranks behind our government.

What is the principle behind this line of reasoning? What but that it is right and proper to protest an error—or what seemed even to President Johnson to be an error, as long as it was a modest one—but that it is unpatriotic to protest an error when it is immense. If this is sound logic, the moral for men in high position is clear. If any policy upon which you are embarked excites criticism, expand it, enlarge it, pledge all of your resources to it; then criticism will be unpatriotic and critics will be silenced. A little error is fair game for critics, but a gigantic error, an error that might plunge us into a world war, is exempt from criticism.

Is this the principle Senators Dodd and Lausche, Kuchel and Stennis, wish to adopt?

Third, there is the now popular argument that whatever the logic of protests, they are intolerable because they might give comfort to the enemy. Whatever may be said for the sentiment behind this argument, it can be said with certainty that it runs counter not only to logic but to history and tradition as well. When George III resolved on war against rebellious colonies, nineteen lords signed a solemn protest against the war; the commander-in-chief of the Army, Lord Jeffrey Amherst, refused to serve; the highest commanding naval officer, Admiral Keppel, refused to serve; Lieutenant General Frederick Cavendish resigned his commission. We do not think poorly of them today for refusing to fight in what they thought an unjust war, and Amherst College is not about to change its name to Lord North.

Nor do we think poorly of preachers and men of letters who denounced the war with Mexico as unjust and counseled civil disobedience. President Polk, who at the last minute found a dubious justification for the war, is remembered a century later as "Polk the Mendacious," while Abraham Lincoln, who called upon him to indicate the "spot" where American blood had been shed, does not suffer in our esteem for his contumaciousness. Henry David Thoreau, who went to jail rather than pay taxes to support a war he thought iniquitous, is one of the glories of our literature and his essay celebrating civil disobedience is read in every high school and college in the land. Does Senator Dodd think it ought to be banned? James Russell Lowell wrote of the warmongers in his day (it is Hosea Biglow who is speaking):

> They may talk o' Freedom's array,
> 'Tell they're pupple in the face;
> It's a gran' great cemetery
> Fer the barthrights of our race.

And he charged that

> Ez fer war, I call it murder;
> There you hev it plain and flat;
> I don't want to go no furder
> They my testyment fer that.

And he concluded with words that are as apt today as they were in 1846:

> Call me coward, call me traitor,
> Jest ez suits your mean idees;
> Here I stand a tyrant-hater
> An' the friend o' God an' Peace.

A grateful government later sent Lowell as Minister to the Court of St. James. And while the war was on, Lincoln's favorite clergyman, Theodore Parker, denounced it from the most eloquent pulpit in America, Sunday after Sunday. He is remembered today as The Great American Preacher.

In 1899 we fought a war that has interesting parallels with that which we are fighting today—a war which we now have almost wholly forgotten, perhaps for reasons that psychologists can understand better than politicians. That was the war to put down the Filipino "insurrection." For the Filipinos—like the Cubans—thought that they were to be liberated, but Admiral Dewey cabled that the Filipino Republic represented only a fraction of the Filipino people and that independence was not to be thought of, and the United States threw her military might into the task of defeating what they called an insurrection. Soon the presses were filled with stories of concentration camps and tortures; soon American soldiers were singing

> Damn, damn, damn the Filipinos
> Slant-eye'd Kakiack Ladrones
> And beneath the starry flag
> Civilize them with a Krag
> And return us to our beloved Homes!

The Filipino war excited a wave of outrage and protest among intellectuals, reformers, and idealists as vociferous as that which we now witness. Mark Twain addressed a powerful letter "To a Person Sitting in Darkness," which asserted that the Stars and Stripes should have the white stripes painted black and the stars replaced by skull and crossbones. The philosopher William James charged that "we are now engaged in crushing out the sacredest thing in this great human world. . . . Why do we go on? First, the war fever, and then the pride which always refuses to back down when under fire." In "To a Soldier Fallen in the Philippines" William Vaugh Moody wrote just such an ode as might be written for a soldier fallen in Vietnam:

> A flag for the soldier's bier
> Who dies that his land may live;
> O banners, banners, here
> That he doubt not, nor misgive . . .
>
> Let him never dream that his bullet's scream
> Went wide of its island mark
> Home to the heart of his darling land
> Where she stumbled and sinned in the dark.

Nor were these men of letters alone in their passionate outcry against what they thought an unjust war. They had the support of a brilliant galaxy of public leaders: Carl Schurz and Samuel Gompers, E. L. Godkin of the *Nation* and Felix Adler of the Ethical Culture Society, Jane Addams of Hull House and President Jordan of Stanford University, and Andrew Carnegie and scores of others. And when the defenders of the war raised the cry "Don't haul down the flag," it was no other than William Jennings Bryan, titular head of the Democratic party, who asked, "Who will haul down the President?"

We need not decide now whether those who protested this war were right or wrong. It is sufficient to remember that we honor Mark Twain and William James, regard Jane Addams as one of the greatest of American women, and still read Godkin, and that Bryan is somewhat better remembered than William Mc-Kinley. Those infatuated patriots who now assert that it is some-how treasonable to criticize any policy that involves Americans in fighting overseas would do well to ponder the lessons of the Philippine War.

But, it will be said, as it is always said, this war is different. Whether history will judge this war to be different or not, we cannot say. But this we can say with certainty: a government and a society that silences those who dissent is one that has lost its way. This we can say: that what is essential in a free society is that there should be an atmosphere where those who wish to dissent and even to demonstrate can do so without fear of recrimination or vilification.

What is the alternative? What is implicit in the demand, now, that agitation be silenced, that demonstrators be punished? What is implicit in insistence that we "pull up by the roots and rend to pieces" the protests from students (it is Senator Stennis we are quoting here)? What is implicit in the charge that those who demonstrate against the war are somehow guilty of treason?

It is, of course, this: that once our government has embarked upon a policy, there is to be no more criticism, protest, or dissent. All must close ranks and unite behind the government.

Now we have had a good deal of experience, first and last, with this view of the duty of the citizen to his government and it behooves us to recall that experience before we go too far astray.

We ourselves had experience with this philosophy in the antebellum South. The dominant forces of Southern life were, by the eighteen-forties, convinced that slavery was a positive good, a blessing alike for slaves and for masters; they were just as sure of the righteousness of the "peculiar institution" as is Senator Dodd of the righteousness of the war in Vietnam. And they adopted a policy that so many Senators now want to impose upon us: that of silencing criticism and intimidating critics. Teachers who attacked slavery were deprived of their posts—just what Mr. Nixon now advises as the sovereign cure for what ails our universities! Editors who raised their voices in criticism of slavery lost their papers. Clergymen who did not realize that slavery was enjoined by the Bible were forced out of their pulpits. Books that criticized slavery were burned. In the end the dominant forces of the South got their way: critics were silenced. The South closed its ranks against critics, and closed its mind; it closed, too, every avenue of solution to the slavery problem except that of violence.

Nazi Germany provides us with an even more sobering spectacle. There, too, under Hitler, opposition to government was equated with treason. Those who dared question the inferiority of Jews, or the justice of the conquest of inferior peoples like the Poles, were effectually silenced, by exile or by the gas chamber. With criticism and dissent eliminated, Hitler and his followers were able to lead their nation, and the world, down the path to destruction.

There is, alas, a tragic example of this attitude toward criticism before our eyes, and in a people who inherit, if they do not cherish, our traditions of law and liberty. Like the slavocracy of the Old South, the dominant leaders of South Africa today are convinced that whites are superior to Negroes, and that Negroes must not be allowed to enjoy the freedoms available to whites. To maintain this policy and to silence criticism—criticism coming from the academic community and from the press—they have dispensed with the traditions of due process and of fair trial, violated academic freedom, and are in process of destroying centuries of constitutional guarantees. And with criticism silenced, they are able to delude themselves that what they do is just and right.

Now, it would be absurd and iniquitous to equate our current policies toward Vietnam with the defense of slavery, or with Nazi or Afrikaner policies. But the point is not whether these policies have anything in common. The point is that when a nation silences criticism and dissent, it deprives itself of the power to correct its errors. The process of silencing need not be as savage as in Nazi Germany or in South Africa today; it is enough that an atmosphere be created where men prefer silence to protest. As has been observed of book-burning, it is not necessary to burn books, it is enough to discourage men from writing them.

It cannot be too often repeated that the justification and the purpose of freedom of speech is not to indulge those who want to speak their minds. It is to prevent error and discover truth. There may be other ways of detecting error and discovering truth than that of free discussion, but so far we have not found them.

There is one final argument for silencing criticism that is reasonable and even persuasive. It is this: that critics of our Vietnam policy are in fact defeating their own ends. For by protesting and agitating, they may persuade the Vietcong, or the North Vietnamese, or the Chinese, that the American people are really deeply divided, and that if they but hold out long enough the Americans will tire of the war and throw in the sponge. As there is in fact no likelihood of this, the critics are merely prolonging the agony of war.

These predictions about the effect of criticism in other countries are of course purely speculative. One thing that is not mere speculation is that American opinion is, in fact, divided; that's what all the excitement is about. We do not know how the Vietcong or the Chinese will react to the sounds of argument coming across the waters. Perhaps they will interpret criticism as a sign of American weakness. But perhaps they will interpret it as an indication of our reasonableness. And assuredly they will, if they have any understanding of these matters at all, interpret it as a sign of the strength of our democracy—that it can tolerate differences of opinion.

But there are two considerations here that invite our attention. First, if critics of our Vietnamese war are right, then some modification of our policy is clearly desirable, and those who call for such modification serve a necessary purpose. We do not know whether they are right or not. We will not find out by silencing them. Second, if government, or those in positions of power and authority, can silence criticism by the argument that such criticism might be misunderstood somewhere, then there is an end to all criticism, and perhaps an end to our kind of political system. For men in authority will always think that criticism of their policies is dangerous. They will always equate their policies with patriotism, and find criticism subversive. The Federalists found criticism of President Adams so subversive that they legislated to expel critics from the country. Southerners found criticism of slavery so subversive that they drove critics out of the South. Attorney General Palmer thought criticism of our Siberian misadventure—now remembered only with embarrassment—so subversive that he hounded the critics into prison for twenty-year terms. McCarthy found almost all teachers and writers so subversive that he was ready to burn down the libraries and close the universities. Experience should harden us against the argument that dissent and criticism are so dangerous that they must always give way to consensus.

And as for the argument that criticism may give aid and

comfort to some enemy, that is a form of blackmail unworthy of those who profess it. If it is to be accepted, we have an end to genuine discussion of foreign policies, for it will inevitably be invoked to stop debate and criticism whenever that debate gets acrimonious or the criticism cuts too close to the bone. And to the fevered mind of the FBI, the CIA, and some Senators, criticism always gives aid and comfort to the enemy or cuts too close to the bone.

"The only thing we have to fear," said Franklin Roosevelt, "is fear itself." That is as true in the intellectual and the moral realm as in the political and the economic. We do not need to fear ideas, but the censorship of ideas. We do not need to fear criticism, but the silencing of criticism. We do not need to fear excitement or agitation in the academic community, but timidity and apathy. We do not need to fear resistance to political leaders, but unquestioning acquiescence in whatever policies those leaders adopt. We do not even need to fear those who take too literally the anguished pleas of a Pope Paul VI or the moral lessons of the Sermon on the Mount, but those who reject the notion that morality has any place in politics. For that, indeed, is to stumble and sin in the dark.

1965

What Is Our Commitment in Vietnam?

As the war in Vietnam escalates, so too has the American commitment. The term, almost unknown in earlier discussions or statements, emerged only with this administration, and it has swiftly taken on an almost mystical character. President Johnson has asserted that our commitment is a moral one, which deeply involves our "national honor," and Secretary Rusk has given us authoritative assurance that it is a binding legal commitment as well. What is more, "commitment" has escalated not only forward but backward. Though the term was not used during the Eisenhower administration, no other than President Johnson has conferred upon it retroactive sanctity. "Our commitment," he said, "is just the same as the commitment made by President Eisenhower in 1954."

Let us then consider the nature and the obligation of this commitment. It is not a doctrinaire or an academic consideration, any more than questions of due process are doctrinaire in the search for justice. Furthermore, it is an issue which may determine the attitude of our seven associates in the SEATO Defense Treaty and, far more important, of the uncommitted members of the United Nations.

Now the odd thing about this commitment in South Vietnam is its elusiveness: it has a quicksilver character about it. Those who insist upon it are quite dogmatic about it, but they are never quite sure what it is. And no wonder, for it never seems to stay the same from one crisis to another—scarcely even from one speech to another. Originally it was President Eisenhower's letter to Diem of 25 October 1954; then it was paragraph 2 of Article IV of the SEATO Defense Treaty; then it was the Tonkin Gulf Resolution of 1964. And now, under prodding from the Senate Foreign Relations Committee, Secretary Rusk, in a remarkable sleight of hand, has gone back to the SEATO Treaty, jettisoned paragraph 2, and substituted for it paragraph 1, just as if we had always relied upon that particular provision. And during all this discussion of obligation and commitment no one—no one in the State Department anyway—seems to have given any consideration to our obligations and commitments under the Charter of the United Nations.

Let us take a close look at some of these "commitments"; let us see if the garments in which they are clothed are real, or are like those which the clever tailors fashioned for the hapless Emperor in Hans Christian Andersen's *The Emperor's New Clothes*.

First, then, the Eisenhower letter of October 1954—the commitment upon which President Johnson so confidently relied in his speech of 2 June 1964. It said four things: First, that "we have been exploring ways and means to permit our aid to Vietnam to be more effective. . . . I am instructing the American Ambassador . . . to examine . . . how an intelligent program of American aid . . . can serve to assist." Second, it said that "the purpose of this offer is to assist the Government of Vietnam in developing and maintaining a strong, viable state, capable of resisting attempted subversion or aggression through military means." Third, it pointed out that "the United States expects that this aid will be met by performance on the part of the Government of Vietnam in undertaking needed reforms." And fourth, it hoped that "such aid . . . will contribute effectively towards an independent Vietnam endowed with a strong government."

Clearly this is not a commitment at all. It is a proposal for an "inquiry," for a "critical examination," into the possibilities of aid, and this only on certain conditions—conditions which, it is proper to add, were not met.

President Eisenhower himself did not regard his letter to

Diem as a commitment. He did not permit the United States to get involved militarily with South Vietnam. Even his aid program was predominantly non-military, and as for military aid, the total American corps of "advisers"—and they were really advisers—was less than one thousand when he left office. To this day Mr. Eisenhower refuses to admit that he made any "commitment" to send fighting forces to Vietnam, and it is out of respect for his position that the State Department has now decided to abandon this much abused letter as the primary sanction for our current commitment.

It is proper to add here a marginal comment. Even had President Eisenhower intended his letter to be a kind of commitment, it would have had no binding force; the President cannot, by private letter, commit the United States to war or quasi-war.

The second basis for our commitment is the SEATO Defense Treaty of 1954. This, indeed, has now emerged as the preferred legal authority upon which Secretary Rusk is prepared to rest his case. It is a shaky authority. It begins by "reiterating . . . faith in the purposes and principles set forth in the Charter of the United Nations." And it adds that

> The Parties undertake, as set forth in the Charter of the United Nations, to settle any international disputes in which they may be involved by peaceful means . . . and to refrain in their international relations from the threat or use of force in any manner inconsistent with the purposes of the United Nations.

But now we come to the heart of the matter, only to discover that there are two hearts and that they are, apparently, interchangeable. They are the two parts of Article IV. The first paragraph asserts that "aggression" against any of the parties to the treaty or against any territory which the parties designate, would endanger peace, and pledges the signatories "to meet the common danger in accordance with its constitutional processes." It also provides that whatever measures are taken "shall be immediately reported to the Security Council." The second paragraph addresses itself to the problem of "subversion." If the integrity of the territory which we undertake to protect "is threatened in any way other than by armed attack or is affected or threatened by any fact or situation which might endanger the peace" of the area, then the signatories to the treaty shall "consult" and agree on measures for the common defense.

Until recently we have, in fact, sought to justify our intervention in Vietnam under this paragraph which deals with subversion rather than aggression. The difficulty here is that paragraph 2 calls specifically for collective consultation, and that this was clearly understood at the time the treaty was adopted. So said Secretary Dulles, who ought to know, since he drew it up. In reply to a question from Senator Green about the nature of the American obligation to put down subversion or insurrection, the Secretary explained that "if there is a revolutionary movement in Vietnam or Thailand, we [the SEATO members] would consult together as to what to do about it, because . . . a subversive movement that was in fact propagated by Communism would be a very great threat to us. But we have no understanding to put it down; all we have is an undertaking to consult together as to what to do about it." And the esteemed Senator George of the Foreign Relations Committee asserted succinctly that "The Treaty does not call for automatic action; it calls for consultation. I cannot emphasize too strongly that we have no obligation . . . to take positive measures of any kind. All that we are obligated to do is to consult together." The requirement of collective action was later slightly modified to permit one party to act if there was no dissenting vote. But at the last two meetings of the SEATO Council, France threatened to veto any action by the United States, so we have not brought the matter up at all.

Now, however, Secretary Rusk has shifted his, and our, position to the first paragraph of the much disputed Article IV. Now, it is asserted, we face not subversion but overt aggression, and are therefore authorized to act unilaterally. But this paragraph, too, if fraught with difficulties. There is first the problem of "aggression." As Vietnam is one nation, not two—that is specifically provided for in the Geneva Agreement and validated by eight hundred years of history—it is by no means clear that "infiltration" of anywhere from twenty to thirty thousand Vietnamese into the South constitutes "aggression." This point was made by George Kennan in his recent testimony on our Vietnamese involvement to the Foreign Relations Committee of the Senate:

> I think the use of the word "aggression" with what we
> are facing today in Vietnam is confusing. . . . The border
> between North and South Vietnam is of a curious quality.
> It was not meant originally to be the border between
> states. This is of course, in part, the invasion of one
> country, if one wants to describe it that way, by forces of
> another country, although all of these things involve
> stretching of terms. But it is also a civil conflict within
> South Vietnam. . . . I do not think we can afford to
> delude ourselves that the Vietcong are simply an external
> force. . . .

Furthermore, there are seven other signatories to the SEATO
Treaty. If what we face is clearly a case of aggression, why is it
that of the seven signatories, only Australia has responded in any
way, and that by what is merely a token force? If our "honor" is
involved, as President Johnson and Secretary Rusk assert, why is
not the honor of the other SEATO nations equally involved? Or
are Britain, France, Pakistan, Thailand, the Philippines, and even
New Zealand without honor? Surely the other alternative is more
persuasive: that these other signatories do not, in fact, recognize
"aggression."

But we are not yet through with the SEATO Treaty. For that
treaty contains two other articles that are relevant to our inquiry.
One (Art. IV, I) requires that "measures taken [to repel aggres-
sion] shall be immediately reported to the Security Council."
(This we have conspicuously failed to do; our belated action of
January 1966 is scarcely retroactive and it was, in any event, not
a report on our own actions, but a complaint of Vietnamese aggression.) A second provision of the treaty (Art. VI) reads:

> This Treaty does not affect and shall not be interpreted
> as affecting in any way the rights and obligations of any
> of the Parties under the Charter of the United Nations
> for the maintenance of international peace and security.

It is the term "obligations" that commands our attention. The
American Bar Association has now asserted that Article 52 of the
United Nations Charter, which recognizes "regional agreements,"
authorizes our Vietnam intervention. Article 52 does indeed authorize "regional agreements or agencies for dealing with such
matters relating to the maintenance of international peace and
security as are appropriate for regional action." But there are two

important qualifications. The first is that such activities be "consistent with the Purposes and Principles of the United Nations." The second, and more important, is set forth in Article 53. "The Security Council shall utilize such regional arrangements for enforcement action under its authority. *But no enforcement action shall be taken under regional arrangements or by regional agencies without the authorization of the Security Council.*" (Italics added.)

There is one more string to Secretary Rusk's bow: The Tonkin Gulf Resolution of 10 August 1964. This is another of those things which have escalated rapidly in the past two years; indeed this resolution has grown to such dimensions that some of its Congressional parents no longer recognize it.

The Tonkin Gulf Resolution was passed without debate, as a gesture of support to President Johnson after the Vietnamese had fired torpedoes (without effect) at two United States destroyers escorting South Vietnamese ships in the Tonkin Gulf. It pledged support to the President, as Commander-in-Chief, to "take all necessary measures to repel any armed attack against the forces of the United States, and to prevent further aggression."

Here, according to Secretary Rusk and his supporters, is the crux of the matter. By firing at our destroyers in the Tonkin Gulf, the North Vietnamese committed an act of aggression—an aggression so flagrant and so prodigious that it justifies the whole of the war we have waged since that day. Was it in fact an act of aggression? Were our destroyers in "international waters"? They were, apparently, within eleven miles of the shore, and Vietnam—like other nations—claimed that her waters extended twelve miles into the seas. Was the fact that the American destroyers were escorting South Vietnamese ships which had engaged in shelling North Vietnamese islands immaterial? A colloquy between Senator Nelson and Senator Fulbright on this matter is relevant:

> SEN. FULBRIGHT: It was testified that they went in at least eleven miles in order to show that we do not recognize a twelve-mile limit which I believe North Vietnam has asserted.
>
> SEN. NELSON: The patrolling was for the purpose of demonstrating to the North Vietnamese that we did not recognize a twelve-mile limit?

SEN. FULBRIGHT: That was one reason given. . . .

SEN. NELSON: It would be mighty risky if Cuban PT boats were firing on Florida, for Russian armed ships or destroyers to be patrolling between us and Cuba, eleven miles out.

The act of aggression was, in any event, determined unilaterally by the United States, though when, a few months earlier, Britain had "retaliated" against Yemen by firing on a fort at Harib, Ambassador Stevenson had denounced the action and the General Assembly had passed a resolution condemning "reprisals as incompatible with the purposes and principles of the United Nations."

Certainly one might conclude that whatever "aggression" occurred in the Tonkin Gulf was mutual, and that to invoke that act of aggression against our destroyers as the legal basis for sending over two hundred thousand men to Vietnam, flying three hundred sorties a day, is stretching things pretty far.

It is relevant, too, that when the Russians moved into Cuba with their missiles, we chose to regard that as an act of aggression, and prepared to retaliate, and learned international lawyers like Eustace Seligman have defended our position. But if Russian missile installations constituted, in themselves, and without any overt act, an act of aggression, what is to be said of the American intervention in Vietnam even before the Tonkin Gulf incident—the presence of the Seventh Fleet, the twenty thousand combat troops, the massive military aid to the South Vietnamese? Aggression against aggression; surely any disinterested observer would conclude that the North Vietnamese had a stronger case against the United States than the United States had against North Vietnam.

Support of this view comes from the report of the International Control Commission of 2 June 1962, two full years before Tonkin Gulf. The report, which condemned North Vietnamese aggression against the South, condemned, at the same time, United States intervention in Vietnam:

> Taking all the facts into consideration [said the Commission] and basing itself on its own observation and authorized statements made in the United States of Amer-

ica and the Republic of Vietnam, the Committee concludes that the Republic of Vietnam has violated Articles
16 and 17 of the Geneva Agreement in receiving the increased military aid from the United States. . . . The Commission is also of the view that though there may not be
any formal military alliance between the Governments
of the United States and the Republic of Vietnam, the
establishment of a U.S. Military Assistance Command in
South Vietnam, as well as the introduction of military
personnel beyond the stated strength of the Military Assistance Advisory Group, amounts to a factual military
alliance which is prohibited under Article 19 of the
Geneva Agreement.

Note that this was not a Communist-inspired report, but that
it was signed by the representatives of two "free" nations, Canada
and India.

There is another angle to the Tonkin Gulf Resolution (it is,
after all, the "hawks" who force it on our attention). Section two
of that resolution proved that,

Consonant with the Constitution of the United States
and the Charter of the United Nations, and in accordance
with the obligations under the SEATO Treaty, the United
States is prepared . . . to take all necessary steps.

If the Tonkin Gulf affair was a clear case of aggression, why
is it that the other members of SEATO have not rallied to our
support, as is required by the treaty? If it was a clear case of aggression, why is it that we did not choose to follow the procedure
laid down by the Charter and submit it to the United Nations?

"We must honor our commitments," President Johnson said,
and that sentiment has been echoed and re-echoed in the debate
over Vietnam. But we have commitments to the United Nations,
commitments which legally and morally take precedence over any
we may have to Vietnam. Let us contemplate these commitments.

First, the Charter obligates the United States—and all signatories—"to settle their international disputes by peaceful
means." Second, it provides that "all members shall refrain, in
their international relations, from the threat or use of force
against the territorial integrity or political independence of any

state, or in any other manner inconsistent with the purposes of the United Nations." And Article 39 of Chapter VII provides that "the Security Council shall determine the existence of any threat to the peace, breach of the peace, or act of aggression, and shall make recommendations, or decide what measures shall be taken . . . to maintain or restore international peace and security."

These words are simple and unambiguous. If their meaning needs to be clarified, we cannot do better than to recall President Eisenhower's denunciation of the military action taken against Egypt by Britain, France, and Israel at the time of the Suez crisis. Granted, said Eisenhower, that the provocations were "grave and repeated," nevertheless "the use of military force to solve international disputes could not be reconciled with the principles of the United Nations to which we had all subscribed." And Secretary Dulles, in rejecting a Soviet proposal for a joint peacekeeping force in the Middle East as "unthinkable," pointed out that "any intervention by the United States or any other action except by a duly constituted United Nations peace force, would be counter to everything the . . . United Nations were charged by the Charter to do." And President Eisenhower added, even more categorically, that "the United Nations *is alone* charged with the responsibility of securing the peace in the Middle East and throughout the world."

It is unnecessary to belabor the point that the Charter of the United Nations—like all treaties made under the authority of the United States—is the law of the land. Every President, every Congressman, is bound to observe that law. No President can set it aside by a letter; no Congress can set it aside by a joint resolution; and it will not be alleged that it was set aside by that SEATO Treaty which explicitly recognizes its own subordination to the Charter.

What, then, is our commitment to Vietnam?

We do not appear to be committed either by the Eisenhower letter of 1954, or by the SEATO Treaty, or by the Tonkin Gulf resolution. Our commitment seems to consist of two things: first, repeated and ever more emphatic assertions by the President, and the Secretaries of State and Defense, assertions which have in themselves no more authority than had the assertion by the Emperor's tailors that his clothes were indeed regal. Second, there is the factual commitment: we are there, whether we like it or not, whether we should be there or not. This is not the kind of argument that can be entertained in a court of law, or in an international tribunal. If President Johnson, Secretary Rusk, and their supporters want to vindicate our presence in Vietnam on the ground of naked power, they are of course free to do so. But that has not been our position in the past.

1966

Vietnam: The Moral Issue

Speaking of one of the greatest of crises Abraham Lincoln said, just over a century ago:

> If we could first know where we are, and whither we are tending, we could better judge what to do, and how to do it. We are now far into the fifth year since a policy was initiated with the avowed object in confidence of putting an end to the slavery agitation. [Let us substitute "to the Vietnamese crisis."] Under the operation of that policy the agitation has not only not ceased but has constantly augmented. (Speech, Springfield, 1858.)

How do we explain the predicament in which we now find ourselves, we the American people and we the people of the entire world? It is not because wicked men plan mischief, because the United States is militaristic, or because clever men in Vietnam or in Peking have planned with diabolical ingenuity to involve us in war. It is because we are caught up in errors, misconceptions, miscalculations, and confusions of our own making, and we do not know how to extricate ourselves from them; like some desperate child, we strike out in anger. Let us try to discover where we are. Let us reflect our current difficulties against the large historical background of the past twenty years—the background of the spectacular emergence of America as the greatest of world powers.

Confronted with the world as it was in 1945—much of it shattered—the United States made a series of decisions and assumptions. It is the assumptions that most concern us. Those were to a considerable degree sound for 1945; they became increasingly less sound with the passing of years, and finally they became those prodigious miscalculations in which we are now imprisoned.

The first of these assumptions was that the world was divided between two great powers or power complexes, the Russian and the American, the slave and the free, and that we and we alone were responsible for the free world. Actually, within a few years, we confronted a world of five or six great power complexes: China, and India, and Western Europe as well as Russia, and possibly others such as Japan, the British Commonwealth, the Latin American, the African, and the Arab worlds. No one nation is, or can be, responsible for the protection of freedom in such a world. The United Nations is responsible for that, in so far as it is able to function, and our most important international obligation is to help it function.

Second, we assumed that communism was monolithic, fixed, and unchanging; that it was not a political system, or even a social or economic system, but a moral (or immoral) system, and that there was no compromise with it, for you do not compromise with sin except to strike it down. We assumed, too, that communism was inherently aggressive and expansionist and we have continued to assert this in the face of a good deal of evidence to the contrary. We have transferred that assumption now from Russia to Communist China. We assumed that the only way we could contain communism was by force, and adopted therefore a containment policy based upon what appeared to be a monopoly of nuclear weapons. We are only gradually learning—some of our Congressmen have not yet learned—that you cannot contain ideas by force and that you cannot even use nuclear weapons without consequences that are self-defeating.

Third, we assumed that there was only one China, that headed by Chiang Kai-shek which ended up in Taiwan, and we are still stuck with that assumption. We insisted that Communist China was not the real China, that it was on the contrary a usurper and an evil force, and was not therefore to be recognized. Not content with this, we went further and blocked recognition by the United Nations. We assumed that Chinese communism, too, was monolithic, militaristic, and aggressive, and that it was therefore our duty to prevent its expansion anywhere in Asia just as we had earlier assumed it our responsibility to prevent its expansion in Europe or in Latin America.

Fourth, we had in 1945 a monopoly of atomic weapons and we assumed that we could retain that monopoly; we were rudely awakened from that dream within a few years. We assumed that our monopoly would permit us to have our own way for some time to come. Of course we would never really use atomic weapons, but we might do so in a righteous cause. Because in 1945 we were the most powerful nation on the globe we assumed that our power was and would continue to be limitless, and that we could impose our will upon the rest of the world. We knew that we were virtuous and our will righteous and we were not therefore worried about the moral implications of this kind of arrogance, though history teaches that there is something corrupting in assumptions of this kind.

Fifth, because we meant well, because the American way of life was part of freedom and progress, and was even identified with the cosmic system, we assumed that those who opposed us were either misguided or wicked or both, and many of us still cherish this assumption, though no longer with the confidence with which we entertained it in the past. Yet we are still astonished that General De Gaulle does not support us in Vietnam, but opposes us. We even delude ourselves that we won a moral victory in the 47 to 47 vote on the admission of Red China to the United Nations, though when we recollect that England, France, Denmark, Norway, Sweden, the Netherlands, India, and Pakistan all voted against us, while eighteen of our votes came from countries of Latin America, we cannot take much satisfaction in the vote.

Along with these misguided assumptions, we made a great miscalculation of a negative character. We failed to understand the nature of what is doubtless the greatest revolution of modern times, the greatest and most far-reaching since the shift in the center of gravity from the Mediterranean to the Atlantic in the sixteenth and seventeenth centuries: the revolt of Asia and Africa against the West, the emergence into modernity of two-thirds of the peoples of the globe. We failed to give sympathetic support to the convulsive efforts of some sixty new nations to catch up, in a single generation, with the progress which the Western world had made over four or five centuries. Materially we did, of course, contribute to this enterprise, but in other and important ways we allowed ourselves to be maneuvered into the position of opposing revolution and what these peoples considered progress. We allowed ourselves to be maneuvered into the position that Britain had occupied throughout much of the nineteenth century and France in the twentieth—that of the stalwart defender of the status quo, of the West, and of the white peoples, as against the under-privileged, the black and yellow and brown peoples of the world.

Now all these were political miscalculations, to be sure, but they were more, they were moral miscalculations. And all of these miscalculations and mistaken assumptions are dramatized now in our misconduct in Vietnam. Once again we see ourselves as the only defenders against communism. Once again we see communism as a moral, not a political or economic issue, and the Communists as enemies so evil that if and when the ultimate confrontation comes we may be justified in invoking the ultimate weapon—or so, at least, many of our respected Senators have recently said. We equate the Vietcong with communism, and communism with evil, and there you are.

Once again we assume that China is what Russia was, only worse; that she is powerful, and dangerous, and diabolical, and that no good can come out of her. At the same time, we pretend that she is not there at all, so we need not talk with her, and we thereby confess what is probably the worst case of schizophrenia in the history of international relations. Suppose Britain had not only recognized the Confederate States of America in 1861, and gone to their aid by blockade, military assistance, and attacks on the Northern States, but had refused for a decade after Appomattox to recognize the existence of the United States, and persisted all that time in the recognition of the Confederate States as the only legitimate government!

Once again, too, we are failing to recognize and cooperate with revolution—revolution in Vietnam, Laos, Cambodia, and elsewhere; that is one reason we have lost the support and confidence of the spokesmen of these peoples. Here as elsewhere on the globe—Cuba, Santo Domingo, Brazil, Guatemala—we have maneuvered ourselves into the position of being the enemy of change and of what the peoples of these countries think is freedom. In the eyes of Asians we are the protagonist of the West against the East, of white people against yellow and brown people, of power against the weak people who are always the victims of power. It is no wonder that we have no effective support anywhere on earth except perhaps in Germany; no support from the two major Asian countries, India and Japan, and that even South Korea and Australia have sent only token forces. We presume to be defending Asia against communism and against Chinese aggression, but not a single Asian country supports us.

Here in Southeast Asia we have assumed, as we had elsewhere, that what we want is what Providence and the Cosmos wants; that our power is limitless; that this is our legitimate sphere of influence (though not apparently China's); and that it is up to us to settle the affairs of this quarter of the globe. And once again many of us appear to assume that to oppose us is immoral and that we must win at almost any cost, even the cost of war with China.

And all to what end?

Not to vindicate international law, for we are pretty clearly violating international law. Not to sustain the Charter of the United Nations, for we are flagrantly violating that Charter. Not to sustain the South-East Asia Treaty Organization which we established, for we dare not take our case to SEATO and have not done so. Not to protect the integrity of Vietnam as is clearly required by the Geneva agreement of 1954—the agreement to which we pledged our support and by which we are bound, which recognizes the unity of Vietnam and provides that the 17th Parallel is a temporary line—for we are attempting to create two countries in Vietnam. Not to protect South Vietnam against outside attack, for so far the major attack has come from us. Only now, almost a year after that extraordinary White Paper of the State Department conjured up an attack coming from the North, have we called such an attack into existence. Only within the last few months have we been told of large scale "infiltrations" from the North into the South. Who, we may ask, was there before? Now apparently there are some 18,000 to 20,000 North Vietnamese (December 1965) in South Vietnam, as contrasted with 175,000 Americans, who do not of course "infiltrate" but who come quite openly.

It is clear that the war in Vietnam was, until recently, a civil war, and that we are the ones who are busily converting it into an international war. Let us remember that President Eisenhower refused to enter the war in 1954, or at any time thereafter; had there been an election in Vietnam in 1956, he said, 80 per cent of the people would have voted for the Vietcong. "I can imagine no greater tragedy than to get the United States involved in a war with Vietnam," Eisenhower declared. Our total build-up in Vietnam, at the end of his administration, was less than one thousand advisers.

Let us remember, too, that President Kennedy had no confidence in a military solution of the Vietnamese problem and that he said, shortly before his death,

> I don't think, unless a greater effort is made by the government to win popular support, that the war can be won out there. In the final analysis it is their war. They are the ones who have to win it or lose it. We can help them . . . but they have to win it, the people of Vietnam.

According to Arthur Schlesinger, Kennedy "realized that Vietnam was his great failure in foreign policy."

We are not there to protect Vietnam against Chinese aggression, as we persistently assert, for there is no Chinese aggression; there is not a single Chinese combat soldier in Vietnam. We are not really there to preserve peace, for we are ourselves conducting the major war, and playing a kind of military Russian roulette with China. We are not there to save Southeast Asia from communism—though we think we are—for everything we see indicates that we are forcing Southeast Asia, and above all Vietnam, to look to China rather than to us.

Nor is there any convincing evidence that, if left alone, China would be able to extend her hegemony over this area. Russia cannot control Yugoslavia, nor even little Albania; we cannot control Cuba; why do we suppose that China can impose her will on all the countries of Southeast Asia? China has in fact been far less insistent on her own sphere of influence in Southeast Asia than we have been in the Carribean or Latin America.

Now we claim to be doing all these things in order to advance the cause of peace in that quarter of the globe. We may delude ourselves that we are advancing the cause of peace but few of the peoples of the globe agree with us. There are even, in some quarters, doubts about our sincerity. We claim to be ready for unconditional discussion but we brushed aside a proposal for discussion which came from no other than U Thant, and we did this for the worst of reasons: that such discussions might interfere with our election campaign, and that at the moment we were not winning the war. Well may we ask, if we refuse to discuss peace when we are not ready why do we expect North Vietnam to discuss peace when they are not ready? Nor for that matter are we really prepared for unconditional discussions, for we proclaim our unwillingness to negotiate with the Vietcong. We have only to ask ourselves, would we have discussed terms with Great Britain in 1778 (when Britain made overtures) if these allowed British soldiers to remain in all seaport towns? Would we have discussed terms with the Confederate States of America which left units of the Confederate army in major cities of the South, or perhaps permitted the British army to keep forces in Virginia? Clearly we would not. You will remember that when Admiral Byng was executed for defeat at Minorca in 1757, Voltaire remarked that this was done *pour encourager les autres.* That is doubtless why we step up our bombing to three hundred sorties a day—*pour encourager les autres.*

Let us look at some of the implications and consequences of our war—not only where we are but whither we are tending.

There is no evidence that our war in Vietnam is designed to achieve the ends which we insist upon, and strong evidence that it will achieve opposite ends. Indeed one is sometimes tempted to wonder if the whole thing was not planned in Peking; perhaps the Birchers who think the State Department is riddled with Communists are right after all!

Consider the claim of "vital interest" in Vietnam. If we have a vital interest there, we have everywhere—and that is precisely what Dean Acheson said recently. Of course in one sense everybody has a vital interest in whatever happens throughout the globe. But we cannot assume a vital interest for ourselves unless we grant similar interest to all others. Does Russia have a vital interest in Cuba because Castro is an outpost of communism? When Russia attempted to display that, we prepared for war. Surely if we have a vital interest in distant Vietnam we must concede Russia a vital interest in Iran, Iraq, and Hungary. And even more obviously, if *we* have a vital interest in Vietnam what are we to say to China's interest: is it something less than vital? What we have here as elsewhere is a double standard—a double standard in political and moral conduct, one for the United States and one for the rest of the world.

And this brings us squarely to the problem of the ethical implications of our enterprise in Vietnam.

We are guilty of violating international law. We are guilty of violating the Charter of the United Nations. We have heard something about our honor being at stake. The Charter of the United Nations is the law of the land, as all treaties to which we subscribe are the law of the land, and our honor is involved in sustaining it. We are guilty of trying to overthrow unilaterally the Geneva Agreement, in trying to create unilaterally two nations where the law, and history, know but one. We are setting the rest of the world—Russia and China included—an example of unilateral action in international affairs—just such an example as we set in Santo Domingo. We are guilty of self-deception in pleading that we are in Vietnam in accordance with formal requests from the South Vietnamese government. Under the Geneva Agreement that government had no authority to make such a request. Furthermore the governments which have functioned since 1956 are puppet governments; the rest of the world knows this if we do not. More, to assume that a request for military aid even from an independent South Vietnam would somehow justify our intervention there requires us to concede that a request for military aid from an independant Cuba justifies the intervention of the Soviet in that island. That was not what we thought in 1962.

We engage in deception of our own people in such matters as the disastrous White Paper put out by the State Department which purports to prove that North Vietnam and China were the real aggressors.

Our very language is corrupted, and corruption of language —as we have so often said of the Communists—is a sign of corruption of mind and spirit. For a long time we avoided the word "war" in Vietnam; now it is at last acceptable and perhaps even respectable. Our soldiers there were not soldiers but "advisers," and even now we hear them so described; never in all history were so few "advised" so much, by so many. The Vietcong engage in "terror" attacks but our bombings presumably do not spread terror, not even among women and children. When we use gas it is not really gas but something our police use every day. Guerrilla warfare justifies bombing at the source: it is a good thing Castro did not take that attitude at the time of the Bay of Pigs. When we land 160,000 fighting men that is open and above-board; when the North Vietnamese send in 10,000 or 15,000 soldiers, they "infiltrate" and everybody knows how sneaky infiltration is. Recently we have had what is perhaps the ultimate in double-talk: when we drop napalm bombs by mistake on a Vietnam village, it is "friendly fire."

We continually escalate a war which we have not yet formally declared, and this despite promises by our President that we would not do so, and we justify ourselves by charges of Vietnamese escalation. We connive at and must therefore take some responsibility for violations of the laws of war, and it is no use saying that the other side is equally guilty: it is our morals we must take care of. We bomb helpless villages—how we condemned that when the Nazis did it—and worse yet spray them with napalm. We destroy crops by pouring chemicals on them; we destroy dams and set back agriculture for years to come. We do not ourselves torture but we support the Vietnamese, who do.

We have said over the years that atomic war is unthinkable but we think about it more and more and talk about it and are even beginning to anticipate it. Let us not dismiss lightly this danger of nuclear warfare. It is very real. Basic to our readiness to consider the use of nuclear weapons is a deep immorality—the notion that somehow Oriental lives are not as precious as American lives, that to rescue some thousands of American soldiers who have no clear business being where they are at all, we would be justified in killing some hundreds of thousands of Vietnamese or of Chinese civilians as well as soldiers. We cannot understand why other countries are fearful that we might use nuclear weapons.

How easy it is for us to forget that so far we are the only country that ever has.

There is no longer any meaningful relation between military gains and military risks in Southeast Asia. If God should put it to us: You may have your way in Vietnam, win the war, put down all opposition, destroy the Vietcong, set up just the government you think right, eliminate communism—all at the cost of nuclear war, would we accept the offer? Is there any one among us who would accept the offer? I think not. Yet we are constantly tempted to do just this. Is it wise, is it statesmanlike, is it moral, to maneuver ourselves into a position where we might be tempted, or forced, to make a choice? Are any conceivable ends worth that price?

But, it will be said, we will not need to fall back on the threat of nuclear force if only we are firm. China would not dare resist. Are we sure of this? If Russia or China threatened us with the bomb, would we buckle under? Why are we so sure that others would? Perhaps the whole thing would be a bluff, perhaps they would think it was a bluff. But bluffs—as any poker player knows —are sometimes called, and sensible nations do not allow themselves to get into a position where they may be required to make good threats which may be suicidal.

The consequences of our Vietnamese involvement to our moral standards are already painfully familiar. It means deception; it means putting out arguments and claims which we do not ourselves believe; it means lying to the American people; it means that we are losing our friends throughout the globe; it means we are coarsening our own moral fiber; getting hardened to bombing innocent people and destroying a country on pretexts that will not stand close examination. It means ever sharper division within our own society, and the upsurge, here at home, of the forces of intolerance. It means the strengthening and consolidation of that "military-industrial establishment" against which President Eisenhower warned us. It means a pervasive indulgence in that sin which may well be the unpardonable sin of the New Testament, the sin of supposing that we are a special people, exempt from those rules of morality which apply to all others.

1966

NOTES

Notes

Democracy and Judicial Review

1 Justice Jackson in *Murdock v. Pennsylvania*, "If we should strip these cases to the underlying questions, I find them too difficult as constitutional problems to be disposed of by a vague but fervent transcendentalism." (319 U.S. 157 at 179.)

2 *Palko v. Connecticut*, 302 U.S. 319.

3 Footnote 4 in *Carolene Products v. U.S.*, 204 U.S. 144.

4 *Introduction to Democratic Theory* (New York, 1960). Professor Mayo teaches at the University of South Carolina. Let us trust his argument carries conviction to the Negroes of that state.

5 For Holmes, see evolution of the clear and present danger doctrine; for Brandeis, see concurring opinion in *Whitney v. California*, 274 U.S. 357; for Hughes, see *De Jonge v. Oregon*, 299 U.S. 353, *Stromberg v. California*, 283 U.S. 539, *Near v. Minnesota*, 283 U.S. 697.

6 Thus *American Communications Assoc. v. Douds*, 339 U.S. 382; *Watkins v. U.S.*, 354 U.S. 178; *Sweezy v. New Hampshire*, 354 U.S. 234; *NAACP v. Alabama*, 357 U.S. 178; *Uphaus v. Wyman*, 360 U.S. 72; *Barenblatt v. U.S.*, 360 U.S. 1081.

In *American Communications Assoc. v. Douds*: "When particular conduct is regulated in the interest of public order, and the regulation results in an indirect, conditional, partial abridgment of speech, the duty of the courts is to determine which of these two conflicting interests demands the greater protection under the particular circumstances presented. . . . In essence the problem is one of weighing the probable effects of the statute upon the free exercise of the right of speech and assembly against the congressional determination." (339 U.S. at 399–400.) And in *NAACP v. Alabama*: "The crucial factor is the interplay of governmental and private action, for it is only after the initial exertion of state power represented by the production order [for membership lists] that private action takes hold. . . . We turn to the final question, whether Alabama has demonstrated an interest in obtaining the disclosures . . . sufficient to justify the deterrent effect which we have concluded these disclosures may well have . . . on petitioners' constitutionally protected right of association." (357 U.S. 449.)

7 *Gobitis v. Pennsylvania*, 310 U.S. 586 (1940) and *West Virginia v. Barnette*, 319 U.S. 624 (1943).

8 *Sweezy v. New Hampshire*, 354 U.S. 234 (1957) and *Uphaus v. Wyman*, 360 U.S. 72 (1959).

9 *Uphaus v. Wyman*, 360 U.S. 72 (1959).

10 *Perez v. Brownell*, 356 U.S. 44 (1958).

11 *Jenckes v. U.S.*, 353 U.S. 657 (1957).

[12] *Dennis v. U.S.*, 341 U.S. 494 (1951).
[13] *Slochower v. Bd. of Education*, 350 U.S. 551 (1956).
[14] *Minersville v. Gobitis*, 310 U.S. 586 (1940).
[15] The Fund for the Republic has nibbled at the edge of this undertaking, and the Center for the Study of Freedom at Harvard University may find it worth attention. But except for some miscellaneous and uncoordinated, though remarkable, individual studies—Leonard Levy's *Legacy of Suppression*; James Smith's *Freedom Fetters*; Russel Nye's *Fettered Freedom*; Harold Hyman's *To Try Men's Souls*; James G. Randall's *Constitutional Problems under Lincoln*; Morton Grodzins' *Americans Betrayed*; Walter Gellhorn's *The States and Subversion*; Zechariah Chafee's classic *Free Speech in the United States*—we want adequate factual information in this important area.
[16] Now, with our involvement in Vietnam, a ninth chapter in the history of intolerance and repression opens upon us.
[17] All this has since been changed. Thanks to the Supreme Court decision on *Baker v. Carr* the principle of one man one vote has been firmly established, and most states have accommodated themselves to the new rule.

Leadership in Eighteenth-Century America and Today

[1] Henry James, *Hawthorne* (1956 reprint), 34.
[2] 8 Julian Boyd, ed., *The Papers of Thomas Jefferson*, 635.
[3] 26 J. C. Fitzpatrick, ed., *Writings of George Washington*, 483.
[4] Thomas Paine, *The Crisis*, no. 13.
[5] Thomas Jefferson, First Inaugural Address.
[6] 9 *Life and Works of John Adams*, 40.
[7] Quoted in R. E. Delmage, "American Idea of Progress," 91 *Proceedings of the American Philosophical Society*, 314.
[8] 26 *Writings of Washington*, 227.
[9] 3 Clarence E. Carter, ed., *Territorial Papers*, 264.
[10] K. M. Rowland, I *Life of George Mason*, 166.
[11] 10 P. L. Ford, ed., *Writings of Thomas Jefferson*, 378.
[12] Quoted in William Tudor, *Life of James Otis*, 144.
[13] Josiah Quincy, *Memoir of the Life of Josiah Quincy*, 289.
[14] "Dissertation on Canon and Feudal Law," 3 *Works*, 448. When in 1785 Adams recommended his son John Quincy to Professor Waterhouse at Harvard College, he noted that while the boy was "awkward in speaking Latin," in "English and French poetry I know not where you would find anybody his superior, in Roman and English history, few persons of his age. He has translated Virgil's Aeneid, Suetonius, the whole of Sallust and Tacitus Agricola, his Germany and several books of his Annals, a great part of Horace, some of Ovid and some of Caesar's Commentaries . . . besides a number of Tully's Orations. . . . In Greek . . . he has studied morsels of Aristotle's Poetics, in Plutarch's Lives of Lucian's Dialogues . . . and lately he has gone through several books in Homer's Iliad." 9 *Works*, 530. An elaborate appreciation of the unifying role of the study of the

classics on this generation is Douglass Adair, "Intellectual Origins of Jeffersonian Democracy," unpublished Ph.D. dissertation, Yale University, 1943.

15 Quoted in Saul K. Padover, *The World of the Founding Fathers*, 173.

16 Karl Lehmann's observation of Jefferson's historical-mindedness might apply equally to most of the Founding Fathers. "Patrick Henry seemed to speak like Homer, and Homer's language could not fail to be imbued with a new and concrete vitality after listening to Henry, with that analogy in mind. General Arnold's famous march to Quebec was a parallel to Xenophon's retreat in Asia Minor as narrated in his *Anabasis*. John Adams, like Themistocles in Athens, had been the constant advocate of the 'wooden walls' of a navy. And the King of England would welcome American-Tory-traitors as the Persian King had given refuge to the fugitive aristocracy of Greece. Burr was the Cataline of the American Republic." (*Thomas Jefferson, Humanist*, 93.)

17 "What does it matter to me," wrote Madame du Châtelet to her friend Voltaire, "to know that Egil succeeded Haquin in Sweden, and that Ottoman was the son of Ortogrul? I have read with pleasure the history of the Greeks and the Romans; they offered me certain great pictures which attracted me. But I have never yet been able to finish any long history of our modern nations . . . a host of minute events without connection or sequence, a thousand battles which settled nothing . . . which overwhelms the mind without illuminating it." It was the *cri de coeur* of that whole generation.

18 Quoted in Carl Becker, *Heavenly City of the Eighteenth-Century Philosophers*, 91.

19 Alexander Hamilton, *The Farmer Refuted*.

20 Quoted in Ernst Cassirer, *The Philosophy of the Enlightenment* (Beacon Press edn.), 216.

21 So John Adams concluded his *Defence of American Constitutions* with the observation that "all nations from the beginning have been agitated by the same passions. The principles developed here will go a long way in explaining *every* phenomenon that occurs in history of government. The vegetable and animal kingdoms, and those heavenly bodies whose existence and movements we are as yet only permitted faintly to perceive, do not appear to be governed by laws more uniform or certain than those which regulate the moral and political world."

22 The comment of Helvetius on the factual evidence which Montesquieu included to support some of his arguments in *The Spirit of the Laws*, illuminates this attitude. "What the deuce does he want to teach us by his treatise on feudal tenure," said Helvetius. "What new forms of legislation can be derived from this chaos of barbarism that has been maintained by brute force, but must be swept away by reason? He should have tried to derive some true maxims from the improved state of things that is at hand." (Quoted in J. W. Thompson, II *History of Historical Writing*, 63.)

23 The literature on this subject is large, but it is sufficient to suggest here Edwin T. Martin, *Thomas Jefferson, Scientist*; Daniel Boorstin, *The Lost World of Thomas Jefferson*; and Gilbert Chinard, "Eighteenth Century Theories on America as a Human Habitat," 91 *Proceedings of the American Philosophical Society*, 27 ff., and the references which they give.

24 L. W. Labaree, ed., *Papers of Benjamin Franklin*, 412 ff.

25 Thomas Jefferson, "Notes on Virginia," Query 14.

[26] *Lectures on History*, 75–76.

[27] John G. Zimmermann, *Essay on National Pride* (London, 1797 edn.), 241 ff.

[28] "History," said the omniscient Dr. Priestley, "by displaying the sentiments and conduct of truly great men, and those of a contrary character, tends to inspire us with a taste for solid glory and real greatness, and convinces us that it does not consist in what the generality of mankind are so eager in pursuit of. We can never again imagine, if we derive our instruction from history, that true greatness consists in *riches*. . . ." And he concluded, "We conceive more clearly what true greatness of mind is, at the same time that our hearts are more filled with admiration for it, by a simple narration of some incidents of history than by the most elaborate and philosophically exact description of it." *Lectures on History and General Policy* (Philadelphia, 1803 edn.), first lecture.

[29] From Pericles' Funeral Oration. Jefferson had four copies of Thucydides' *History* in his library.

[30] *Ibid.*